CRISIS-PROOF
YOUR PRACTICE

A Norton Professional Book

CRISIS-PROOF YOUR PRACTICE

HOW TO SURVIVE AND THRIVE
IN AN UNCERTAIN ECONOMY

Lynn Grodzki

W. W. NORTON & COMPANY
NEW YORK • LONDON

For information about permission to reproduce selections
from this book, write to Permissions,
W. W. Norton & Company, Inc., 500 Fifth Avenue, New York, NY 10110

Production Manager: Leeann Graham
Manufacturing by

Library of Congress Cataloging-in-Publication Data

Grodzki, Lynn.
Crisis-proof your practice : how to survive and thrive
in an uncertain economy / Lynn Grodzki.
p. cm. — (A Norton professional book)
Includes bibliographical references and index.
ISBN 978-0-393-70611-6 (pbk.)
1. Psychotherapy—Practice. 2. Psychotherapists—Marketing.
I. Title.
RC465.5.G762 2009
616.890068'8—dc22
2009021710

W. W. Norton & Company, Inc.
500 Fifth Avenue, New York, N.Y. 10110
www.wwnorton.com

W. W. Norton & Company Ltd.
Castle House, 75/76 Wells St., London W1T 3QT

1   3   5   7   9   0   8   6   4   2

CONTENTS

ACKNOWLEDGMENTS

For the past 10 years I have worked with thousands of therapists, coaches, consultants, healers, and other service-oriented professionals who seek to improve their practices. In seminars, classes, and individual coaching sessions, I watch as these reluctant entrepreneurs—professionals who did not intend to become businesspeople—learn to own and operate a practice with integrity, purpose, and profitability.

Today's economic situation has made this process much more challenging; as a result, my coaching approach has changed as I have adopted a crisis-proofing plan to help my clients further their goals during an uncertain time. This book defines the plan that is helping my clients today. These clients, who are on the front lines of practice building, are the co-creators of this plan, in that they report back what works, what doesn't, and why, continually teaching me what I need to know to help them and to pass along to others. I appreciate the feedback and efforts of this community of clients more than I can say. My mission as a business coach has always been to help those within the helping and healing professions stay viable, since their services are so needed. This need is amplified during times of crisis.

I asked business and marketing coaches across the country for their thoughts about the recession and what they are suggesting to clients that works best in this challenging time. Many responded and generously contributed ideas and specific strategies, making this a fuller effort; they are cited throughout the book and I thank them for their input. I have also had the good fortune to continue to work with a great publisher, Norton Professional Books, and appreciate Deborah Malmud, Director, and her staff who welcomed this book as an important one for readers to access today.

My husband of 20-plus years, Tad, gave me the gift of

uninterrupted time for months' worth of weekends and evenings to complete this manuscript. I consider myself lucky to always have his unconditional support and encouraging presence for the projects that attract me.

As always, I welcome readers to join the dialogue. Feel free to e-mail me (see my contact information at the end of this book) and respond to the material presented. We are all in this together and I believe that what helps one, helps many.

CRISIS-PROOF YOUR PRACTICE

PART I: REVIEW

Your best teacher is your last mistake.

—*Ralph Nader*

CHAPTER 1

From Surviving to Thriving

Economist Paul Romer once said that a crisis is a terrible thing to waste. Any crisis, global or personal, becomes a defining moment in time. It is fraught with difficult challenges but also filled with a remarkable opportunity for making major, important changes. As I write this book, much of the world is facing a deep economic recession. My clients—therapists of all types, healers, coaches, consultants, and many other service-oriented professionals in private practice—are justifiably worried. They ask: How can I manage the problems that this crisis is causing within my small business? With so much to do, what should I attend to first? I may be okay today, but what about tomorrow? And the most determined wonder: Is it possible to not just survive during a crisis, but to thrive?

This economic crisis is global, but during the course of your business ownership you may also face a crisis of a more micro or personal nature. Illness, an unexpected need to relocate, a professional setback, the breakup of a partnership, or a change in the need for your specific services can bring your practice to the brink and leave you feeling scared. In times of fear, we tend to contract our awareness and develop a kind of tunnel vision, seeing just a small slice of the big picture. Flooded with our own feelings, overwhelmed by the needs of our small business, and trying to work with the ongoing needs of our clients, it's hard to regard a crisis as any kind of gift.

But buried within every crisis, often veiled by the multiple daily worries and tasks, is a hidden jewel: the rare opportunity to stop and see your private practice and yourself with new eyes. With the proper framework you can use a crisis, any crisis, as a jumping-off point to reexamine your business, shift its direction, and make it more purposeful and more profitable. Many small businesses get better at what they do *only* during bad times. Many business owners only take action when their back is against the wall, and their old way of working *stops* working.

Therapists I coach find that the challenges created by the current recession, while anxiety-producing, are also highly illuminating. (For purposes of brevity, I will often use the generic term of *therapist* in this book to refer to readers, although I know that many of you are working in other helping or service-oriented professions. Please adapt or adjust this term and any references to one profession versus another in the case examples I offer, so that the information fits your professional situation.) In a crisis, everything good, bad, or indifferent about your private practice and yourself as a business owner is exposed for evaluation.

A crisis is like a low tide at the ocean. When the ocean recedes you can walk far out on the sand and see all manner of debris littering the ocean floor; but you also spot the occasional treasure—a pristine, glimmering shell buried in the sand. Today's crisis, the recession, has stripped away the surface gleam of business and society. We now see all the weak links and vulnerabilities. But if you know where and how to look, you can also see potential. There are countless prospects for new business within all healing and helping professions.

You can approach a crisis with trepidation, standing on the shore and nervously looking out, horrified at the debris and confusion. Or you can learn to be a savvy beachcomber, walking among the litter, scouring the sand for shells, scanning the horizon so that you don't overlook prospects for business development. In the pages of this book, I will help you unearth the business opportunities right in front of you. Dig deep enough, and you may discover your own latent entrepreneurial capacity to increase your profitability, resilience, and leadership. All of these half-buried treasures are laid bare by a crisis; they are yours for the taking. Ignoring them is, as Romer says, a waste.

Time is a factor in a crisis. You need to move quickly. I know some believe, as Nietzsche said, that that which does not kill us makes us stronger, but I am a realist: Everyone has a breaking point, as does every small business. In this book I will work with you in two ways, to show you what to *do*, effectively and quickly, to save your practice, but also to suggest how to *be*, so you can stay resourceful and calm. As with my earlier books, I will be speaking to you as though we were in a private conversation, with me as your personal business coach. I will offer examples and ideas gleaned from years of coaching thousands of your colleagues. I will combine a healthy dose of tough love with compassion and optimism. My hope is that this will be the right book for you at a critical time, but also a book to keep on your bookshelf and refer to when needed.

For those readers who have picked up this book but are not faced with a current crisis, reading this for prevention is a wise move. Knowing how to avoid risk and act more strategically helps you stay successful over time. Think of this book as a fire drill—without the danger of smoke and heat at your back, I will show you how to take steps and make changes that can reduce concerns about your future. Regardless of your current situation, I offer you what I believe every small business owner needs: a crisis-proofing plan that can light your way in times of darkness or help you to avert disaster altogether.

TRIAGE

I am a psychotherapist in a solo private practice that I have operated successfully, free of managed care, for over 20 years. Before that I worked for 7 years in the family business, as general manager of a multimillion-dollar scrap metal business, and I also started a few small businesses of my own. In a move to marry my fascination about business with my love of helping people change, a decade ago I began working as a business coach and consultant with an international clientele. From this combined experience in my own private practice, my experience spent coaching others, and understanding the world of small business ownership, I know that in a crisis your job, as the owner of the practice, is similar to a surgeon on a battlefield: you must do triage. You need to do assess the damage, stop the bleeding, stem the worst of the pain, and start treatment where it will help the most. Any crisis is destabilizing; trying to figure out the first steps to take can be bewildering. If your practice is hurting, you need triage in the form of a crisis-proofing business plan.

Being without a business plan is common. During good times, a plan is helpful but not critical. But in a crisis, having some kind of plan is essential, not just to keep the practice afloat but also to keep you, the practice owner, calm. You may be flooded with fear or anxiety. Fear causes a strong fight-or-flight impulse and it's a dangerous impulse for a business owner. Instead, you want to slow down, think clearly, conserve your energy, and take well-considered steps. Having a plan, a way to formulate your thoughts and actions and a way to put the situation in perspective, can make the difference between your practice's success or collapse.

This book comprises a business plan that works well in a time of crisis or can be used as a resource to protect you against crisis. It is comprehensive and addresses the major areas of a business plan: overall direction, finances, marketing, administration, and business positioning within the marketplace. It is easy to understand and implement. But it is different from a traditional business plan in that it has four sequential stages that help you navigate a crisis. Each stage of the plan corresponds to a section of the book. The early stages and chapters of the plan focus on immediate steps to help your practice get on a solid footing quickly; the later stages and chapters consider longer-term ideas and strategies that can help you maintain and sustain an ideal practice over time. You can read the book progressively, stage by stage, to have the complete plan, or you can customize the plan as needed by jumping ahead to the sections that seem most relevant.

Here is an overview of the crisis-proofing plan, stage by stage:

- *Review*: In the first section of the book, we quickly determine your starting place and assess any damage. I will lead you through a streamlined evaluation of your situation, so that you can analyze your assets and liabilities, set and then prioritize your goals. You will read a long case example of the crisis-proofing plan in action to see exactly what is possible to correct and improve in a small business with guidance. In each chapter, I give you exercises to help you take next steps and also to clarify your situation, so that you can see the big picture of your practice within the context of a crisis. Step-by-step, you will learn to regain control of your situation and feel supported.

- *Recommit*: Next we focus on strategies to help you recraft your practice. I explain the ways to minimize risk in a small business and how to break free from unhealthy dependencies that are obstructing profitability. I will show you specific ways to affiliate and collaborate, pursue better opportunities and options, so that over time your practice becomes healthier. We look at your financial situation and how you handle money. I will walk you through the ins and outs of cutting expenses to trim unnecessary fat from your budget, but not starve your practice. Using a crisis-proofing marketing plan, you will see how to generate referrals even in a down market and attract quality clients. We will retool your systems and operations so that your practice management improves and you operate a more efficient business—one that reflects the best of who you are today.

- *Rebrand*: With your practice moving toward a healthier position, it's time to rebrand—to make it more visible. People who need your services have to be able to find you. You will see how to make the best use of the Internet in order to generate clients and develop multiple streams of income. We will refine your future practice direction by analyzing the top four business models for a private practice during a tough economic market. Then you will integrate all the earlier sections and formalize your turnaround plan, setting specific goals to help you move forward and stay motivated.

- *Reinvest*: The final section of the book looks beyond surviving to thriving. I will show you how to build a practice you can sell, not just own, so you can consider retirement options. You will also see how to invest more in yourself, since you (the owner) are the most valuable asset of your practice. We will look at the emotions and beliefs that can sabotage your success; your mind-set is often the difference between going the distance and giving up. With exercises and case examples, I will help you shift from feeling victimized by a crisis to claiming a sense of leadership, empowerment, and choice.

CRISIS-PROOFING MANTRAS

Starting right now, I want you to think about your practice the way a successful entrepreneur thinks: with a balanced combination of optimism and pragmatism. You need some business mantras, short phrases, repeated often, that keep you focused and on track. I have six mantras that my clients hear me say again and again. Each one addresses an important crisis-proofing perspective that I want you to consider before you act.

1. "Focus on Profit, Not Growth"

Profit and growth are not the same. In a crisis, the smart way to operate is to keep your eye on your profit (your income minus your expenses). Stop daydreaming about new ideas and services for new or different markets; come down to earth and think about ways to make your existing practice and services as profitable as possible. Even though you may be bored or yearning for newness, this is not the time to expand impulsively. In a weak market, don't overburden your small business with unnecessary expenses. Adopt a tough love approach to your business spending. The best ways to focus on profit include the following:

Lower input costs: Negotiate to cut expenses on office rent, advertising, supervision or mentoring, printing, mailing, Web site hosting, office equipment, phone lines, and outsourcing billing. Leverage these same expenses by sharing them with colleagues or affiliates.

Increase productivity: What work do you do that is not billed? Begin to examine billing in these areas that involve your time and effort. Set boundaries on your unbilled activity. Increase productivity. What will help you do more with less?

Systemize: Organization is key in being more profitable. Match your business efforts to your business needs. What can you clean out, fix up, delegate, or automate? Start with small steps and make inroads into clutter and filing. See Chapter 7 for ideas and software that can help you run a leaner, more efficient practice.

2. "Small Steps Count"

You are a small business, so the loss of one or two clients can be a hard hit. But the opposite holds true as well—one or two new clients can keep your practice humming. A small increase in savings or a small reduction of spending can make a real difference. Let your small business help you to think in small steps. Consider short-term goals and small action steps. Avoid losing yourself in daydreams of big visions; keep your objectives specific and doable so that you don't get discouraged. Small is beautiful in a crisis. One way to think small is *chunking down*. *Chunking down* is a process-oriented term that means going into detail to find smaller and more specific elements of a system. It's a useful strategy to combat feelings of being overwhelmed, when a task seems too large to comprehend, or a goal is too complex to implement.

For example, rock climbers facing a daunting mountain climb will chunk down the difficult climb to ease both their psychological and physical ordeal. They will mentally divide the huge mountain climb into a series of shorter climbs; it's similar to driving a long distance in your car and, instead of trying to do the drive in one long haul, stopping every few hours to stay refreshed and see the drive as a series of destinations. Try this with your goals. As your mind learns to see a task in smaller elements, you will feel calmer and in better control. You can use a back-and-forth mental process of *chunking up*—seeing the big picture—and then chunking down to manage change and create more understanding and focus for developing an action plan. For example, David Straker (2008) suggests this process:

- Define the problem in one all-encompassing sentence (chunking up).
- Chunk down to find possible project goals.
- Chunk up to review the strategy as a whole.
- Chunk down to build an even better understanding of the relationship of the problem and the steps.
- Chunk up to look for problems in the overall system.
- Chunk down to find specific actions to address.

Here is how this works: A therapist complains of feeling paralyzed. She complains (chunking up): "There is a huge amount of tasks that I need to do for my practice right now. I am overwhelmed." It's time to chunk down to make it manageable. To get her started, I ask her what, specifically, needs doing first. We look at a series of steps and 10 goals for the next 3 months. She gets clearer about the details and begins to feel calmer.

Now we need to review her goals by chunking up, so I can make sure that she is fully on board with this plan. I review by reading her list of goals out loud, for both of us to hear, and then ask: Will this list of goals take care of the problems? She sits quietly and then says that it seems complete, but she is not sure. Time to chunk down again to make sure it more precise. I go over each goal in detail with her and we discuss her steps. After each goal, she says, "I get it. I am clear."

But we are not done yet with this back-and-forth thinking. Time to chunk up one more time. I ask her to get up from her chair, walk around the room, and then come back and look at the plan. "How does it make you feel?" I ask.

"Tired," she says. Uh-oh, a problem with the system: The plan to fix her overwhelm is overwhelming her! We stay chunked up, discussing the big picture of her goals and look for ways to revise it. First, I reverse the order of all the goals, so that number 1 is now number 10 and vice versa. Her take on this? She is somewhat less tired. Then I ask her to order the goals by putting the easiest goals first, hardest last. Her take now? She says she feels energy. Easiset to hardest shifts her motivation from exhaustion to "I can do this."

With the big picture feeling better, we chunk down one more time to finalize her now revised to-do list for just the coming week and to set up the time for the next coaching appointment. This process of chunking down and up, going from big picture to small steps, back and forth, helps her to feel in control and reduce the initial overwhelming feelings and exhaustion.

3. "Don't Resist, Assist"

Change always occurs fastest in a tough environment. History shows that the most difficult survival conditions (think the Ice Age) encouraged the fastest evolution. In the same way, a crisis will force your business (and you) to change faster, just in order to survive. As a result, today's recession is causing a lot of small business owners to play catch-up, as their practices change faster than they are emotionally and psychologically prepared to handle.

How to cope? Stop fighting it. Instead, grease the wheels of your own evolution. As the owner and operator of your practice, help the necessary, inevitable change to take place without the friction of added resistance such as fear, doubt, or anxiety. Of the many therapists and other service providers I coach each month, the ones who are doing the best right now are those who are willing to allow themselves and their practices to change quickly—with their blessing. Darwin said, "It is not the strongest of the species that survive, nor the most intelligent, but the one most responsive to change."

Stop resisting and start getting curious. Look around you to see examples of new, better, easier, smarter ways to operate your practice. What is working for others? Borrow solutions and adapt them to make them fit for your situation. Who are your models for success today? Learn from what others are doing. Business consultant Barry Moltz (2008) wrote that a recession is the time to challenge all of your dearly held business assumptions. "If your business can be done in another more efficient way, then adapt—or die," he said, adding that cockroaches (who are very flexible insects in that they eat almost anything and live almost anywhere—including in the North Pole!) do extremely well in bad times. Darwin would agree.

4. "The Most Flexible Practice Wins"

When I was at an NLP (Neuro-Linguistic Programming) workshop about 25 years ago, the trainer, John Grinder, explained that the most flexible element in a system will have the most influence or choice in that system. For example, during a negotiation, the person who can see more sides to the argument and adopt multiple strategies can get others to a "win-win" agreement faster than a person who can only see one point of view. Flexibility has always been a bonus of being a small business. A private practice can quickly change course, adapt to a new market, stop an unprofitable program, or start up a needed program.

In a recession, flexibility is a key survival strategy. The more choices you have in the way you operate, the greater the chances you will be viable and profitable. That's why I see, over and over, that the most flexible practice wins. Can you dance with the current changes in the market? Flexibility in business is similar to ballroom dancing. Your partner is the economy. You are dancing the tango—but right now the market has the lead. Can you follow, light on your feet, and find ways to stay in the flow? Just because you have operated your practice one way your entire career doesn't mean you have to continue down that same path if it no longer serves a purpose.

EXERCISE: FLEXIBILITY

Pick one area and enhance your practice's flexibility now.

- *Pricing*: Can you lower your price point? How about adding low-cost, very small groups to fill in empty hours? Can you discount those times that don't fill easily? Could you partner with another practitioner to run ads, sharing the expense? Perhaps you can offer a discount for prepaying, or take credit cards to help with the price issue. If pricing is not an area of flexibility for you, how about . . .

- *Accessibility*: Can you add Friday evening or weekend hours to capture more clients? Agree to see clients less frequently and still help them make progress? Turn around new clients to see them within 48 hours of contact? Find additional ways (Internet, social marketing, audiotapes, videotapes) to reach clients from an educational position? If you can't be more accessible, how about . . .

- *Services*: Can you add a new service, see a different population, expand your normal session times from 50 minutes to 75 minutes, offer a menu of services to give your clients more choices, become an independent contractor for a busier office in your off hours, move into a corporate setting with your programs?

Here's how this works: A life coach complains that her practice needs more clients, and I ask about her degree of flexibility. Because her expenses are low (she does not maintain a formal office space and instead works from a home office), she could consider lowering her fee. She does accept credit cards, but decides that she could also offer a discount for those clients who prepay two months' worth of coaching sessions. She can also be more accessible: Although she works primarily by phone with clients, she has had some recent requests for meeting in person at a very busy client's office. This would require her to commute about 30 minutes to get to the client. In terms of services, the life coach is already offering the coaching services for which she feels best trained, so this is an area that will not change; but now she has two other ways (pricing and accessibility) to reach out to clients who may be interested, but not completely sold, on working with her.

A counselor is also considering flexibility for his addictions clinic. He can't budge on prices ("I have done my budget and if I lower or discount my fees, I will not be able to make the profit I need"), and he can't relocate, but he can be flexible when it comes to services. "I am going to offer couples counseling, family sessions, and even play therapy for children." This will become a helpful additional income source.

5. "Stretch, Not Stress"

You are just one small business owner. You are carrying multiple roles and need to have a full life. Although I will recommend many strategies and ideas, no one does all of these at once. This program is not intended to cause more stress—the last thing you need in a crisis. But it may ask you to stretch some, to tolerate a little discomfort as you learn a new way of operating, thinking, or even feeling about your practice in a crisis. For most of us, the opportunities that can help us transform our practices exist just outside our traditional comfort zone. Think about stretching more into new actions. My personal trainer reminds me that when I stretch, I feel a few seconds of discomfort, maybe even pain. But quickly my body adjusts and I can soften into the stretch. When I stress my body, the pain persists and worsens. I have asked too much of my body and caused harm. Don't try to do everything I suggest in this book. Slow down, stay curious, consider all your options, *then* select just one or two changes to start with. Don't go far outside your comfort zone. Select those changes that require a comfortable stretch, not damaging stress.

6. "Detach From Results"

How your business responds to a crisis is not a referendum on who you are as a person, a clinician, or even a business owner. You need to detach from the *results* of your practice building and stay focused on the *process* of practice building. With a small practice, results can take time. You still need to stay in process, work your plan, take action, move forward. Tapping into your internal resources can help you stay in process. Attend to the process of change. Note your starting place today and your goal. But focus on the space between the two points (present and future), which I call "the gap." Observe the qualities of the gap. If the gap is too big, you will get discouraged. If the gap is too small, you won't move enough. If the gap is vague, you will feel confused. If it's too narrow, you will feel constrained. Just like Goldilocks, you will know when the gap between where you are today and where you want to be feels "just right." I find that the perfect-sized gap can become its own motivating force. Try this exercise adapted from my earlier book with coauthor Wendy Allen, *The Business and Practice of Coaching* (Grodzki & Allen, 2005.)

EXERCISE: CLOSE THE GAP

Complete the following exercise to help yourself take initial steps.

- What change is needed now in your practice? Think of a general statement that defines it. (Example: "My practice needs more clients.")
- What is the smallest goal you could set to resolve this? Pay attention to the size of the gap. Does the goal excite you or bore you? (Example of small goal: "I will call one colleague to see if she has any ideas for me.")
- What is the largest goal you could set to resolve this? Pay attention

to the size of the gap. Does the goal seem compelling or impossible? (Example of large goal: "I will contact every physician, attorney, and human resource director in my city within the next 15 days.")

- What's the right-sized goal and gap for you at this time? Evolve by stretching just beyond your normal comfort level, but not so far as to put yourself into a state of stuckness or terror. (Example: "I can send letters of introduction plus a follow-up call to all the family law attorneys within 5 miles of my practice. I actually feel excited about this plan. I can do this without too much anxiety. I have been wanting to meet more attorneys for a while.")
- Anticipate: What will change as you close the gap? Do you see a benefit to evolving this way? (Example: "To make those calls, I will have to verbalize better what I do. I will learn to be less shy when talking about my practice to strangers. That will benefit me as a person, and probably be good for my practice.") If so, close the gap quickly. Write an action plan with next steps. Get moving. Celebrate each win. Get support for every setback. Assist your evolution and change things now.

THE VALUES CONVERSATION

Each week in my coaching practice I hear smart, caring, resourceful therapists grappling with how to cope with the effects of crisis and ending up reviewing what in life and work is most important. These conversations about values are one way to reorient or reprioritize during a difficult time. A psychologist who works with adolescents says: "With my practice in free fall, I have had some time to think about who I am and what I want. I am realizing something essential. This is not the direction I wanted for my practice. Early on in my career, I just began to get referrals from a school for emotionally disturbed teenagers. Within two years I had a waiting list. But I have never really liked this work. It just happened. Now that my client count is falling, I am going to get motivated and build the practice and services I want to offer now."

Another coaching client, an executive coach, has a similar breakthrough: "My husband lost his job and we are making some hard financial choices. We never had a household budget, but now we do. We are talking about all the elephants in the room, all the things that we never discussed when money was flowing. His spending, my nagging, our lack of savings. It has been tense, but we are getting closer as a result. This crisis is making us grow up, as a couple, and get more serious about our future."

When a crisis occurs that threatens your work, your relationships, or your well-being, you can let it bring you back to your core values. What is really important to you? How can you reorient your life and work around these values? Use the following list of values to see what you want to emphasize in your practice.

EXERCISE: CORE VALUES CHECKLIST

Note your top three core values on this list or add your own if it is not shown.

Health	Patience	Contribution
Strength	Fairness	Advocacy
Fun	Compassion	Respect
Sexuality	Freedom	Power
Sensuality	Spirituality	Influence
Love	Service	Honor
Kindness	Sacredness	Trust
Grace	Security	Creativity
Understanding	Home	Invention
Beauty	Family	Openness
Adventure	Community	Imagination
Courage	Partnership	Planning
Risk	Growth	Building
Leadership	Enlightenment	Challenge
Inspiration	Happiness	Discovery
Change	Joy	Learning
Honesty	Support	Self-Expression

Feelings	Peace	Nurture
Nature	Quiet	Wholeness
Action	Calm	Vitality
Rules	Inner Strength	Communication
Persuasion	Intuition	Happiness
Encouragement	Intellect	Profitability
Mastering	Play	Helping Others
Accomplishment	Truth	Family

After identifying your top three values, answer these questions:

- What would a practice and/or a personal life based on these values look like?
- What would need to change about you or about the way you currently operate your practice or live your life?
- How would you, your clients, and others around you benefit from your having made these value-based changes?

FIRST THINGS FIRST

Integrity issues get my first attention as a coach and they need to have your immediate attention as well. Only after they are addressed will I move on with a client to discuss the needs of a practice and then the business owners' wants, such as new carpeting or an updated Web site. Integrity issues are those glaring or subtle cracks in the foundation of your practice that are crisis-oriented and need your first attention. These include financial, clinical, legal, or policy-based concerns that must be resolved to keep the doors open and stay professional, licensed, and legal. Sometimes integrity issues appear like minor cracks in a wall—small enough to ignore, but indicators of the problem underneath. They may appear as inconsistencies, contradictions, or irregularities in your actions or policies that signal that something is wrong on a deeper level. Sometimes your feelings are the first indicators or integrity issues. Feelings of resentment can be a signal that some aspect of your business is on shaky ground. Feelings of secretiveness, shame, or embarrassment about any aspect of your practice often point to real problems. Look at anything that bothers you, anything that feels wrong or "off."

Here is another quick checklist to make sure you are noticing anything that would fall into the integrity category of concern.

EXERCISE: INTEGRITY CHECKLIST

Check the items that are true for you at this time.

Obvious Crisis Indicators

❑ I can't pay my bills.

❑ I will soon be homeless or without an office.

❑ I feel blank or numb when I try to come up with solutions.

❑ I (or my spouse) have a major health issue that is affecting my ability to work.

❑ I am losing money, losing clients, losing sleep, and/or losing confidence.

❑ I don't want to ask for help (supervision, coaching, peers, other experts or consultants.)

❑ I don't have a plan, I don't like to think about the future of this problem, and I just hope for the best.

❑ I haven't been able to pay myself a salary or take money out of the practice for my own use in months.

❑ I make money but not a profit.

❑ When asked how my practice is going, I find myself telling white lies because I feel embarrassed at my lack of success.

❑ My office space is a mess.

❑ I have relationships with clients that my colleagues (if they knew) would think were inappropriate.

❑ I don't bill on time and many of my accounts are months in arrears.

❑ I have no idea what direction my practice will be going one month from now, much less one year from now.

❑ I have no plans for the future, other than hoping I survive in this business.

❑ Talking about my work is a drag.

❑ I am secretly worried about all or some important aspects of my practice.

❑ I won't invest any money to deal with this issue, even though it makes sense to get some help.

❑ This business problem is making me feel quite depressed.

❑ I am isolated and don't have anyone I can talk to.

❑ I feel embarrassed or ashamed that I have this problem.

❑ My practice (or some aspect of it) is worsening and making me feel like a failure.

Subtle Crisis Indicators

❑ I get good advice, but can't seem to follow through on any of it.

❑ I am in a reactive mode, feeling a lot of fear and anxiety, not a proactive mode.

❑ I forget to return phone calls from clients and/or colleagues.

❑ I quote different fees to different clients for the same service, without well-thought-out reasons.

❑ I am behind in my important paperwork—taxes, treatment reports, letters, etc.—and I have no idea when I will get to it all.

❑ I make repeated mistakes with clients, like double booking sessions or making errors on their bills.

❑ I am not clear about my policies regarding missed sessions or cancellations, so I end up being inconsistent.

❑ I am terrified when clients talk about leaving therapy, and I make them feel guilty or defensive when they say they are done.

❑ I have dual or even triple relationships with certain clients.

❑ I barter for my services with others.

❑ Clients call me anytime, night or day. I am always on call.

❑ I can't take a real vacation because my clients can't handle my being gone.

❑ I feel like falling asleep during sessions, I am that bored.

❑ I don't know what my practice earns or what I really make.

❑ I don't rely on anyone else to advise me about business. I prefer to keep my own counsel in all matters.

❑ I'm exhausted, I work too much, and I have too little to show
for it.
❑ I have goals, but I don't follow through on them.
❑ My family, friends, and colleagues are tired of hearing me
complain about the same issues in my work.

INTEGRITY REPAIR

If you checked one or more items in either section of obvious or
subtle crisis indicators, you need to take some corrective measures.
Make a written daily, weekly, and monthly plan to resolve the integrity
break—even a brief list of goals will qualify as a plan—and then follow it. Look at it every day. Modify it. The more structure you put in
place when you are in crisis, the better. This is the time to write a list
of good habits and productive actions that you will take each day and
each week, and then follow them, no matter what.

Along with the plan, you will need willpower, and you get that by
connecting to a higher purpose, via your broadest intention. Review
your list of core values above. In crisis, you will normally feel discouraged; your confidence is shaken. Fear makes us see in tunnel vision,
with a narrow, tight focus. Take time each week to broaden your
perspective and see the big picture, by remembering your intention.
Use affirmations, meditation, professional support, and anything else
that helps you to feel connected. Go for daily nature walks, pray, sing,
chant, draw, find time to be with others. Be as creative as you can for
an hour each day. Use this energy to remotivate yourself on behalf of
your business.

In addition to having a plan and intention, you also need to make a
big commitment to your practice right now, even though you feel like
pulling in and pulling back. Reach out to those who have been through
business ups and downs and can help you put your business back on
track. You may need to let someone from outside your immediate system help you spot integrity breaks—someone in your advisory circle,
a coach, a colleague, supervisor, or even a business-oriented friend.
Join a professional group and go to the meetings. Let others who are

wiser in business help you think through a plan, set goals, and then ask if you can be accountable to them, in order to get yourself and your business back on track. Make whatever changes you need so that your practice has high standards and then notice how you feel and what energy is restored to you. As you proceed with this book, I will offer you specific strategies to address many of the problems you may have checked. But start thinking about what needs to happen right now.

EXERCISE: INTEGRITY ISSUE REPAIR

Fill in these sentence stems, to help you correct any integrity issue.

- *My daily action*: One step I take each day is: _____
- *My intention*: I stay in a positive mind-set by: _____
- *My commitment*: The resources I am giving to my practice are: _____

CONGRUENCE

Crisis or not, therapists and other service professionals in private practice do two jobs at once: You deliver services and you operate the business. Most often, therapists feel split: They love only one of these jobs. To be truly successful in private practice, you need to be congruent and enjoy the practice of your craft *and* the business of your craft. I have identified three premises: Premises are not absolute truths, but if you adopt these premises as though they were true, you can balance your feelings and benefit from the business of therapy.

1. You Are Not Your Business

You may be a sole proprietor in your business and be doing it all— providing the therapy services, paying the bills, even emptying the trash—but I strongly suggest you see your private practice as a separate entity. A major cause of hating business comes from overidentifying with one's practice. You probably have blurred boundaries between yourself and your private practice. In psychological terms, we call this *fusion* and it usually provides great strife.

Imagine that a couple comes into your office and the wife says, "I'm angry at my husband." The husband immediately says, "If you are angry with me, then I am angry with you, too."

The wife says, "What are you angry about?"

The husband pauses, then says, "I'm angry at you because you are angry with me. Whatever you feel, so do I. If you are happy with me, I am happy with you. If you are mad at me, I am mad at you." This is fusion, and it makes a relationship difficult, if not impossible. Everything feels personal.

Fusion and overpersonalizing are the number one reason that therapists hate business. You feel like you and your business are one and the same. You business is full, you feel full and good. Your business is slow, you feel lethargic and empty. To be a better (and happier) business owner, you need to defuse. See your private practice and *relate* to it as a separate entity.

Differentiate yourself from your business. Think of it as a child you birthed who has a lot of you in it but is not you. Your small business has its own needs (much like a perpetual toddler, it is always wanting something from you) and even its own nature and its own (business-like) behavior. As a good parent or good business owner, it's your job to give your business what it needs, but not to confuse its needs with your own.

For example, my business needs between 24 and 27 client hours each week to stay highly profitable. I understand this and try to keep my practice full, in order to give my business what it needs. But I personally don't need to see that many clients and work at that pace in order to be happy. I could spend my days being very happy by seeing only 2 or 3 clients. I keep a fuller schedule for my business's sake. It needs this full schedule to thrive, so if I want to keep my business viable, I do what it takes to keep its calendar full.

My business also has its own nature, which does not match my personal nature. It is much more linear than I tend to be, and moody. It goes up and down. I tend to stay much more even in my mood. My business loses its steam during the summer as clients go on vacation. I don't. Summer is often a time of great energy and productivity for me personally. Seeing the nature of my business accurately helps me not to take its behavior personally. My business is just doing what all businesses, large and small, tend to do. Noting this, I don't need to feel depressed; I just have to plan accordingly. In spring, I increase my marketing so that the summer brings in new clients. I have an ebb and flow strategy, to boost income when the business starts to dry up and to even it out when I get too much activity. As a good business owner, it's your job to give your business what it needs to stay viable, but not to confuse its needs with your own.

EXERCISE: DIFFERENTIATION

Answer the following questions about your practice to become more differentiated.

- What are your various roles in the practice (owner, administrator, janitor, technician, clinician, etc.)?
- Which roles do you prefer? Which would you rather delegate?
- What are the roles that feel most disconnected to you (clinician/bill collector, or administrator/creative development)? How can you reconcile these roles best?
- What defines the nature and behavioral patterns of your practice (seasonal, frequency of ups and downs, hours it operates, need for cash and energy, etc.)?
- What defines your personal nature and your personal behavioral patterns?
- What are the differences between your personal nature and the nature of your practice?
- What will you give to the practice to help it flourish?
- What boundaries do you set so that the needs of the practice don't overwhelm you personally?

2. Your Business Reflects Your Strengths and Weaknesses

Even though you are not your business, your business will mirror aspects of you. For example, if you have strong boundaries regarding time, have always been a prompt person, and manage your time well, this will probably be reflected in your business; your sessions probably start and stop on time; your business calendar is clear and exact. You schedule the weekly administrative tasks and follow through without a problem. If you are very disorganized and live with clutter and chaos, chances are your business mirrors your disorganization. Your paperwork is hard to find and file; your treatment reports are late. If you have a good relationship with money, your business reflects that as well. Your finances are up-to-date and you can talk easily to your clients about fees and their financial responsibilities. You pay your estimated taxes on time without a problem.

Recognizing that your business is a good reflection of you means that when you want to make a change in your business, you may be able to address this change easier by making it in yourself. Now as therapists, some of us are so tired of working on ourselves that we will groan at this, because it signals an AFGO (another frigging growth opportunity). But others of us will see this as a saving grace: "Thank goodness I can work on myself. I know how to do that!"

One of my coaching clients had a goal to find more focus in his practice that was extremely diversified. He had five separate, very small businesses operating under one roof—a publishing company, a therapy practice, a bookstore, a coaching practice, and a clothing store. All of them were doing poorly and he told me that the only solution he could see was to add one more into the mix: a recording studio to help other therapists create and sell podcasts. I disagreed with this idea and tried to get him to see the bigger picture, but he was stuck on it and we had a nonmeeting of the minds.

Rather than trying to work this issue through in the business, I asked him to take a look at what was driving his personal need to diversify this way. The next time he said: "I realized that my problem in business comes from inside me. I am always going in all directions and can't settle on one. This is the story of my life. I have three different academic degrees, have lived in six different states as an adult, and have been in four marriages. I see now that until I work some of this out on a personal level, I won't be able to find a focus for my business." He was wise to see that the easiest path was for him to first work on his own lack of personal cohesiveness, rather than having to try to tame his many-headed business.

EXERCISE: THE FACE IN THE MIRROR

Answer the following questions about your practice to see the reflective nature of your practice.

- What strengths that you possess are reflected in your practice?
- How does this benefit the practice?
- What weaknesses that you possess are mirrored in the practice?
- How does this harm the practice?
- What needs work inside yourself in order to better the practice?
- What are the areas of your practice and yourself that get ignored or that you resist addressing? What patterns do you notice about this that need to change now?
- What are the first steps of your plan to help your practice improve?

3. All Actions You Take in Business Are Fear-Based or Love-Based

In a crisis, fear is in ample supply. Anxiety, worry, and panic are almost palpable. If you feel flooded by these feelings while taking an action for the improvement of your practice, you will resent your practice. For example, you may need to make several marketing "cold" calls to potential referral sources. You do it, unhappily, with a sense of dread, thinking: "If I don't make this call, my practice won't survive. And it's not just making the call. I have to get results, and soon. If this doesn't go well,

I will be out of work for good." Imagine the pressure that kind of thinking places on you as you try to develop professional relationships. Who could love a business that puts them into this kind of a spin?

If you take action from a basis of love, you make the exact same call, but do it from a different perspective. You think, "Yes, the situation is dire, but in this moment I will call this person to let him know how much I love the work I am doing. I will see if there is something I can offer, to not just get but also give. I will suggest a win/win suggestion of how we can support each other since times are hard all over. Even if no results come from this call, I can feel good about making this call. Then I will call the next person and the next." Same action, different basis, different experience of marketing, different feeling about the actions needed to keep a business operating.

According to author Neal Donald Walsch, "Fear is the energy which contracts, closes down, draws in, runs, hides, hoards, harms. Love is the energy which expands, opens up, sends out, stays, reveals, shares, heals" (1996, p. 19). Every time you take action in regard to your practice, see if you can do it from a basis of love—love of self, love of others, love for your business, or love of the profession. This feeling of love makes you feel expansive and openhearted, a good way to proceed in business.

EXERCISE: FEAR TO LOVE

Answer the following questions to help you shift from fear to love.

- What business actions bring up fear?
- How could you do the same action from a basis of love—love for yourself, love for the business, or love of the profession?
- How will it benefit you when you shift from fear to love?
- How will it benefit your practice?

During a crisis, our practices get tested. The market changes, and you will see the results. Remember these three premises. If your practice has fewer clients or less income than you need, you may think that the problem is you—that you are a failure or not smart enough in business. Not true. Every business owner is challenged in a down market. But you can make some internal changes to shore up your practice in various ways. Take those actions from a place of love so that you don't resent the business you have built. Think of your practice as one of many small boats trying to stay afloat in a stormy sea. My goal is that you will know how to set course and sail through these waters. You can survive, find new opportunities for business, and grow stronger.

Now I want you to read Dina's story, a case example of the crisis-proofing plan that is the basis of this book. Through her experience, you will see what is possible and ways to improve your practice, step-by-step.

CHAPTER 2

Crisis-Proofing in Action

For some during a recession, hiring a business coach may seem extravagant. But when Dina left a message on my voice mail late on a Friday afternoon, she sounded determined and desperate. "Lynn, you don't know me, but I have one of your books," she started. "It sits on my nightstand and I have been reading it when I wake up anxious in the middle of the night. As you might imagine, it's bad here in Michigan where I live and work. A lot of my clients lost their jobs and can't afford to see me each week, so my client count is way down. I am trying to stay calm, but if I can't shore up my practice soon, nothing will be left. Please help me!"

At our first phone-coaching session, Dina told me she'd been working as a marriage and family therapist and seeing individuals for 17 years. "I take some insurance and used to work a caseload of about 25 client-hours a week. But this week, I saw only 11 clients, and last week, 8. I'm really worried," she sighed. "I need help *yesterday!*"

I explained to her that engineering a turnaround in her practice would take time, but if she could commit herself to business coaching every other week for the next 4 months, I felt confident that she could greatly improve her practice. My coaching plan for her included the four distinct phases mentioned in the previous chapter: review, recommit, rebrand, reinvest.

REVIEW: TAKING AN HONEST INVENTORY

During the review process, we needed to assess Dina's practice quickly. I asked about her overall profit picture: gross income, expenses, net profit. What was her biggest expense each month and why? Which services were the most profitable? Which the least? How long did the average client stay with her? What was her average fee per hour? How much time did she spend on unpaid tasks (answering phone calls, doing administrative work, taking notes)? What was the breakdown in profits between those who paid with managed care or insurance and those who paid out of pocket? Dina's initial response was what I expected: *she didn't know.*

"I really don't track these things, Lynn. I wait until tax season for my bookkeeper to tell me the bad news," she joked.

This was her first piece of homework, I said: to get to know her practice inside and out. I requested that she use any type of system that made it easy for her to produce an overview of her practice—software-generated reports, paper-and-pen analysis, a spreadsheet—so she could learn where her practice stood today and track the progress of our work during the next 4 months.

I likened her disregard of this practice information as a form of dissociation: "Dina, you won't be comfortable taking action if you feel you don't have enough information to make the right choices." She promised to have the analysis completed by our next session and put a positive spin on the work required: "It'll keep me busy when I have no clients to see."

I knew from experience that this first step—setting up a process for tracking her practice, even as she felt it was falling apart—would be both informational and motivational. A therapist I was already coaching had just reported that tracking clients on a spreadsheet allowed her to see, in black and white, that she'd been shifting the balance away from managed-care clients toward private-pay clients. Without keeping track, she'd have been too anxious to follow a plan that might cost her *any* clients, especially during the early months, when the ratio between managed care and private pay was barely moving.

At Dina's next session, she reported her financial news, much of which proved distressing. Her income, client count, and referral base were all seriously down. I saw the full picture of her problems, but I needed to help her define her business strengths. As with most therapists, she protested that she had none: "I'm awful at business, and I hate marketing! Please don't ask me to make any cold calls."

I quickly put her at ease. "Great! I'm glad you told me that. Please don't do anything that gets you too far out of your comfort zone. I want you to stretch some, but not get stressed. Let's look at what you're already doing and good at, in regard to your business."

With questioning from me about a range of ordinary business activities, Dina began to identify her strengths. She liked to have her office clean and well organized, enjoyed tidying her desk, and took pleasure in paying attention to detail with her calendar and files. "I've written thank-you notes to every referral source over the past 10 years and kept track of them all," she added. *Aha!* I thought, *an untapped resource we'll use later!* By the end of our second session, we had a clear snapshot of her challenges and strengths as a business owner. We were ready for the next step: developing a custom-designed turn-around plan to which she could commit herself.

RECOMMIT: FORMULATING A TURNAROUND PLAN

Before playing with the nuts and bolts of the plan, I wanted to be sure Dina had the energy and commitment to execute it. Clearly, she was exhausted: She'd been working for more than 17 years and had just come through a discouraging year. Was she really up to carrying out a comprehensive business-turnaround plan? Or would it be better for her to find another career? Before we ended the second session, I asked, bluntly: "Why do you want to be in private practice at this point? Is it for the money? your clients? your mission? or fear of doing anything else?"

"Lynn, I've always loved having my own practice because it's *mine*, and I really love the work I do as a counselor," she said. "Being my own boss allows me to work directly with my clients. I wish I didn't need to accept managed care, because that gets in the way of my work, but at least I can be in charge of whom I see, why and how I work with them, and what direction the counseling will take."

"What's it worth to you to stay autonomous?" I pressed. Dina paused for a full minute, and I could hear her breathing quietly. "It's worth everything to me," she said. We both heard the commitment in that statement.

During the next few months, I'd find myself returning to this statement several times to remind her of what was at stake and help her keep going when she felt lonely, drained, or burned out. As a business coach, I try to work within a partnership model, rather than adopting the authoritative attitude of a business consultant.

At our next session, starting the second month of our coaching, I wanted Dina to take ownership of any plan we created: "After last month's review, how would you identify the major source of weakness in your practice?" Dina said that after studying her finances, the spreadsheets, and the clients she saw, she thought the major problem was how complicated her practice was—how many different services she offered. She was spread too thin; she wasn't well-enough known as an expert in one or two areas for people to think of her for specific kinds of work. Also, she said, there were things she loved doing—weekend, personal-growth workshops, body-psychotherapy training—but they took up time and energy, and made almost no profit.

Dina's parenting consultations and couples counseling sessions were her most profitable services. Over the past decade, she had developed a small reputation in her local community as a couples counselor. To help her focus her work around only those services that were profitable and backed by her reputation, I asked her to stop her weekend personal-growth workshops altogether (they rarely filled and took days of preparation) and to eliminate the body-psychotherapy training and methods she used (a distraction to her brand) and, instead, keep open more slots for couples counseling sessions. I suggested she continue to make time for one unprofitable service that still fit her focus: Dina taught parenting classes each semester for her local county recreation center. I would show her how to enroll clients from her teaching during the rebranding stage, to make this a better marketing tool.

With her focus on services in place, we planned her budget. Looking at her past expenses, I asked her to defend each expense as necessary to the practice. All unnecessary expenses were eliminated. We examined and wrote down all the small and large changes she needed to make, with a timeline for implementing them. We worked with a 6-month timeline for accomplishing all her changes, since she needed to show progress as soon as possible. We looked at her systems to see which she could automate to reduce her administrative time. Small businesses have advantages over large companies in that they can turn on a dime, making decisions and changes quickly, without having to pierce layers of bureaucracy. I asked Dina which areas of her practice were flexible enough to change in ways that would provide better "customer service" and more choices to clients, and she identified four:

Payment: She received payment from three insurance panels, but half of her clients paid out of pocket. For those clients, she added the capacity to take credit cards and, for those who paid for 3 months of therapy up front, she created a discount payment package.

Services: The usual couples session was 90 minutes. She added a 60-minute option for a reduced price.

Frequency: Sessions could be as often as once a week, or spread out to once a month.

Location: Since Dina's office was in a suburban area, she sublet space in a downtown office one evening a week, so that instead of asking clients to come to her, she could go to them.

These steps provided the appeal of consumer-based choices to potential clients. Dina liked this plan and was eager to implement it. She agreed to track the finances and other measurable aspects of her practice so she could see the progress she was making. To offer emotional support, I set up a series of weekly check-ins by e-mail between our coaching sessions so she could, as she said, "feel that she had her coach at her back."

REBRAND: MARKETING A UNIQUE SELLING POINT

Now it was time to develop a marketing plan to promote the business model. Dina needed to increase income quickly and attract the most profitable clients to her retooled practice. But, again, some preparation was required. I asked her to sum up, in a sentence or two, who she was and what she offered. This simple piece of articulation, which I call a "basic message," is at the core of branding. It's the most difficult task for therapists and others who sell invisible, intangible services. In her message, I needed Dina to define her USP—her unique selling point. What about her services made her different from the competition?

After much thought, Dina e-mailed me her basic message: *I offer short-term counseling for couples with long-term results. Whether couples want help fixing their marriage or parenting their children, we move forward on their goals quickly.* I complimented her on the clarity of this message and the USP of brief, goal-oriented therapy, but I suggested she include a sentence highlighting the flexibility of her practice. She added: *My practice offers a variety of services, pricing packages, and locations in which I can see you. I strive to stay flexible so we can work together successfully, even during these tough economic times.*

Now she needed low-cost business materials to emphasize her message. She highlighted the phrase "short-term counseling for couples with long-term results" as the slogan beneath her name on her business cards and brochure, which she produced within a day on VistaPrint.com, an online do-it-yourself printer. Next it was time to utilize one of Dina's untapped resources: the referral sources to which she'd sent thank-you notes but never contacted further. I asked her to list each source, when each had last sent her a client, and the results of her work with the client. Then she drafted a letter to each source, to be followed up with a phone call. I helped her write a script for each call to reconnect with the source, ending with a request for business: "I have some openings in my practice right now and prefer to fill them with clients who come from referral sources I trust, such as yours."

Dina set a goal of 10 letters and follow-up phone calls each week. She was nervous and hesitant, but I reminded her of her commitment and what she'd said—that her practice was "worth everything" to her. My job was to hold her accountable, and she reported to me each week by e-mail about how the calls were going. It was hard and awkward the first week and better the second week, and she got one "great" response the third week—a potential affiliation with a law office to train their staff about difficult marital dynamics during custody depositions. By the fifth week, she'd gotten two new clients from referrals.

She then updated her Web site, using simple optimizing techniques to draw more traffic. I showed her how to "enroll" clients (persuade audience members to become paying clients) when she taught parenting classes—not by promoting herself, but by demonstrating her skills with parents from the front of the room. She'd been playing the role of teacher, but now I encouraged her to act in her true professional role, that of therapist.

REINVEST: EMPOWERING THE BUSINESS OWNER

Even during a recession, a business needs an infusion of money and energy. Administrative, phone, billing, and computer-tracking systems all need continual upgrades. For Dina, the most important area of investment concerned her health and well-being. Like many therapists in private practice, she worked and worried long hours; she suffered from compassion fatigue—a lack of physical and psychological self-care that's common among caregivers. She was isolated as a solo entrepreneur and had little collegial business support.

I asked her to select each week an item from a self-care checklist (see below) to accomplish as a way of maintaining her emotional and physical resilience. I also asked her to let go of nonessential activities—resign from volunteer positions, for example—while we worked together. Building a practice is hard and time-consuming work, and I wanted her to have some breathing space.

After 4 months of coaching, much was accomplished, with still more to do. During this period, Dina lost three clients through attrition, but gained eight new clients, all of whom were, in her words, "good clients—couples ready to work and invested in their therapy." She'd had her first meeting with the law firm about training lawyers to understand and cope with the dynamics of couples in custody battles, and she'd reconnected with three dozen old referral sources. She felt excited and empowered that she was taking clear actions. Because her practice remained less profitable than it needed to be, I encouraged her to begin saving money for a cash reserve to help reduce her financial risk.

Dina was galvanized by the recession to retool her business to survive, but her plan would help her stay profitable, even when economic times improved. She learned how to assess her situation, prioritize her services, find a focus, cut unnecessary expenses, develop better referral sources, and systemize and manage administrative tasks. She took steps to build her brand and her connection within the public and professional community. She managed, with support, to stay calm, resilient, and clearheaded, so she could continue to take action in a planned way rather than a chaotic one. Most important of all, she felt a new sense of confidence in herself because she now knew that, rather than see her practice wither away, she had the business skills and entrepreneurial mentality to continue building it up, in spite of gloomy economic forecasts.

SELF-CARE

Dina focused on the need to take care of herself while she took care of her practice. This is a good time for you to begin this practice as well. You are the primary asset of your practice. Use the following checklist as a reminder for the process of extreme self-care. Find two items from the self-care survey that you have not checked. Work on them this month. Define the specific action steps necessary to achieve each item. For instance, if you want to work on the item "I rarely rush," what specific actions do you need to take this month to make this true?

EXERCISE: SELF-CARE CHECKLIST

Check those items that are true for you. A majority of these items checked indicates that you have ample care of self; checking less than half means that you will need to improve your self-care, to have the energy you need to enhance your business.

❑ I get a good night's sleep each evening.

❑ I eat foods that promote my physical well-being.

❑ I exercise several times each week to stay flexible and resilient.

❑ I have quiet time each week for myself, doing things I love, so that I feel refreshed.

❑ I have friends and family who I can talk to whenever I need a sense of connection.

❑ I make time each week to engage in activities that give me pleasure.

❑ I live in a home that feels nurturing, safe, and pleasing.

❑ I get all my personal needs met outside of my practice.

❑ I am on a strong financial track.

❑ I get clinical supervision, peer support, and business consulting/coaching as needed.

❑ I actively seek solutions for the complaints I have regarding my life and my work.

❑ I maintain a high level of personal and professional integrity.

❑ I know how to forgive and/or feel compassion for myself and others who have hurt me in the past.

❑ I let go of my guilt over my past mistakes.

❑ I keep clear, consistent boundaries regarding my personal and professional life.

❑ I rarely rush; I go through my day being on time.

❑ I have a reserve (more than enough) of money, time, friends, space, love, and information, fun, and affection.

❑ I carry the insurance and protection systems I need to feel and stay safe and protected.

❑ I take action based on feelings of love instead of feelings of fear.

❑ I am part of a community that gives me a sense of purpose.

❑ I live a life based on choice and meaning.

In the following chapters, I will take you through the same steps that I guided Dina, but in more depth and with more customization, so that you can find the best path and plan for your practice. Are you ready to get started? It's time to begin the review by taking an honest inventory.

CHAPTER 3

Taking an Honest Inventory

Depending on your background, the concept of taking inventory may be either a business or a moral task. Those who have worked in business know that taking inventory means the tedious and exacting task of checking on goods sold versus those that are still stored in inventory. But participants in a 12-step program know the phrase from the internal rigors of the 4th step: taking inventory of one's flaws to be accountable for one's current situation in life.

For our purposes, I want you to take an inventory that combines the best of these two concepts: I want you to become part accountant, part accountable. I want you to know the ins and outs of the finances of your practice. But I also want you held accountable for the strengths and weaknesses of your business. This is not punishment, although some of you may be groaning and ready to lay this book down right now, frustrated with what I ask. Instead, think about this as being a camera. You are going to record, in an unemotional but accurate snapshot, the truth of your practice as it stands today. Only you can do this task. To complete this first step in your recession-proofing process, the review process, you need to step back, with a quiet, courageous attitude, and note (on paper) the realities about your private practice.

I will ask questions that direct you where and how to look, but the process of looking carefully and closely, without fear or judgment, is yours. Honesty relieves stress. Relieve your stress by knowing what is true for you today: the energy your practice holds, even if it is untapped; the financial power you have, even if it is small; and the potency of your assets and strengths as the business owner. Our goal is to gather information and then analyze some key points, to know what actions and plans need to be put into place to help position your practice to ride out the economic storm.

So please, get curious. When was the last time you took an honest inventory of yourself, your life, and your business? What would you learn about yourself and your practice if you looked at your current situation with open eyes? I want you to recognize what you already have in place, as well as what you lack, so you can make good decisions about what you do and don't need to change. The first is the Strong Start Survey. I ask everyone I coach to fill out the Strong Start Survey, because it helps me to quickly understand patterns and clues that explain each person's current situation in private practice. As I read over a Strong Start Survey, I group the answers into four major topics: energy level, motivation, direction, and action.

EXERCISE: THE STRONG START SURVEY

Answer each question fully. Take your time.

1. Where do you get your energy from?
2. Where are you most personally limited?
3. What do you love about your work—being a therapist, coach, healer, consultant, or other type of service provider? What are your unique strengths and talents? What is going well in your work right now? What are you proud of in regards to your work?
4. What motivates you to take action?
5. What challenges and problems regarding your practice are you currently facing?
6. What challenges and problems regarding your personal life are you currently facing?
7. Of these challenges, which need attention immediately? Which are low priority that can be corrected over time?
8. What are the five business opportunities that you are currently not making the most or anything of?
9. What are the 10 goals you want to accomplish in the next 90 days?

10. If you have an existing support system (friends, colleagues, mentor, coach, peer group, etc.), what should they know about you in order to best understand the challenges you face now? How can they best support you (strong feedback, gentle encouragement, listening, direct suggestions, advice, accountability)?

EVALUATING YOUR STRONG START SURVEY

I want you to go back through your survey and evaluate it based on four criteria: energy, motivation, direction, and action. For assessing your energy level, look over the answers to Questions 1, 2, and 6 and think about your current energy level. Is your work listed as a source of energy in your life? Are your limitations draining you? What are you doing, or will you consider doing, to build your energy as you get ready to build your business?

For example, Tom, a psychologist with a group practice in Arizona, sent me his Strong Start Survey. In our first conversation, he told me that I would find his problems obvious. He had poured everything into this practice, which employed six other therapists, but in today's market, he could not make it profitable. He paid the other therapists, but had not drawn a salary for himself for over 6 months. "My wife says that my practice is basically a nonprofit or my personal charity. I work for free to support my staff and my clients."

I listened carefully to how he answered the three questions that pertain to energy level. Under Question 1: Where do you get your energy from, he wrote: *I don't know. I am tired all of the time.* Under Question 2: Where are you personally limited, he wrote: *I don't understand why I can't make this practice work. I try the best I can. I guess I am not good enough.* Under Question 6 regarding personal challenges, he wrote: *I have sunk all my time, money, and energy into this business. It is failing and I think that is representative of me. I am a failure as well.*

My first question to Tom was to ask him why he was taking the failure of his business so personally. "Tom, if you didn't give your car the right kind of gas, who would be to blame when it wouldn't run?"

He bristled at this. "Well, whose fault is it when my business is ailing? I am not one to blame others or the economy. If I had the goods, this would work."

I stuck by my point. "I don't think it is a problem of you not being capable. I think you are missing the needed fuel to take care of things. When was the last time you had a good night's sleep or spent a day without thinking of the office?"

When work drains you, you need a way to recharge. A business in a recession is like a hungry, needy toddler. You can't put a smile on its face if you, as the parent, show up exhausted, angry, and without personal resources. As strange as Tom found it, my first coaching request was that he remember how to recharge himself and to begin gathering energy. This included finding the aspects of his work that energized him in previous years. He loved working with clients, but had let that go as the administrative needs grew. I asked him to take walks each day, take long time-outs when he put the needs of the business on hold, and to reclaim his passion for his work by taking on a few clients. During the walks he thought about himself, his goals, and his life. He began to shift his perspective and see the big picture. His practice, while problematic, was not the totality of his life. As he began to feel lighter and more optimistic, he was in much better shape to begin the hard work of rethinking the practice.

To see your motivation, look at Questions 3 and 4, which explain a person's natural motivation, passion, and current success, important components for fueling further change. What helps you to take action? Does your love for your work help motivate you to build your practice? If not, why not? Are you motivated primarily by fear? What positive motivators can you add to your list?

For example, if you feel passionate about baseball and are motivated by competition, I will want you to use that sporting energy to help you design a gamelike quality to your practice-building efforts, perhaps keeping score and competing against yourself so that you stay naturally motivated and passionate about your efforts. Like many entrepreneurs, Tom was motivated by creating new things, but in his practice he had little novelty. With the recession inhibiting his ability to start new projects, his motivation waned even further. Part of his plan would need to include some novelty to help him find the motivation to go forward. I hoped this would happen as he adopted a new business model, one that could be more profitable in the current market.

Questions 5, 7, and 8 are strategic questions that help formulate the direction for you to take in the short- to midterm. What challenges and tasks do you need to attend to and clean up in the short term, to make more space for your bigger business goals? What do you think the short-term direction of your practice will look like? What opportunities are you ready to pursue this month?

These questions pinpoint what needs to get done now, including what opportunities are right in front of you that you tend to overlook. Tom had a long list of challenges that needed immediate attention, including addressing the unequal payment plan that allowed him to pay his independent contractors but not pay himself. He also had a good business opportunity that he had been slow to pursue: to bring in a business partner, who had a lot of energy, experience, and motivation and was willing to add some much-needed cash to the practice. Together, we began to prioritize the steps of evaluating the partnership agreement.

Questions 9 and 10 define your 3-month goals, the specific actions you will take, and the support you need to take them. Will these goals add to your sense of energy or do you get tired just looking at the list? If it's the latter, add to and change that list so that you have some goals that create a feeling of energy within you, even if the goals are not directly related to building your practice. Your level of energy and desire will be contagious, and it will assist in your ability to achieve the harder goals. What support system do you have in place, or could you begin to put in place, to help you take action for your business? How do you best like to receive support? Prioritize your list of 10 goals from easy to difficult. List the easiest ones first and commit this month to achieving the 3 *easiest* goals.

FOLLOW THE MONEY, HONEY

Even those of you who hate talking and thinking about finances must have guessed that a part of the review would be about money. First, here are the business terms we will be using for this review:

Gross income or *revenue*—all of the money that you earn in your practice.

Expenses—the costs you incur from doing business. There are two types of expenses I will look at with you:

- *Direct expenses*—the essentials that must be in place to allow you to run your business (office space rental, utilities, telephone, licensing, supervision, billing, accounting, postage, supplies, malpractice insurance, self-employment tax, etc.).
- *Indirect expenses*—those expenses that you may write off to the business that are nonessential, but helpful (travel, publications, office decorations, meetings, conferences, etc.). Some therapists have low direct expenses (they work out of their home, employ no staff, don't advertise, have few equipment needs) and others have more overhead (high rent and utilities for multiple offices, advertising budget, direct-mail campaign, staff, billing service, subcontractors to pay, equipment).
- *Net income* or *profit*—what's left of your revenue after you pay your direct and indirect expenses.

Your next steps include:
1. Look at your financial data to determine your profit or loss to date (for this year).
2. Measure this against your profit or loss from last year.
3. Analyze your data.

Now some of you are going to be stuck on Step 1 and are thinking, what financial data? If you don't have immediate access to evaluate your profit and loss, this is the most important step of all. You will need some type of accounting program in place so that you can see your budget and the profit picture of your business at a glance. You can do this with software or just a pencil and a ledger, but you must have information about your practice finances to keep it recession proof. Itemize your data so that you can see, on a weekly and/or monthly basis, how much money you earn in all categories of services and how much you spend and for what items.

Table 3.1 gives you some recommended guidelines for tracking your expenses as a percentage of your total revenue. Most small business owners create a monthly report, so that they can see the arc of their earnings month by month. An annual report, retained in your records, will allow you to analyze your income against previous and future years.

TABLE 3.1

Sample Basic Business Budget

Income	
Clients sessions including:	
Individual	
Groups	
Classes	
Consulting	
Reports	
Speaking	
Workshops	
Product sales (audiotapes, books, etc.)	
Other income:	
Total Income	
Expenses	
Accounting	
Advertising	
Automobile	
Books and publications	
Cleaning	
Consultants	
Dues	
Education	
Equipment	

Furnishings	
Insurance:	
Malpractice	
Disability	
Medical	
Landscaping	
Meals/Entertain	
Parking	
Phone and Internet	
Postage	
Printing	
Repairs and maintenance	
Rent	
Salaries	
Supplies	
Taxes and licenses	
Training	
Travel	
Utilities	
Web site	
Other	
Total Expenses	
Net Income or Profit (or Loss)	

EXERCISE: ANALYZE THE NUMBERS

Answer these questions to help you make sense of your data.

- What services are most profitable for you?
- Which are least profitable?
- How much time do you spend in your practice that is not billable time (answering phone calls, administrative tasks, writing, etc.)?

- What financial cycles does your practice go through each year (highs and lows)?
- If you wanted to increase your profit by 10 percent, what line items of income need to increase?
- If your want to decrease your expenses by 10 percent, what line item expenses could I eliminate?
- When was the last time you raised your fees?
- What was the best month for you last year? What was the worst month?
- When should you plan to take your vacation time based on your business plan?
- How long does the average client stay with you?
- What does the average client yield in terms of income and profit?
- What is your average hourly fee?

ASSETS AND LIABILITIES

Next I want you to list your assets and liabilities. *Assets* mean:

- your physical business belongings (property, furniture, money, equipment, client list, and
- anything else of a real, tangible nature)
- your resources of people (network, referral sources, contacts)
- your materials (programs, advertisements, manuals, written policies, newsletters)
- your products (books, handbooks, audiotapes, workshops, seminars, talks)
- your reputation (credentials, affiliations, connections, perceived value).

Liabilities mean:

- debt
- unmet responsibilities

- clients who are a financial or emotional drain on the practice
- poor business policies or a lack of policies
- any real, situational issues that must be dealt with for you to stay safely and ethically in business.

As you list your liabilities, think about what worries you the most late at night when you can't sleep. List those worries that are real and concrete here. They might include: no cash flow, lack of equipment, inadequate billing system, money owed, issue with co-therapist, no plan for future, big credit card bill, or not enough referral sources.

Also note your "gains" and "drains." *Gains* mean:

- all of your personal strengths
- everything about you or your business that could be seen as an advantage, benefit, or resource, even if you don't currently take advantage of it. This is where you can list the intangibles, such as "optimism" or "persistence." Include your level of physical well-being and overall resilience, if that is a gain.

Drains mean:

- intangible aspects (vague feelings, concerns, worries) about yourself or your business that reduce or restrict your rate of progress. intangibles may be existing or projected, such as "lack of self-confidence" or "nervous that i will look foolish."
- current circumstances or problems that sabotage your efforts. Drains may be physical or situational, such as "dealing with chronic back pain" or "no time available in a too-busy schedule for marketing."

YOUR TIMELINE FOR CHANGE

No plan can work without a timeline. You need to decide, given your resources (energy, money, support, time, staff, etc.) when each goal needs to be completed. The crisis-proof plan in this book works on a faster timeline because of the crisis nature of many practice situations, but you may need to adjust your goals to your specific circumstances. Some practice owners have more time to spend on their plan and the results happen faster. Others need to go slowly and balance the changes with other priorities in their lives. Sometimes there are extenuating conditions (intense competition, breaking into a new market) that can slow down results. But in general, I would expect to see a practice owner with a practice that needs clients and more profits making changes according to the following timelines:

- Within the first 3 months, I want to see evidence of those individual actions that the practice owner can control: better review of business, improved organization of finances and paperwork; attention to business identity—brochure, Web site, business cards); a working budget in place that keeps track of income and expenses; a regular practice of stress reduction and self-care—exercise, meditation, time in nature. As the coach, I look for internal changes in the attitude of the business owner and a sense of calm as we develop a crisis-proof plan. I may not see any evidence of new business at this point, but I hope to see that the business owner is trying new behaviors, inside and outside the practice.
- Six months into the plan, I look for evidence of new business: With increased networking and a marketing plan, the business owner should have new contacts and an expanded community; we usually see new referrals and opportunities for affiliation or partnership. The practice is usually more profitable at this point and running leaner due to cost cutting—reducing or sharing expenses. I see changes in the practice owner as she becomes more focused and confident in her business acumen. Often the practice is up by at least 10% in income and down by the same amount in expense. The rise in income may be due to seeing the same number of clients but increased by a rise in fees, new clients from marketing efforts, or additional services or products that are in place.

- Nine months into the plan, I expect that the practice is operating with a crisis-proof direction based on one of the Ansoff business models (see Chapters 10 and 11); the practice owner has a number of new behaviors in place that are repetitive—marketing, networking, producing new income streams. The practice is profitable and administratively easier. The owner shows enhanced status— she feels good about her changes and empowered by her efforts. Just like a baby, in 9 months the new, crisis-proof practice has been born.

Achieving this timeline often requires coaching or working with a peer group. The practice owner needs to track changes, take consistent action steps, stay accountable, process obstacles and inevitable setbacks, and then just keep going. I have seen hundreds of "reluctant entrepreneurs"—therapists, healers, coaches, consultants, and other non-business-oriented professionals achieve this timeline with the support of coaching, and witnessed their delight that they can control the outcome of their practices, even in a difficult market.

CHAPTER 4

The Big Picture

Maybe you wear eyeglasses, as do I. Instead of struggling with different pairs of glasses for distance viewing, midrange viewing, and reading, I sighed with relief when I found that one pair of eyeglasses could offer multifocal or progressive lenses that adapt to each type of sight. In tough economic times, you need clarity in three distinct areas.

- *The big picture*: Scan the horizon to see how the society at large and your community are responding to the economy, so you can anticipate trends and determine your next move.
- *The fine print*: Focus close at hand, to keep an eye on your business operations and data, to make sure that you are organized and on task.
- *Between the lines*: Using self-reflection, check in with your personal thoughts and feelings. You want to know if, under stress, you are behaving well, taking appropriate action, or procrastinating based on fear or anxiety.

I want you to be able to switch back and forth with this type of business perception. See the big picture by looking at trends that are happening in your profession to stay current and position your practice. Shift focus to note your practice closer at hand: Are your bills paid this week, calls returned, clients invoiced? Then note your feelings: Any intuitive sensations, gut reactions, emotions, beliefs, or attitudes that need attention? What follows is a further exploration into these three ways of seeing to help you further review your practice.

SPOT TRENDS

In a crisis, what you can (or can't) determine about the future—of your profession, the local region in which you practice, or society at large—will directly affect your ability to stay viable. The way to see into the future is to learn to spot trends. Trends are not wishes about reality. Trends are an extension of current reality—changes in the world that are determining the course of our lives. Look at what is already happening around you and mentally follow it to a logical conclusion. How will this present reality look 6 months or 1 year from now? Trends are not fads. A fad is a momentary interest in something new, a flash in the pan that won't last. Trends are broad movements, sometimes subtle at first, but eventually they pick up momentum and shape daily life. Today's trends are not optimistic ones; but even bad economic times require that we stay conscious, to anticipate how to respond. Since many readers combine services and work within multiple and diverse roles, I offer summaries of macro trends as well as professional trends in psychotherapy, coaching, and consulting.

First, the macro trends. We might call 2009 the Age of Anxiety. Gerald Celente, author of *Trends 2000* (Celente, 1998), is one of the more extreme predictors of bad news. His Trends Research Institute alerted readers to an impending economic crisis he named the "Panic of '08" in 2007. What does he see for the future? "The Collapse of '09," which in turn will spiral into worse economic conditions. He predicts that we will all be on a spending diet, an "economic Slim-Fast." According to Celente, medicine may become more hands-on for patients and clients, as the consumer model turns into a do-it-yourself affair with more focus on education and self-help. Celente sees trends that indicate that selling will get localized, with a move away from large shopping centers toward a resurgence of small-town commerce. Finally, he predicts that escapism will prevail. We will lift our spirits via entertainment; drugs, and alcohol will be big business and major pastimes.

Another view of macro trends is offered by Faith Popcorn, popular trend-spotter, author, and consultant for an impressive list of major corporations. Popcorn predicted that we will face a year marked by unprecedented fear, anxiety, and uncertainty (Popcorn, 2009). She proposed a new set of priorities: changing the power relationship with big companies to shift from consumer mentality to citizen responsibility. Popcorn forecasted that businesses that demonstrate empathy through an understanding of the consumer plight will survive best. "It's going to be a combination of messaging, price, and purchase continuity programs that offer progressive refunds, as just a few examples. The strategy is simple—be with them when they're down; they'll remember you when they're up"

What these trends may mean for your practice: If these predictions are correct, you will have a large market for your services who need help and empathy to deal with their feelings of anxiety, fear, and anger. Services that are easily understood, and build community and continuity among your target market are a good bet. Staying creative and flexible in how you offer services will also be key to attracting clients. A top 10 trend list of macro trends cited at the Internet blog *Toptrends* cites "anxiety" as number one. People will need help staying calm. But Toptrends' list includes other issues that will play to your services: an increase in anger, a desire to get back to basics, unplugging from technology, and longing for community building.

Now let's look at some specific professional trends that reflect the current crisis.

TRENDS FOR PSYCHOTHERAPISTS

Spending on health care, which is not a luxury for most, is not recession-proof. Although 1 in 2 Americans has a diagnosable mental disorder in any given year, fewer than half of all adults and one third of children seek help. Not all of this is recession-based. The public acceptance of mental health treatment is low; too many fear treatment or consider it taboo. Mental health therapists in the United States have been in a professional recession since 2000, according to at least one survey, as the demand for services is dropping. Since 2000, the reliable *Psychotherapy Finances* survey has tracked a 22% loss in income for social workers and counselors. Not even psychologists' earnings are keeping pace with the low inflation. Managed care has severely cut its spending for mental health. In 1992, insurance dollars for mental health services were 10% of managed care's budget. In 2007, insurance dollars for mental health services have dropped to 1.5%, according to insurance experts.

But incomes vary for those in private practice. Therapists in large metropolitan areas on the East and West Coast are doing better financially, as they are more protected from the incursions of managed care, with more white-collar workers. Many in small towns and in the middle of the country are having a very difficult time. Expenses of a private practice are up. The average therapist in private practice still spends 30% to 50% of income on direct expenses of running the practice (rent, utilities, dues, staff, billing, etc.).

Competition among mental health professionals is up. With 30,000 new social workers graduated each year, statistics point to a pool of 500,000 psychotherapists (social workers, psychologists, counselors) in the United States, of whom 60%–70% work in private practice. While some in private practice will close up shop due to hard times, a large percentage of therapists are in practice part-time, as a second or third profession, and not dependent on their practice for their family income. There is more bad news for therapists as we look at three additional trend lines.

The first trend line is our age. We're a graying profession. The average age for a marriage and family therapist (MFT) is 56, and the average age for a social worker is 50. Our profession attracts those seeking a second or third career. As a result, many regard their practice as something between a hobby and a way station to retirement, and they are less likely to embrace technical innovations that improve efficiency. The second trend line is our demographics. Where have all the men gone? In most professions, feminization means a lowering of pay, and, unfortunately, that's been true of psychotherapy. A survey of the profession in 2000 found female MFTs reporting incomes of 59% of their male counterparts, down from 99% 3 years before. Female psychologists' incomes dipped during that period, too, from 91% of men's in 1997, to

78% in 2000. One reason for this trend is that male clinicians negotiate more aggressively with insurance companies and EAPs (employee assistance programs), charge self-pay clients more, and work more hours per week than their female counterparts. The third trend line is our view of our work. Many therapists in private practice wrestle internally with the question of whether psychotherapy is a vocation or an occupation. Is what we do a service (assisting those less fortunate) or a business (selling our skills for a profit)? To resolve these problems, we need to rethink our philosophy about the business of therapy.

What this means for your psychotherapy practice: Today, more than ever, therapists do not have the luxury of ignoring the business end of private practice. Keeping an eye on practice management (which we will look at in this chapter) and knowing how to stay proactive toward marketing and building a community of referral sources and satisfied clients is imperative. You need to reach out for clients, continue networking and marketing, and stay flexible (reread Chapter 1) to make sure that your practice fills up.

COACHES

Approximately 30,000 coaches of all types (life coaches, executive coaches, etc.) operate globally. An October 2008 Marketdata Enterprises Inc. report noted that personal coaching pulled in almost $1.3 billion in revenue nationally. According to the International Coach Federation (ICF), the coaching industry is holding steady for the moment, and the industry is choosing to see the silver lining in the current economic cloud. Even more so with the recession, Ann Belcher, ICF marketing manager, said, "Clients are looking to reduce stress in their lives" (Houppert, 2008,)).

A recent ICF study (2008,) continued to indicate an average annual revenue of $50,000. The numbers have not improved much over time. Five years ago, an earlier ICF survey (2003) showed that 70% earned less than $50,000 per year of gross annual income. Thirty-seven percent earned less than $10,000. Only 1 in 10 earn the magic number of $100,000 annually. One interesting trend noted by the Sherpa Executive Coaching survey (2008) is that while earnings for coaches have remained steady for 5-year veterans, annual revenues have actually dropped for coaches in business less than 5 years. This validates my findings that despite promises of a lucrative business, coaches report that the coaching business functions similar to any small start-up, with slow growth and slow earnings in the first few years.

But the studies suggest that there are many underpaid coaches in the ICF. There are several reasons why: A majority in the 2003 survey reported not charging a full fee, instead offering a sliding scale, pro bono sessions, or bartered sessions. Over 50% said it took them up to 2 years of marketing to get their first paid coaching client. Fifty percent said that they are only working with 1–6 clients per month. From this, we can surmise that a coaching business is similar to most other types of small service-oriented businesses. According to small business statistics, most small businesses take 3 years to show profitability. Three years may also be a fair assessment of how long it will take to develop a full-fee coaching practice. Filling a coaching business can be a slow process, and regardless of what you may be promised by a training organization, you may need a day job or substantial financial reserves in order to supplement your coaching in the first several years. Many coaches have existing or prior experience as business consultants or managers, and a smaller number have some experience as teachers, counselors, psychologists, or mental health professionals. Seventy percent have prior experience as consultants, executives, or managers, and 20% of coaches report a background in mental health. Coaches are, as a rule, well educated: Forty-four percent report a graduate degree.

What this means for your coaching practice: Have a business plan and recognize that it takes time to develop a market niche and make good money. Stay knowledgeable and current about the ways to generate clients and best business practices as a coach, as outlined in my earlier book, *The Business and Practice of Coaching* (Grodki & Allen, 2005). Be patient. Learn to network, find the right specialty, know how to target a profitable market, and become an organized and efficient entrepreneur. Be sure you have adequate financial reserves. Don't quit your day job too soon.

HEALERS

Studies show an increase in public acceptance and use of complementary alternative medicine (CAM) services such as massage, acupuncture, herbal therapy, homeopathy, naturopathy, and chiropractic. According to a nationwide government survey released in May 2004, (Barnes, 2002) 36% of U.S. adults aged 18 years and over use some form of CAM. CAM use occurs among people of all backgrounds. But, according to the survey, some people are more likely than others to use CAM. Overall, CAM is used more by women than by men, and by people with higher educational levels and people who have been hospitalized in the past year.

But because most of the services require out-of-pocket payment, CAM growth is based on a strong economy (Faars-Jones, 2001). With a recession, providers can anticipate a decrease in demand as clients' disposable incomes dwindle. People get sick regardless of economic cycles, and the publicly funded safety net programs ensure that people who need care get it. Yet if you look around the health system, what you see looks suspiciously like a recession: low single-digit pharmaceutical cost growth, a collapse in high-tech imaging and cardiovascular sales and clinical volumes, declining hospital admissions, and rising bad debts. Even when alternative health care is covered by insurance, it isn't recession-proof. Employers, who through their private health plans provide the industry most of its positive cash flow, also have a predictable response pattern to declining cash flow. When corporate cash flow dries up, health benefits get restructured. According to Jeff Goldsmith (2008), who writes about health care issues, the restructuring of private health insurance coverage in the past decade has made the industry much more recession-sensitive, and exposed the industry to price and use sensitivity we have not seen before.

What this means for your healing practice: As you get more successful and have a full client load, continue to reserve at least 10% of your overall working time for business-related activities. Get ready to wear a number of hats: CEO, healer, marketer, administrator, program designer, manager, maybe even bookkeeper. Develop an entrepreneurial mind-set to make this pleasurable.

CONSULTANTS

For the past decade, despite the September 11 attacks, economic setbacks, and corporate reengineering, training investments held their own. "Despite many serious economic issues, organizations in ASTD's [American Society for Training and Development's] Benchmarking Service did not show a marked decline in total training expenditures as a percent of payroll since the last *ASTD State of the Industry Report*," said Tina Sung, president and CEO of ASTD (Homer, 2003). "What's even more encouraging is the projection by Benchmarking Service organizations that their training expenditures will continue to increase in the near future. This positive signal indicates that business leaders realize that employee training and development is critical to sustaining a competitive advantage, for growth and innovation, and for the long-term success of the organization," she noted.

Trainers and OD (organization development) consultants working in corporate settings are also feeling the pinch. Recession fears have affected training budgets and lead to cancellations of leadership classes, executive seminars, and other training downturns (Laff, 2008). According to several association reports, vulnerable sectors, notably retail and the government, are cutting back on training. Some of the cutbacks won't be felt for a while due to budgetary process, which may cushion some trainers, but it also means that it takes a while for corporate spending to recover. It usually takes 2 years from the time a recession hits for training budgets to return to previous levels (Thompson, 2002). Training budgets are a lagging indicator that come back in increments, not in one fell swoop, according to the training and development publication *T + D*.

What this means for your consulting practice: Dr. E. Ted Prince, author of *The Three Financial Styles of Very Successful Leaders* argued that "recessions normally see a reduction in leadership development programs and spending since companies typically do not have confidence that these programs can provide short-term solutions to the financial issues that must be addressed. However, companies have an unparalleled opportunity to transform both leadership development programs and the way that they are viewed by their companies by rapidly introducing programs to modify financial behavior, including business acumen programs" (2009, p. 8). Trainers who can make a case for their continued importance may focus on the need to keep employee communication and morale high as well as looking for a way to justify return on investment of programs.

SURVIVING NEGATIVE TRENDS

In a recession, many trends look bad. Here are four things to remember:

1. *You are not the problem.* If your practice has fewer clients or less income than you need, you may think that the problem is you—that you are a failure or not smart enough in business. Not necessarily true. Every business owner is challenged in a down market.

2. *You are not alone.* You are one of the tens of thousands of professionals affected by today's recessionary, economic market. Think of your practice as one of many small boats trying to stay afloat in a stormy sea. My goal is that over time, you know how to set course and sail through these waters. You can survive, find new opportunities for business, and grow stronger.

3. *Most of us hate change.* It's ironic that those of us who profess to be masters of change (as long as we are changing others) often don't handle change well ourselves—especially when it is a change that is affecting our own bottom line. This is normal: Our brains much prefer homeostasis. But businesses change and evolve, even when times are good. The task for those of us who own and operate a small business is to learn to welcome change and take advantage of the many opportunities that change creates for profitability. Make change your new normal.

4. *Find the need in the market.* During difficult economic times, people will purchase based on need. Remember your purpose and understand who is in pain and what you can do to help them. Do some research—find out who needs your help. Ben Dean (2000), founder of MentorCoach (a coaching training organization for mental health professionals), suggests these considerations when assessing your market:

- *Burning need.* If there is an intense, perceived need for the niche in the minds of your prospects, the more quickly will the niche respond to your efforts.
- *Underserved.* All things being equal, a practice will grow faster in an underserved industry than in a highly developed one that has many vendors trying to meet the given need.
- *Precedent.* Are there already successful businesses operating in this niche? Some of the risk is reduced if you know there are others that are successfully targeting the niche on a local level.
- *Be first.* Take a successful concept and narrow it further, to be seen as first in the field.
- *Discretionary income.* Can your prospective clients pay for your services out of pocket? Does your niche fall under the list of services that sell, even in a down market? (See Chapter 6.)
- *Coherent group.* If members of your proposed niche feel they belong to a coherent group, you're more likely to have niche members forward your promotional material to others and generate word-of-mouth marketing.
- *Temporal dimensions.* Is the niche's need for your services short-term or enduring? It's far easier to serve existing clients than to have to continually acquire new ones.

PRACTICE MANAGEMENT

Okay, now shift your perspective and focus more closely on your practice and your practice management. Some therapists approach their private practice as a hobby, not as a serious business. Turning a therapy practice that is essentially a hobby into a business feels like growing up. It's time to take your practice by the hand and, like a responsible parent, give it some tough love to help it mature. Review your policies to remove all the hobby elements or inconsistent aspects of your practice management using the Practice Management Checklist below. Feel free to adapt this checklist so that it resonates with your particular practice, adding or subtracting items as needed to make it relevant for your business. There are 20 items on the checklist that signify good practice management. If you can check off every item as "true," you have a professionally managed practice. If you leave many items unchecked, use the checklist as goals to help you evolve and mature.

Adopt higher professional standards. Take a long, hard look at what you do during a day or a week or a month. What business aspects are you proudest of? What creates embarrassment or shame? Those shame-based aspect need your attention now. They are the hidden vulnerabilities that can topple a business or, at a minimum, undermine your productivity or profitability. Feeling brave? Let a trusted colleague or a business coach review your practice operations and help you correct the areas that are weak and inconsistent, so that you can have the professional feel of a larger company, even though you may be a small business.

EXERCISE: PRACTICE MANAGEMENT CHECKLIST

Check each item that is true for you. This checklist functions as a guide for optimal management. Complete the fieldwork that follows this checklist, and return to this list during the next several months until you can check off all the items and have an efficiently managed practice.

❏ I have a written business plan with my objectives and goals that I use to guide my practice.

❏ I know my top five business goals for this year and the action steps to take in order to accomplish each one.

❏ I continually look and ask for ways to upgrade my administration systems, including billing, record keeping, and filing.

❏ I have an accountant, lawyer, and business coach who I can turn to for advice.

❏ I am in control of my day-to-day operations.

❏ Each working day I take one action designed to strengthen my business.

❏ I return calls promptly and follow up on information in a timely manner.

❏ I devote one specific time each week to handling all my business paperwork.

❏ My office is well organized and set up to let me do my best work.

❏ If I employ staff, we have first-rate communication. They know how to please me and perform their job with minimum input from me.

❏ My office is a pleasant environment for both me and my staff.

❏ I have a client policy sheet that states all my policies in writing. It is openly displayed in my waiting room and given to each new and prospective client.

❏ My clients know that I will hold firmly to the boundaries of my policies.

❏ I educate my clients about how they can get the most out of our working relationship in therapy and become my ideal clients.

❏ My time at work is a valuable commodity and I manage it carefully.

❏ At least 75% of my total time at work is spent doing what I do best—seeing clients and delivering service.

❏ No more than 10% of my time at work is spent handling paperwork or unbilled calls or meetings.

❏ I reserve 10% of my working time for training, reading, writing, contemplating, networking, or learning so that I stay energetic, interested, and on top of my field.

❏ The remaining 5% of my working time each week is spent working *on* the business—improving the overall health of my practice.

❏ I discuss my practice management policies with a coach or colleagues that I trust, so that I can get feedback and advice to continually improve my business.

❏ I use software and technology to help make my practice
operate easily and inexpensively (see Chapter 7 for high-tech
resources and tips).

ALICE'S BUSINESS MATURITY

When Alice, a counselor in private practice for 15 years, cornered me
after a workshop, she admitted that her practice was disorganized. "I fit
the profile you mentioned of a hobbyist," she said. "I struggle with the
idea of whether I really want to make a commitment to my business, or
continue to treat it like an expensive hobby. I need you to coach me on
how to take my business more seriously." Alice, like many therapists
who have full-time jobs or are full-time parents, set up a home-based,
part-time practice. She worked hard, but her lack of policies and organization meant that she never earned over $55,000 per year. She rational-
ized it this way: "My family came first and the practice came second.
But now that my children are in college, I have to put up or shut up! I am
going to have to grow larger during this recession, or call it quits."

Alice felt uncertain about her ability to get tough on her practice
and wrestle its unwieldiness. I asked Alice to take the practice management checklist and her score was zero. She felt embarrassed, but
I was motivated.

"Alice, this is fine. We know where we are starting from. What do
you want to tackle first?"

For Alice, her practice felt like a very personal, very private enter-
prise. In the same way that it's hard for your clients to open up their
lives for your examination, it's often very uncomfortable to allow
someone to really look into your business. We reviewed her checklist
to note all the ways that her practice operated as a hobby instead of a
business. Most of the "hobby" aspects involved her inconsistent practice management.

Alice started with the lack of files, and at my insistence she agreed
to hire a neighbor to help her clean out and organize her home office.
It took 3 days and cost Alice $525 to pay her neighbor and buy sup-
plies, including filing cabinets. Alice was thrilled. For once, her office

looked professional. She could find all of her papers and client notes. "This is money well spent," she reported.

Next, she formalized her client policies, including her cancellation policy. "I have one, but I never follow through. My clients know that they can get me to back off."

We determined a fair policy, one that Alice could stand behind and commit herself to uphold. When I help therapists determine their practice policies, I don't have a formula about cancellations or any other policies. I want them to find what works for them, at any given time in their practice. Your policies and protections are a chance to allow your practice to become more solid, to reduce risk, and to ask yourself some hard questions: What is important to me about running my practice? Where do I hold resentment and how do I remove it by instituting a better policy? What feels vulnerable in my practice and how can I correct it by setting better boundaries?

Like Alice, you can determine the operation, look, and results of your practice by first deciding how to become a better manager of your practice.

EXAMINING MONEY BELIEFS

One more shift in focus, up close and personal: What are your personal attitudes and beliefs about business and money?

Many high-functioning people who are mature in every other area of their lives struggle with money. But you need to resolve this struggle in order to succeed in business. As an entrepreneur, your developmental task is to develop an adult relationship with money.

Failing financially in private practice is not always due to the economy. In good years and bad, I witness many therapists underearning or showing a negative profit picture; even having a full caseload does not signify financial success. Some therapists work hard but sabotage their profitability based on their own irrational financial behaviors, which are rooted in their core beliefs about money and profitability. The subject of money is loaded, not just for therapists, but for most people, and can carry the weight of unexamined emotions. The problem is that these beliefs and emotions can harm the profitability of your practice. So it is essential that you become aware of how you think and feel regarding money, become aware of any tendency to act out these beliefs within your business. Here are the four most common money attitudes that get in the way of financial success.

Deprivation Attitude

Maybe you grew up with money deprivation. There was never enough money for your basic needs as a child. You still believe money is in short supply and watch every penny, reluctant to spend on anything "unnecessary." You won't attend major conferences because they cost too much. You irritate the colleagues who share office space with you because you refuse to pay for simple amenities like magazines, flowers, or even bottled water to add ambiance to the waiting room. You don't join associations because it's not cost-effective. As a result, you fail to give your business the resources it needs to flourish. You miss networking opportunities, skimp on training that would benefit your work, and don't see the collegial resentment building up due to your lack of sharing.

As a result, you fail to give your business the resources it needs to flourish.

You believe:
❑ I can't make money.
❑ I am just one step away from being on the street.
❑ I can't charge what I am worth because no one will pay my full fee.
❑ Money doesn't grow on trees.
❑ Other: _____

How your belief plays out in your practice:
❑ I won't attend major conferences because they cost too much.
❑ I annoy my colleagues who share office space with me because I am so cheap.
❑ I don't join associations because it's not cost-effective; who needs it?

❑ I fail to give my business the equipment, advertising, or other resources it needs to flourish.

❑ I miss networking opportunities and skimp on training that would benefit my work.

❑ Other: _____

Deification Attitude

Maybe you grew up in awe of money; in your family, money came first and trumped love or concern. You think a lot about money, compare your finances to others, feel envious of others who make more, and judge others and yourself based on money alone. In your practice, you'll see clients you don't like as long as they will pay your full fee. You build up resentment but work an exhausting caseload of 50 hours a week to see your bottom line advance. Money is the driving force of your business; you feel pressure to keep increasing your fee and earning more each year, giving rise to complaints about the rigid or elite nature of your practice.

You believe:
❑ The only bottom line that matters is the profit line.

❑ I must increase my revenue every year, no matter what other situations may be occurring in your life or work.

❑ My self-worth is tied directly to my earning ability.

❑ Each client has a dollar sign in front of his or her name.

❑ Other: _____

How your belief plays out in your practice:
❑ My clients are interchangeable as long as they pay my fee.

❑ I have no flexibility regarding any of my policies, regardless of the client situation.

❑ I don't spend adequately on staffing or other office expenses.

❑ I work a bigger caseload with longer hours than anyone I know, and am proud of this fact, even though I am burned out on my work.

❑ Other: _____

Dissociated Attitude

Maybe you grew up believing that money was mysterious, because no one in your family understood how to make it or save it. You ride an emotional money roller coaster. When your practice goes through a slow time, you are down and self-critical; when it's up you feel great. Mostly you are confused because there is so much about money you don't comprehend. In your family, money magically appeared and then, just as randomly, was gone. Your family spent wildly when money was present, then panicked when they got into debt. You alternately feel blessed or panicked based on your financial bottom line and clueless about how to bring the situation under control. As a result, your practice swings from positive to negative cash flow. You feel exhausted from the ups and downs, unable to take the steps necessary to keep your practice on an even financial keel.

You believe:
❏ Nice people don't talk about money.
❏ I only care about my craft; money isn't important.
❏ If I don't pay attention to money, it comes when I really need it.
❏ Money isn't everything; in fact, it isn't anything.
❏ Other: _____

How your belief plays out in your practice:
❏ I don't discuss money issues with clients, even when they act out financially.
❏ I don't bill on time.
❏ I carry the debt of uncollected accounts when I do bill.
❏ I don't know what I make, what I owe, and why I am so broke.
❏ My practice swings from positive to negative cash flow.
❏ Other: _____

Demonized Attitude
Maybe you believe money is inherently wicked. You watched anxiety on your parents' faces when they talked about money, so you feel scared or impure when you have to deal with it, too. You hate to

raise your fees, negotiate with a landlord, or hold your boundaries about your established policies. You find all aspects regarding money unpleasant and suspect. Maybe you believe the topic of money is tawdry or dirty; you wish you could disregard it altogether. You are too frightened to negotiate a better office rent or hold your boundaries about your established policies. You find all aspects regarding money painful and difficult. As a result, you attract clients who pay too little and demand too much, or you work for others for a split-fee arrangement, letting someone else handle your billing so that you don't have to confront money issues with clients. You end up wishing you could have more autonomous control over your practice but feel too fearful to handle the business finances yourself.

You believe:
❑ Money is the root of all evil.
❑ I can't have money and have integrity, too.
❑ Only greedy people think about money all the time.
❑ Money is dirty and corrupting.
❑ Other: _____

How your belief plays out in your practice:
❑ I don't raise my fees when justified.
❑ I don't hold my boundaries about my established policies.
❑ Clients take advantage of me.
❑ I sacrifice (unfair split-fee arrangements, managed care
   agreements, sliding scale for most clients) so that I don't have
   to deal with my money anxieties.
❑ Other: _____

The solution? Resolve any beliefs and behaviors that impede your business development. Take time to do an honest inventory about your financial beliefs and note the policies and behaviors that you enact that are unprofessional or out of the norm. Correct them all. Get support from others (a supervisor, peers, a business coach) so that you can operate a more adult, ethical practice. Don't sabotage your progress with undeveloped money beliefs and behaviors.

Part II: Recommit

Test fast, fail fast, adjust fast.

—*Tom Peters*

CHAPTER 5

Protecting Your Practice

In this second section of the book, I want you to consider the essential question about your practice regarding commitment: Are you willing to do what it takes to keep your practice alive and thriving?

The answer probably varies, depending on your definition of "what it takes." Commitment to one's work involves three distinct areas (Myer and Allen, 1991):

- the emotional ties or attachment you have to your practice (the hopes and dreams you developed about your practice)
- the financial investment you have incurred
- the obligation or moral and ethical responsibility you feel toward continuing your work.

I add a fourth commitment that I see in therapists in private practice: a bond with the core values that your profession represents.

Given these four areas, I hope you can find at least one to help strengthen you to do what it takes to keep your practice viable. If you can't find a way to make a commitment now, in terms of your energy and resources, if you don't seriously invest in your practice even as it is failing, you may not have a practice left to discuss. The investment can be in the form of time, energy, money, training, supervision, coaching, support, or any other resource that will help you to build or rebuild your practice. Commitment follows several steps. To commit you need willpower, support from others, a sense of purpose, and a clear plan.

EVALUATING RISK

Building a small business is hard and risky, even in the best of times. A large percentage of small businesses fail, and the creation of a business built on "intangibles"—services that are hard for the public to define, explain, or measure—adds to the difficulty. You have to do double duty as the owner: create a market and then sell them your services. You need to be part educator, part salesperson, part leader in the field—and be ready to demonstrate coaching to people you meet, at a moment's notice. This takes assurance. You have to become articulate. You must impart the value and consequent expense of your coaching services primarily through your words, written materials, and presence. You have to hone your language and your speaking. This takes preparation and poise. As if this weren't enough, you need to be a skilled in your craft. Clients, many of whom pay for their therapy, coaching, consulting, or healing services out of pocket, want to see results. You need to be good at what you do. Your services and programs must add clear, tangible value. This takes know-how. Because you have so much of yourself, your skills, and your finances tied up in your practice, it is important to evaluate risk.

When the market is tough, it's essential that you evaluate your level of risk. By risk, I mean both what you *do* and what you *don't do* that can threaten the survival of your private practice. Some therapists work hard to steer clear of all business risk, but risk avoidance is a two-edged sword. You may think that curtailing all investment into your practice right now is the best way to avoid the risk of economic failure. But *not* investing in your private practice or *not* giving it enough time, money, energy, opportunities, or brainpower is a way to threaten its survival.

Three ways to consider managing your business risks include risk reduction, risk retention, and risk transfer. Let me explain:

1.Risk Reduction

Risk reduction is a way to evaluate the dangers to your practice and then minimize the severity of the loss or potential loss. For example, one basic method of risk reduction in your home is smoke detectors that will warn you of a potential fire. Risk reduction in your business includes:

- A written business, marketing, and financial plan that will help you evaluate and track the state of your practice at any given time.
- A cash reserve to cushion the operating expenses of your practice. Each practice needs a minimum of 6 months' cash reserve to help you sail through especially tough months and still pay your basic operating expenses.
- Self-care for the business owner so that you—as the primary service delivery person—don't get sick, exhausted, and unable to work, unable to market, and unable to fulfill responsibilities to clients.
- Complete record keeping by the service professional and written treatment planning. Data counts. Know your limits and strengths with clients. Transfer those who are not a good fit for your strengths.
- A brain trust of advisers so that you have others you use for professional support as a sounding board and to help you strategize your next steps, especially when you are tense or anxious.

2. Risk Retention

Risk retention means having a way to accept and survive a business loss if and when it occurs. Let's say that you have a private practice in a cold climate, and an unusual series of snow and ice storms put you out of business for a month. This risk of weather is one that can't be avoided, reduced, or transferred, and is "retained" by you, by default. Risk retention requires that you:

- Plan for worst-case scenarios and then try to average out losses over time (the bad winter month gets incorporated into the overall profit and loss statement for several months or a full year, to try to amortize the loss).

- Anticipate slowdowns and losses as a normal part of the ups and downs of doing business and keep a reserve of clients (waiting list), cash (savings), or opportunities (networking or marketing possibilities) so that you have more than enough to keep you busy in slow times.
- Focus on staying flexible in how you deliver service; if clients can't come into your office when their child is ill or weather is bad, can you do the session by e-mail or by phone? Or can you send them an audiotape or written report that you have created specifically for them during the session time to use as a substitute?

3. Risk Transfer

Risk transfer means that you transfer a loss to another party, by contractually having agreed to the risk. In this way, the risk doesn't fall entirely on your small practice, but is either shared or taken on by someone else. Risk transfer includes:

- Enforcing cancellation policies that you and your client have agreed to. If the current policy is too harsh, set one that you can live with and enforce without discomfort.
- Negotiate with landlords or other vendors for a reduction in price or payment terms when circumstances cause a loss of income. Often a landlord, credit card company, training company, or other vendor is willing to work out some temporary terms of payment rather than lose your business altogether or see you go bankrupt.
- Maintain insurance, including malpractice insurance, rental insurance, and life insurance on partners or associates if their income is critical to the operating income of a practice.

BEST BUSINESS PRACTICES

During a down economy, clients are quicker to feel dissatisfied with your services. You can minimize the risk of unhappy clients or client dissatisfaction with the way you conduct your business, starting with your initial contact with a client. As the business owner, it is your job to create clear guidelines around your services, so potential clients can easily understand what to expect when they hire you. Your clients need to know, ahead of time, what therapy, coaching, or consulting with your practice is and is not. Since you are a professional for hire, they need to know how to get their money's worth from their experience. They also need to understand and value the rules and policies that make for an optimal therapy, coaching, or consulting experience. Here are four guidelines for best business practices:

- *Don't overpromise results.* Unfortunately, some therapeutic and personal growth professionals promise miracles. This is the first and most obvious way to incur risk, by setting expectations that can't be met. Even though you may feel very confident about your ability to resolve a client's problems, you need to couch your results in terms of what you can guarantee. Outcomes that therapists and coaches have posted on Web sites and even in yellow page ads have promised potential clients to "overcome all your issues in your life and work" or "have loving relationships" or even "remove all symptoms." If a client believes these results are a promise of your services and these claims never fully materialize, you are liable for problems. What can you promise instead? Some of the skill-based behaviors that we tend to overlook are important to our clients. For example, perhaps you can promise to listen carefully with an open mind, to reflect back honestly what you hear, to be a sounding board without a hidden agenda, to stand behind the client's goals when possible, to stay constructive and practical. Underpromise, and then overdeliver.
- *Watch your written claims.* Offer only what you are sure you can provide. Many clients can move forward and take big steps in life as a result of some very basic skills that you may undervalue. A life coach I worked with made a list of the basic skills she could guarantee to deliver to all

her clients and spent 6 months keeping notes of current client outcomes. She then translated this data into straightforward statements, such as: I will offer ways to structure your goals into manageable action steps. I will contact you weekly to check on your progress. My clients say that they gain clarity by getting a chance to talk openly in our sessions about what is most important to them, while I provide a safe and nonjudgmental environment.

- *Don't take on multiple roles with the same client.* To lessen your risk, stay with one role. Be your client's therapist, healer, consultant, or coach. Don't take on conflicting functions, such as being both coach and close friend, or psychotherapist and employer, or healer and employee. Keep your business dealings with clients as uncomplicated, aboveboard, and professional as possible. Maintain professional boundaries. While mixing socially with clients may be essential and part of the culture in which you work if you are a consultant or coach, avoid all situations, especially sexual or financial situations, that could lead to a conflict of interest. In the same way that you would not have a romantic or sexual relationship with a client, you should also not profit from a client with any additional business dealings. Refer out to others at the hint of complications in role. If you are a life coach and your client needs a therapist, or a financial adviser, refer to others. If you are a therapist and your client needs a coach, refer out. Give at least three referrals each time, not just one. That way, you don't have any vested interest in whom your client chooses to hire.
- *Document your sessions and phone calls.* Even today, in our litigious society, some therapists, coaches, consultants, and healer feel that their discussions with clients are organic, that in session they simply follow a conversational flow, and as a result they take few notes. But documenting what you do and say is essential and can serve to reduce your risk with legal situations if a client distorts reality, makes

false claims, or decides to sue. Use technology. Create a system that allows you to take notes on each session easily. Some therapists take notes at the end of a session, with a client, to make sure that the client concurs with the issues and results of a session. Date your files, and save copies of your notes on disks and store them safely. Bob is a personal trainer at an upscale spa and health club. He makes recommendations to his clients regarding nutrition, exercise regime, and lifestyle changes. He keeps scrupulous records about his advice, and gives each client a written summary at the end of each session, with weekly goals. "Since I am working with health-related coaching issues, taking careful notes and then making the notes immediately available to my clients ensures that we take a partnership approach. There is nothing hidden, and I am not the sole expert. We are both on the same page, literally," he said. One of Bob's clients sustained an injury at the spa during a workout and sued the spa. She did not name Bob, in part because she had copies of his weekly summaries and felt that, after reviewing them carefully, she could find no fault with his suggestions or approach.

- *Maintain straightforward payment policies.* Whenever you have a fiduciary relationship, it's safer and less risky to keep business finances uncomplicated. Some new therapists or coaches, hungry for business, accept bartering as a way to avoid losing a client who can't pay their fee. This is a bad idea. Resist the temptation to try to equate your intangible services with other more tangible services in order, to avoid feelings of resentment. Keep your dealings with clients legitimate. Don't set yourself up for a conflict of interest by investing with clients or complicate your fee with additional financial transactions outside the realm of your professional services. Follow accepted billing and accounting procedures. Don't barter or slide your fee without giving this careful thought. Check your licensure and code of ethics regarding payment. Don't find yourself in a conflict-of-interest situation by having any financial dealings with your client other than what is considered normal and usual.

EXERCISE: PROTECTING MY PRACTICE

Fill in the following statements to determine the level of your risk management.

My level of risk is reduced by taking these steps: _____
My plan for worst-case scenarios includes: _____
My risk is shared with this cancellation policy: _____
My insurance protects me from these potential problems: _____

RISK VS. REWARD

Even during a crisis, your business needs to incur some risk as a result of growth. Business risk is a combination of your investment (money, time, energy, resources) and your tolerance of possible loss of that investment. Ask yourself the following questions: Am I taking enough risk this year, in terms of how I invest in my business? What are the risks inherent in my business and my investment? What is the right balance for me now, so that my business and I stay healthy and viable?

As you evaluate your efforts and your results to build your business, sort out your short-term aims from your long-term goals. For example, if your goal is more clients now, and you judge all your marketing and advertising investment against the flow of clients generated this month, you will probably be disappointed and, even worse, may stop your investment too soon. Marketing, networking, and advertising are long-term investments. Industry standards say that it takes a person a minimum of six times to see an ad before contacting the advertiser.

Networking usually requires four to six contacts before producing referrals. Direct mail yields about a 1% success rate. These strategies are important and need to be ongoing, but you have to give them enough time (usually years) to really produce. Track your results, but be realistic about the timeline. Successful business owners tend to be as interested in the top line (dramatic growth from new markets and innovation) as the bottom line (the accounting fiction of profits).

RETURN ON INVESTMENT

Most of us in private practice work hard. We are devoted to our craft and continually train and learn to improve our skills. We do our best to administer and manage our small businesses, including taking time to build our practices. No wonder then, that at some point we all stop to ask ourselves the following kind of questions:

How do I know if my efforts are worth the trouble?
When will my marketing pay off?
Am I doing enough, too much or too little to stay viable?

If these questions seem familiar, than you are thinking about how to measure your return on investment (ROI). This is a good thing and shows that you are being entrepreneurial. When you are the owner and operator of a small service-oriented business, measuring ROI is different from the traditional method of looking only at your profit line. Traditional ROI is a mathematical formula that divides net profit of the business by assets or total worth of the business. Return on investment isn't necessarily the same as profit. ROI deals with the money you invest in the company and the return you realize on that money based on the net profit of the business. Profit, on the other hand, measures the performance of the business.

But in a small business such as a therapy, consulting, coaching, or a healing practice, ROI is measured with additional factors. You need to factor into your investment things such as time, energy, and knowledge, not just money. Your return may need to chart some factors other than profit, such as referral sources, opportunities, reputation, or enhanced value of your services. This is not easy to reduce to a mathematical formula or to chart directly. In a service-oriented practice, results may require months or years to materialize. It doesn't mean your efforts aren't working: It means that your goals require more time than you know.

But you still need ways to evaluate your expenses and efforts, to know what is useful in achieving your goals and what is not. Here are useful markers for ROI that may make more sense when trying to determine the right balance between effort and effect in your practice.

EXERCISE: MY ROI CHECKLIST

Each item on this checklist can help you track your efforts to see if you are profitable over time and meeting your goals.

❑ I keep my profit and loss statement updated each month (income minus expenses).

❑ I also track my investment of time (hours with clients as well as nonclient hours spent doing administrative tasks, returning phone calls, marketing, etc.), knowledge (training, supervision), and money (practice expenses).

❑ I keep two kinds of tracking: all expenses minus my time, and all resources including my time.

❑ If my practice is a start-up to 5 years in business, I expect my investment to far exceed my income and net profit.

❑ If my practice is 5 years or older, my investment should be less than my net income.

❑ I measure all results (income, profit, number of referrals each month, how long clients stay, opportunities, etc.).

❑ I understand the ratio of investment to return may take years to accomplish, yet I have ways of measuring and tracking this over time.

❑ I approach this measurement with absolute honesty, so that I can know my business and my investment accurately.

ECONOMIES OF SCALE

Economies of scale is a business term that refers to reducing costs by spreading them out over increased production. Here is an example: Imagine you love to bake cookies, but your recipe takes a lot of time and some expense to create. In fact, the last time you baked a dozen cookies it cost $25 for ingredients and took 3 hours of preparation and baking time. Now imagine that you expand production, to make a lot more cookies, and find that for only $25 more, you make 100 cookies in the same 3 hours. How? Well, you buy flour and chocolate in bulk, you repeat the same recipe 10 times and develop expertise, and you organize your cooking area so that you can be more productive. You have just achieved economies of scale.

But how can this concept of increased productivity and lowered expenses apply to a small service-oriented business? Let me offer you some quick coaching so you can leverage your operating expenses and increase your output. Here are threee ways to increase scale in your practice:

1. *Lower input costs:* If you are baking cookies, your input costs are your ingredients. By using volume as leverage, you buy in bulk to reduce costs. Your therapy, coaching, or consulting practice can shift this strategy a bit and, by affiliating or combining your input costs with others, you can approximate volume and reduce expenses. Common big-ticket expenses for a private practice include: office rent, advertising, supervision or mentoring, printing, mailing, Web site hosting, office equipment, phone lines, and outsourcing billing. To leverage volume, one group of therapists decided to form an association without walls. They have separate practices in separate offices but find that they can join together to share some of these expenses: They join together when advertising and marketing, to list all their offices under one name and divvy up the cost of running ads in a local new-age magazine each month. They all want some supervision with a senior therapist to improve their skills; they buy 2 hours a month of her time and share that expense. They coordinate their direct mail efforts so that they can use bulk mailing rates. A psychologist contacted four colleagues who all needed part-time help with billing. Together, they negotiated a discounted full-time rate with a bookkeeper. She goes office to office each week, spending one day with each practice. An acupuncturist doesn't use her

office and equipment on weekends or mornings; she sublets her space during those times and charges an extra fee for use of her administrative equipment: computer, copier, and fax machine (which her subleaser is happy to pay). If you think cooperatively, you can find creative ways to share expenses.

2. *Increase productivity*: A management consultant I coached complained of his long office hours, but when he analyzed his time carefully, he saw that he spent hours each day on the phone and at his computer, doing unbilled research for his clients. I asked him to either find a way to bill for that time or eliminate it. He decided to bill for it, but was worried that his clients would balk at extra charges. Together, we developed an updated explanation of his services, and research topped the list. His clients had no idea of the work and benefit that the research yielded, and with the information he provided, most were eager to have him include this new service, for the added price. He increased his profitability by 18% over the course of a year. What work do you do that is not billed? How can you set boundaries on your time and activity to increase productivity? What will you say or explain to clients about the additional services you can provide, and the benefits?

3. Systemize: Organization is the key to economies of scale. You need to match your business efforts to your business needs. If you are baking hundreds cookies, you need to organize your kitchen so that it becomes a production line. If you are a therapist, coach, or consultant, your tasks need to be systemized in a similar way. Look at your office. Does it lend itself to productivity? If not, organize your space. Set up your desk so that you can do one thing at a time, and so that task naturally leads to the next, and the next. When I was bothered by the big pile of paperwork on my desk that never got filed, I called a colleague to ask how she approached filing. Her method was simple, but smart. She kept her "to be filed" papers in a plastic box, right above the filing cabinet. One task led to the next. Ask for help. Learn from others. Look for the easiest way possible to achieve your business goals. Find colleagues with whom you can share information, technology, support, and expertise.

SURVIVAL OF THE FITTEST

We know that we continually evolve as human beings, both internally, in our consciousness, and externally, in the things we create. But you may not yet recognize that your private practice also goes through evolutionary stages. If you are like most small business owners, you are consumed with the details of your work and focus on the daily tasks that are necessary to help you stay afloat. Who has time for thoughts of evolution?

But viewing your practice from the perspective of evolution lets you see a pattern of undercurrents and emerging phases that develop in similar ways for all businesses. If you understand the ramifications of the particular stage you are in right now, you will know what tasks you, the business owner, need to attend to in order to make sure that you and your practice not only survive, but thrive. For a moment, think of your private practice, the business you have birthed and nurtured, as a child. Just as it makes parenting easier to anticipate the tantrums that occur during the "terrible twos" or the sullen behavior of a preteen child, it helps to know what stage your practice is in, what is going to happen next, and why. Businesses go through early survival phases, midlife stages where matters of organization, achievement, and affiliation dominate, and mature phases where the matters of integrating core values, defining legacy, and reinvention take over. It helps to become independent by recognizing that business as an ecosystem develops in stages. The four stages are:

- Birth
- Expansion
- Leadership
- Self-renewal (or death)

EXERCISE: MY PRACTICE EVOLUTION

Answer the following questions to determine where you fit in this developmental model.

- Birth: When did you start my practice? Is there a common, repetitive topic or theme in your concerns or worries about your business? (Can indicate Birth stage)
- Expansion: Have you grown and developed the business? What would help your business the most: more cash, more information, more infrastructure, or more professional support? (Can indicate Expansion stage)
- *Leadership*: Are you taking steps to set course and direction? Do you feel like a fully mature, high-functioning adult in your response to your business challenges, or do you regress to a younger version of yourself? (Can indicate Leadership stage)
- *Self-renewal*: Will this be the year you reinvent yourself and your practice? When you daydream about the future you want, do you see yourself working more or working less? (Can indicate Self-renewal stage)

Here is a metaphor that can help you see the evolution of your business path. Close your eyes and imagine that you are taking a journey. It might be by foot, by horseback, or in a vehicle. You pick the terrain: on land, over water, in the mountains, through the forest, or across the desert. Imagine that you look forward to your journey; it is one of choice, a journey based on your desire to reach a great destination. The journey is not dangerous, but it is challenging and you need to stay alert. Imagine how you use your existing strengths and inner resources to stay safe and enjoy the experience. What do you need to bring or have with you to make sure that you feel as calm and alert as possible? What is your mind-set? What helps you to take pleasure in the journey?

Now open your eyes and translate this imagery to your current business journey. For each item or resource in your imagined journey, find a correlation in your real business process. Use your imagination and creativity to generate resources that can make your business journey feel calmer and more enjoyable. Make a list of the resources currently at your disposal to smooth your journey. Make it real. What do you need to add to your life in terms of both tangible and intangible items to help you self-soothe and further reduce any generalized business anxiety? Create a plan for obtaining these items.

CHAPTER 6

Cutting Unhealthy Dependencies

In 12-step programs, a story is told to motivate newly recovering addicts about a person who walks down a street absentmindedly and falls into a pothole. If the person is an unrecovered addict, he or she keeps walking down the same street, falling into the pothole, evoking Einstein's definition of insanity: "doing the same thing over and over again, but expecting different results." An addict further along the recovery process sees the pothole and tries to circumvent it, sometimes successfully, sometimes not. The paradigm shift in recovery occurs when the addict decides to walk down a different street.

Can a private practice walk down a different street? The new street might be named "Autonomy." Because so many of us trained in the medical model, we tend to operate our practices much like addicts operate their lives, with a lot of obvious and hidden dependencies.

DEPENDENCY

Dana Ackley, author of the pioneering book *Breaking Free of Managed Care*, sees the challenges therapists in private practice face as a potential blessing. "This might be the best thing that could happen to those in private practice," Ackley said to me, "if it forces psychotherapists to redo their relationships with the insurance companies and rethink their way of interacting with the public" (Grodzki, 2007).

Ackley cautions, "Those who tied themselves to the medical model have now reaped what they sowed. Private practitioners have become dependent upon insurance companies. This relationship has become abusive. Just as in abusive marriages, dependency relationships are maintained out of the false belief that 'I can't get along without him or her.' Therapists need to think about what they'd tell an abused spouse about giving up dependency relationships, and then take their own advice."

Autonomy for a therapy private practice would mean:

- No more hand-holding with insurance companies or accepting their low fees as fair trade for meager referrals.
- No more self-identifying with the medical model.
- Finding other ways to define ourselves, perhaps "necessary human education" or "the prerequisite for wellness."
- Dropping the jargon and diagnosis codes while we decide if we want to present our product as an art or a science.
- Learning to face the public squarely, on footing equal to that of other service-oriented professionals, and find the words to explain who we are, what we do and why psychotherapy is important.
- Appreciating that being a small business allows us to be flexible, respond to feedback, and routinely measure client results in order to create practices that follow consumers' needs and desires.
- Seeking ways to increase market share for everyone within the profession, building alliances among therapists for advertising and PR efforts and putting more pressure on our associations to help educate the public about the legitimacy and value of counseling.

EXERCISE: GOOD AND BAD DEPENDENCY

Ask yourself the following questions to determine your level of dependence or autonomy.

- What are my unhealthy dependencies right now (insurance panels, EAPs [employee assistance programs], etc.)?

- What are my healthy dependencies right now (peer support or supervision groups, good referral sources, business organizations)?
- How do I explain my practice and my services without jargon or medical/therapeutic terminology so that the public can understand what I have to offer?
- What ways do I have to meet the public on a regular basis (community events, associations, networking, marketing, advertising)?
- What feedback do I get regarding my business and my services (comments from clients, reputation within the professional community, word of mouth from others)?

By now, the solution may be obvious. If you have an unhealthy dependency, you need to get free. If you are on managed care, you need a plan to eventually (and gradually) become less dependent on insurance. This may mean that you need to get off of the panels that pay the least and move toward a practice that has a limited amount of insurance clients, or that you need to get off of all panels. If you are insurance-free, but too many of your clients pay a discounted fee, you will need to eventually (and gradually) raise the fees of the lowest clients so that all of your clients pay you a standard, full fee. If you are tied to a contract, you may need to renegotiate the contract to help you be more profitable and competitive.

As you can see, I am suggesting no sudden moves here when it comes to changing the financial structure of your practice during a recession. Instead, create a plan and then go step-by-step so that you don't disrupt the status quo of your business. I have helped many therapists create and implement financial plans to get free of managed care, diversify, leverage with more groups or classes, and find other ways to increase their incomes. First, make sure that your practice is operating in a professional manner.

EXERCISE: HOBBY TO BUSINESS CHECKLIST

Put a check next to each statement that is true. Try to check off more statements as true over time.

❏ I assess and correct any unprofessional, unethical, or amateurish policies and procedures in my business.

❏ I surround myself with other entrepreneurial colleagues who want me to succeed.

❏ I am becoming more pragmatic and optimistic in my thinking about business each month.

❏ I know how to set a future goal and not be deterred by negative, self-sabotaging beliefs.

❏ I have created and have regular contact with an advisory board of people who can offer me good business advice (see Chapter 15).

❏ I am accountable to others for achieving my monthly business goals.

❏ I am comfortable talking about the positive aspects of my work (my strengths and talents).

❏ I understand the difference between a fear-based and a love-based practice (see Chapter 1).

❏ I educate existing clients how to get the most from therapy so that they can become my ideal clients.

❏ I organize my calendar to reflect a balance of work and quality nonwork time.

❏ I set monthly goals and enjoy achieving them.

❏ I model the strategies of other successful businesspeople.

❏ I collaborate and link with others to make operating my business more fun.

❏ My practice operates from a model of abundance (enough time, money, clients, opportunities, ideas, referral sources to help me succeed) instead of deprivation.

HEALTHY DEPENDENCIES

Now let's look at four strategies used widely within the market right now, during this recession, that are keeping practices strong. Freely adapt or adopt any of these to help you stay autonomous and be optimally positioned with your market and other referrals sources.

- Need-driven niches
- Services that sell
- Affiliation
- Client connection

THE ITCH TO NICHE

I talk with professionals who ask: Why should I narrow my services or my audience, rather than appeal to a broader market? What if by targeting my market I miss out on potential clients? It sounds counterintuitive to narrow your pool of clients by having a niche, even a niche based on needs in the marketplace, just when you are desperate for clients. But targeting a niche is actually effective in a recession because it helps you to conserve your energy, your costs, and your time.

In bad economic times, don't make the mistake of trying to be all things to all people. By focusing clearly on a niche, you can tailor your professional message so that it has maximum impact. You won't spend time going to the wrong networking meetings that yield little in the way of results. You won't spend money unwisely, mailing announcements to uninterested recipients. Instead, you can anticipate where to get the biggest bang for your marketing buck, so that you only show up and promote your practice where it makes the most sense. When you focus, you can target people who are also focused—those potential clients who know what they want and need, and are looking for what you have to offer.

If you research your market and in the process find out that there are others working within your niche, don't get discouraged. Competition is often a good sign. It means that there is work available in that market. Don't let the fact that others are mining the same niche stop you from entering it. In fact, many marketing experts say that if there is no competition in a market, it's because others have already investigated that niche and determined it to be a total waste of time. Sometimes it's good to follow the crowd. Just figure out a way to stand out in that crowd.

Multiple Ways to Niche

You can niche in more ways than you might think: by services and population (what you offer and to whom); results and outcomes (what you achieve and how); and logistics (where and how you practice, what you charge). To niche by results or outcomes means that you highlight the end point of your work, rather than the population or even issue that you address. Here's a short list of possible outcomes. Notice that they are broad enough to allow you to work with several populations, but specific enough to allow you to develop a reputation for offering your special brand of therapy:

- Improve decision-making ability.
- Maintain a healthy balance between work and family time.
- Manage difficult emotions with integrity.
- Set strong personal boundaries.
- Communicate more assertively with friends, office mates, or family.

You can diversify and build a program around any well-articulated outcome. Notice that this list of outcomes uses ordinary, everyday language so that a potential client can feel drawn to the outcome. Using outcomes as a niche can help you to distinguish your work from others. You might become a "relationship-enhancing" social worker or a "total relaxation" massage therapist. One family therapist I know routinely says, "I teach kids how to raise good parents" instead of the other way around, which is an amusing description of his niche.

Your niche is anything that gives you a unique selling point, helps you stand out, or addresses a need in the marketplace. You can niche around logistics by focusing on:

- your fee (reduced fee; cash only with a price point that is affordable)
- your location (inner city; accessible; small town where you are the only working therapist)

- your accessibility (available after hours; on call for crisis; makes house calls to the elderly, ill, or disabled clients)

SERVICES THAT SELL

The services that sell in an up market often change during a recession. Here are services that are in demand despite a down market, according to my research of industry publications, interviews with professionals around the country, and an examination of my own network:

Services for children: attention-deficit disorder (ADD), learning/emotional disabilities, sensory integration, autism spectrum, educational psychological assessments, high-risk teens, anorexia and eating disorders, multiple birth children (i.e., twins), sleep problems, needs of gifted children, consulting to summer camps on mental health issues, bullies, drug, alcohol, sex, computer addiction.

Marriage savers: premarital counseling, divorce prevention, financial and debt-related counseling, parenting (including programs for stepfamilies and blended families), relationship mediation, counseling for new brides under stress, dating advice or therapy for singles, specialized couples counseling for gay, lesbian, bisexual, and transgendered couples, faith-based couples therapy, parents with bereavement issues.

Career savers: court-referred therapy, anger management, out-patient addiction treatment programs including Internet or sex addiction, crisis intervention, work-related critical incidence or post traumatic stress disorder (PTSD) from violent workplace situations, career- and unemployment-related counseling, debt and money counseling, workplace employment screenings and personality tests, conflict resolution.

Health-related: cancer-related counseling, stress reduction, depression, middle-age eating disorders, dual diagnosis of depression as related to other illness, smoking, aging, postpartum depression, compulsive shopping, hoarding, panic, social anxiety (shyness).

Coaching and consulting niches that are attracting and retaining clients in this recession include:

- *Corporate*: executive coaching, improving morale, productivity, peak performance, management skills, executive coaching, corporate retreats, time management, internal entrepreneurship, global leadership, best business practices, teamwork, staffing, hiring, firing.
- *High net-worth individuals*: family business, financial and inheritance issues, gifted adults, peak performance.
- *Entrepreneurs*: all phases of business development—marketing strategy, profitability, product development, communicating with clients, and strategic planning for the business, staffing, productivity, evaluation, and consulting to prepare owner to foreclose or sell.
- *Nonprofits*: executive coaching, staffing, generating donor contributions, executive burnout.
- *Individuals*: career, transition, work–life balance, skills, relationships.

AFFILIATION

The old business maxim, "It's not what you know, it's who you know" might well be changed to "It's not who you know, it's how many you know" for the small businessperson today. In his book *The Tipping Point*, writer Malcom Gladwell (2002) looked at the business and social power that is inherent in the quantity, not quality, of relationships you can develop. The power comes not from the depth of your relationships, he wrote, but from their sheer numbers. Using a series of studies, he showed that those individuals who know the most people, *especially superficially,* have a much greater chance to gain business success.

Gladwell (2002) referred to the "strength of weak ties." Superficial acquaintances will actually provide you with more reach and success than friends and family because the acquaintances who operate outside of your natural social or business world are more likely to know things or other people you don't, hence the far-reaching power of the broad network versus the limited power of a close inner circle. The new definition of poverty is not deprivation, Gladwell concluded; it's isolation.

Therapists in a sole proprietorship are often the most isolated businesspeople I know, and, in this way, impoverished. Therapists tend to be isolated by the type of work they do, which is private and confidential; isolated by the nature of their often introverted personalities; and isolated by the lack of networking within and between various therapy professions. Today, affiliation is a powerful strategy to help you eliminate unhealthy dependency by using a "we, not me" approach.

Cultivate diversity in your professional network. In your professional networking, affiliate with those who are not in competition with you, but those who revolve around your target market. If you are a social worker treating children with learning disabilities, develop closer ties with those who diagnose but don't treat the condition: psychologists, university programs, educational programs, any other adjunct professionals (e.g., one therapist treating adults with ADD networks with an organization that helps learning disabled prisoners get back into society). Make a list of all the possible organizations that surround your target market and how you might affiliate or connect with them. What can you offer (mentioning them on your Web site, stocking their business cards in your office, giving free talks to their audience, writing for their monthly newsletter)? If you offer these services, what might you ask for in kind (be part of their advisory board, sit on a committee, have your business cards on their front desk, be mentioned on their website or in their newsletter)? Goals of affiliation are to make a small practice feel larger and have a larger audience, by borrowing the network of a like-minded or complimentary organization. Your networking efforts might include connecting with groups of businesspeople, teachers, community activists, and a variety of therapy professionals to give you access and reach within some other pockets of your local community. Take a day a week to have lunch with business owners who are clearly outside your field. After one year, you will have 50 new sources for ideas, expanded thinking, and referrals. You can also network professionally online, using the Internet to join the e-mail lists of professional groups.

Take a risk. It's easy to isolate yourself professionally and socially. If you are isolated professionally, start with a baby step within your existing professional network. Seek out difference. Gravitate to any committee or activity that is new to you. If you are a massage therapist who specializes in working with women, and your tendency is to go to meetings of the American Massage Therapy Association and sit only with your friends, begin to network with those who you don't know, especially those who practice massage differently. If you are a social worker and always end up volunteering time for the legislative action committee of your local National Association of Social Workers chapter, sign up to be part of the committee that organizes the next benefit picnic. You will be meeting a wider circle of people and expanding your network from the inside out.

Increase the number of worlds you belong to. My friend Kay is an outgoing person with strong ties to her community. She seems to know everyone and is a great source of referrals for everything from the best place to get a moderately priced haircut to a top-notch financial planner. When we first met many years ago, I asked her how many "worlds" she belonged to. She counted eight—the parents and teachers at schools her children attended, her synagogue, the neighborhood pool (she sat on the board and knew all the members), colleagues from jobs she had years ago (she stays in touch with lots of people), her husband's professional colleagues (he is a lawyer), the local Democratic political organization (she was a committed participant), and the chamber of commerce (her husband was past president). This doesn't include the world of her close friends, neighbors, and family members. How many worlds do you inhabit? Increase your spheres of operation and broaden your ties to society.

I've Got People

H&R Block, the tax preparation company, promoted a successful advertising campaign on TV a few years ago using the phrase "You've got people." Too often, those of us in private practice feel isolated and without people. The isolation may be that we tend to be introverts, or work in isolation, or feel independent—we don't like to ask for help. Here is a simple exercise, suggested by psychotherapist and writer's coach Susan Borkin (author) of *When Your Heart Speaks, Take Good Notes* (2000), to help you think through who you currently lean on or could ask for support during a time of crisis. She does this using a "mind map," a diagram that represents words, ideas, tasks, or other items as linked to and arranged in a radius around a central key word or idea.

EXERCISE: MY PEOPLE

Diagram your support system so that you know who you can turn to in a time of need.

- *Create your map.* Using pen and paper or software (see http://www. xmind.com), create a mind map, putting yourself in the center.
- *Define your categories.* Have a series of categories of your support team. Susan Borkin suggested these options and more: business coach, editor, best friend, therapist, supervisor, office colleague, office assistant, staff, mentor, family, friends, and other support people in your life and world.
- *Fill in your categories.* List the name and contact information of all people in your support team, whether they are active or inactive in your life right now. You may have someone listed whom you have not seen or talked with in years, yet you are certain if you reached out, that person would immediately be on board to help you. This counts as support, even if you are not ready to activate this resource. Include any other important information: nicknames, most helpful moment with this person, what this person is best at offering to you, a private joke between the two of you.
- *Take in the pleasure of support.* Look at your map and appreciate the pleasure and richness of the support you have. Notice the gaps in your support. This year, make it a priority to fill in any gaps and find more people to have on your team who can also count on you.

CLIENT CONNECTION

Loyal clients are the best defense against a recession. Outstanding service is a sustainable competitive advantage in any economy. Clients who know that you are giving them very caring and expert help will tend to stay with you long enough to complete their treatment or program.

What does customer service mean for you? One therapist works from multiple locations so that her clients don't have to travel far to see her. She does the commuting, not them. Another answers calls within 24 hours and says so on her voice mail.

When you are a small business, one way to act like a larger practice and, as a result, take better care of your clients, is to know when to refer them to other professionals and then make the referral sooner rather than later. If you make a referral quickly and decisively, rather than waiting and hoping things will work out, you will be taking better care of your client. This strategy holds true for referrals of all kinds, including referring a client who is clearly not right for you to another therapist or referring a client you see to others for adjunctive services.

This strategy requires you to detach from a client and recognize that you are just one therapist with one approach. While your approach may be right for many clients, it certainly can't be right for everyone. Take a deep breath, let go of anxiety, and think about this client's best interests. I think you will find this strategy has long-term, positive effects, on both your relationships with clients and your relationships with the other therapists in your network.

In the coaching community that I belong to, it is standard procedure to ask each new client to interview two other coaches before deciding to hire you, so that the client can be sure they have found the right coach. This is a good idea for therapy clients as well, but it may be more difficult for them to effect since most often therapy clients come in at a low point in life and are not at their most resourceful level. Knowing this, you can take on the resourceful role for clients because you are in a better position to know if you will be a good match. If you have a sense that you are not quite right, or that they need other services in addition to seeing you in order to make this a successful relationship, make the referral.

You can build a solid connection with clients if you have a way to help existing clients remember the value of the ongoing work, the gains they have already made, and the process they are engaged in. Do you talk with your clients about the results you see over time and the nature of the process of therapy? Too often therapists don't have this kind of discussion with clients until the termination process. But this discussion is needed to provide a holding space or a container for the changes that the relationship goes through. Identifying results gives clients a way to chart their progress. It's easier for your clients to feel trust when they are clear about their results. Make the process of therapy less mysterious. Help your clients to articulate their gains and put into words how and why the process is working, on an ongoing basis, so that they really understand the effectiveness of your services.

Communicate your boundaries and policies. As a business owner, you need to provide safety for clients by having clear boundaries in the practice that are firm, yet responsive. Boundaries signal a well-run practice and translate into a feeling of safety and professionalism. Check your business boundaries next to see if they contribute to a good client connection.

EXERCISE: BUSINESS BOUNDARIES CHECKLIST

Check the following statements that are true for you. Checking a majority of these items means that you have strong business boundaries. Checking only a few signals a need to identify and strengthen your boundaries.

❑ I have clear policies about the way I work (time, fees, cancellation, missed sessions).

❑ I don't see everyone who calls. I have limits based on diagnosis, symptoms, preference, my skill set, and my ideal client profile.

❑ I have a solid referral network so that I can refer clients I don't want to see, or can't see, to others who will be able to see them.

❑ I practice confidentiality, do not engage in dual relationships, and adhere to the highest standards of my profession, its ethics, and my licensure.

❑ I know how many hours I am willing to work in a week and the settings in which I will and will not work. I don't go beyond these boundaries.

❑ I am aware of the policies, boundaries, and procedures that, if followed, allow me to do the best work I possibly can. I put them in place and keep them there.

❏ Exceptions I make to my boundaries, policies, and procedures that weaken my connection with clients are: _____

❏ Exceptions I make to my boundaries, policies, and procedures that strengthen my connection with clients are: _____

After reviewing this list, correct any boundaries, policies, or procedures that don't promote a strong client connection.

Lifetime Customers

If clients decide to leave your practice, as a business owner you want to set things up so they can comfortably return if they so choose. Businesses call this creating "lifetime" customers—customers who will stay with a company over the long term, repeatedly purchasing services and products, coming and going as need be.

You can consider clients lifetime clients, whether they are active clients (someone you currently see) or inactive (past clients who could return) if you can find ways to keep a line of communication open and hold a space for them in your heart and mind. The skill that is essential to developing lifetime clients is the ability to end therapy well, so that a client can easily return. Helping clients to end well furthers advocacy and trust. It can be hard to let go of clients gracefully, when you don't think the work is completed, when each client represents a portion of your weekly income, or when you don't have a waiting list. Even when you have mastered your feelings of anxiety, not every client will leave well. Some insist on leaving with anger, abruptness, and in a hurtful manner. But you can do your best to try to have good endings with those who are ready. Here's a checklist to help you put the steps in place.

EXERCISE: ENDING WELL CHECKLIST

Check the items that are true for you. Circle the items you have not yet included in your policies that would help you to promote better endings with clients.

- ❑ I help clients leave with an absence of guilt, embarrassment, or shame.
- ❑ In the first session with a new client I say, "I want you to know that one of my policies is to support all termination, for whatever reason. When you are ready to leave, I would like to help you to leave well. Here are my suggestions to make that happen."
- ❑ I have my policy of supporting termination written in my client policy sheet.
- ❑ I educate clients about their role in making a good ending.
- ❑ Although a client has announced that he or she is ready to leave, I take the time to anticipate, with the client, what the next piece of work would be if he or she chose to stay longer.
- ❑ When a client has decided to leave, I do not look for new issues to explore. I allow the process to begin to wind down.
- ❑ I spend the final session talking about how far the client has come, what he or she got from therapy, and what didn't get accomplished this time. I allow time for both my client and me to express appreciation for working with each other.
- ❑ If I feel anxious about my finances when a client leaves, I practice all the anxiety-reducing techniques I know and use a business affirmation (see Chapter 16).
- ❑ If I am worried about my client base, I take action to generate new referrals and do more marketing (see Chapter 8).
- ❑ I consider appropriate ways to stay in contact with old clients, such as keeping them on my mailing list and sending them my periodic newsletter.

Note the items that you circled and begin to incorporate these policies into your practice immediately to support all termination. Let new and existing clients know that you want to support them in ending therapy, their coaching, healing, or consulting well. Add to your policy sheet your thoughts about leaving or find a way to educate all new clients about how to leave.

CHAPTER 7

What to Charge, When to Spend, How to Save

Some service-oriented professionals are uncomfortable with the entire concept of profit. Profiting from your clients can feel especially wrong during a time of recession. You may think: "How can I be a person who helps others and at the same time take money from them? How can I raise my rates if others' resources are low?" This internal dialogue between the need to offer service and yet earn a profit can become a battle. You need to reconcile profit and service in a way that makes sense to your heart and your mind. Possible ways to reconcile these two concepts are to:

- Separate the caring and affection you may have for your clients from your skills, recognizing that you charge for the skills, not the caring
- Think about the time and value you provide, and the viability of your business (if your business doesn't make a profit, you will no longer be able to provide services)
- Track your income and expenses. You will see that a small service-oriented practice is an expensive business to operate.

The definition of a business is an entity that makes a profit, but a normal response to an economic crisis is to become more flexible in terms of pricing. During this recession, consumer spending has dropped precariously. Even though the market of people in distress who need helping and healing services has expanded, your practice client count may be low. If your clients are reluctant to purchase your services, you may want to cut your fees in reaction. But there are many ways to become flexible regarding pricing. If you are dependent on managed care or an external contract to determine your fees, there is little choice but to accept the amount determined. If you have a fee-for-session or out-of-pocket policy, you need to think carefully about your financial decisions. Before taking any steps, read this chapter in full.

Cutting your fees may seem essential to attract new clients, but it overlooks an important point: Whether you are a sole proprietor or part of a group practice, whether you work from home or out of a fancy downtown office, a therapy business is considered an *expensive* business to operate; your expenses will always be a substantial percentage of your gross income. It may not seem that way when you have a small practice because there is relatively little start-up expense, especially with a home office. But when you look at your expenses as a *percentage of gross income*, you see the true picture. For example, as a sole proprietor of a therapy business, your product is likely to be your therapy sessions; you may only bill based only your contact hours with clients. You can't send in a lower-paid "substitute therapist" to deliver therapy. You also can't mass-produce your sessions. Your time and energy is limited—there are only so many client sessions you can conduct each week. Based on this limitation of time and delivery of service, a private practice can't easily match the high profit ratios of a manufacturing or consulting business. You simply can't produce as much product.

If your primary revenue stream is generated by delivering hourly sessions, your profit potential will always be capped. Since you have some set expenses that must be in place in order to operate, your ratio of expenses to profit will always be relatively substantial. In order to be as highly profitable as possible, you need to carefully consider how to charge for your time, what to spend to help your practice survive, and how to cut or control your expenses to keep it viable. We will look at how to keep your fee strong enough to safeguard your practice, and then explore additional strategies, such as multiple income streams and other packaging ideas that can increase your profits without turning away clients.

YOUR FEE

If your fee represents the basis of your earnings, you want to have it based on your overall business plan. Keep in mind the following six criteria for setting a fee:

1. *Your vision for the practice*: Your fee needs to reflect your philosophy of service and your vision for the practice. Match your fee to your market. If you want to work with senior citizens with fixed incomes, your fee must be low to reflect that market. If your service is extremely specialized and of very high value, your fee needs to be high. If your vision is to create a practice that stays full with a big flow of clients, your fee needs to be priced in the middle of the market, to keep you competitive.

2. *A desire to adhere to your business goals*: Look at your business budget (see Chapter 3). What do you need to earn this year and why? What do you need to cover your expenses and ensure a profit? What are your goals for the year? If you are in the expansion phase of your business and need some cash reserves, consider raising your fees. If you are concerned about retaining your existing clients, keep your fees at their existing level.

3. *Market forces*: It's helpful to know what others charge in your local area, as well as what your market can pay. For example, therapists in a rural area generally charge less than those in a major metropolitan city, based on market forces. Therapists with corporate clients need to stay current with other training companies and charge enough to be taken seriously. Most professionals I meet talk about their fees informally; many licensing and professional associations caution against fee setting. In my workshops, I will ask participants to establish the range of fees: What is the highest fee they hear of and the lowest? We always hear of very large ranges, sometimes hundreds of dollars between highs and lows. Many professions track average or median fees in their annual surveys for members. If you can determine the range of fees normally charged within your profession or local area, then you

can decide better where you want to position your practice—on the high, middle, or low end of what is normally charged.

4. *Perceived value*: The unwritten rule of business pricing is that you can charge what the market will bear, based on your real or perceived value. Perceived value is a felt or intuitive sense of what something is worth, based on the benefits offered. Two therapists in the same city can offer the same type of therapy, but one will be able to charge twice what the other one does. The one who charges more has clients who perceive that his or her skill and talent are top quality and therefore they are willing to pay top dollar.

5. *Your timeline to fill your practice*: In an earlier recession during the '80s, my husband was laid off from his job. I was leisurely building my practice and immediately rethought the timing of my business plan. I needed to move quickly and decided to start several groups at a low fee so that they would fill without a long wait. Over time, I raised the fee of the groups to bring them into line with the going rate of therapy groups in my local area. If you need to fill hours fast, you will probably set a lower fee. If you have no money pressures and are in no hurry to add extra clients, you can wait for those clients who can pay full fee.

6. *Professional courtesy*: Sometimes you will set your fee as a courtesy to another therapist. I had a colleague who was seeing a wife and asked me to see the husband. She also asked if I would match her fee, which I agreed to do out of professional courtesy. This includes setting your fee to work with a referring organization or a sponsoring group. One therapist worked out a relationship with a local church, where she offered church members a discounted rate for the first three sessions.

Now that you know six *right* criteria to use when setting your fee, here is a list of *wrong* ones:

1. *Anxiety*: Emotion doesn't have a place in deciding how much to charge. Decide on a fee that is fair, meets the right criteria, and reflects

your business objectives. While it is good to be flexible, that doesn't mean to be reactive. Don't raise or lower it based on your worries or fears of keeping or losing a particular client. Your fee must be based on logic. If you need to negotiate a discounted fee with a client, make sure you put some time conditions on it so that you can keep renegotiating the fee in short intervals.

2. *Guilt:* Some therapists feel guilty about charging what they are worth or charging a high fee during a recession. Your expenses are not going to drop during the recession. You need to keep your bottom line in sight. Rather than feeling guilty, see your practice through the eyes of a business owner. Make sure that you stay profitable. Set an example of fiscal responsibility for your clients. Be fair to your clients and to yourself. If you have feelings of fear regarding success or confusion about reconciling profit and service, often the source of guilt, get therapy, coaching, or supervision to help you resolve your feelings about money. Don't sabotage your practice by acting out your feelings with your fee.

3. *Zero-sum game mentality:* This mind-set says that there is only a fixed amount of money in the world. If I take more, you get less. If I win, you lose. This is both illogical and demeaning to your clients. Instead, see your decision to set a fair fee as a win-win scenario. With the right fee, you can become a better therapist and better serve those clients you choose to see. If you can't stay in good shape and keep your office door open, you can't help clients.

4. *Love:* Some clients confuse love with the caring or affection with which therapy is often delivered , and they feel offended at having to pay for love. You are not selling love. I heard a senior therapist in New York explain it to a client this way: "You pay me for my skill. The love I choose to give is free."

5. *Anger:* Sometimes therapists will set a fee based on anger or resentment with a specific client or a certain type of client. For example, a therapist might say, "I don't like to work with that type of diagnosis. It's too difficult. If a person comes in with that diagnosis, I'll see him or her

but charge double." This is not a good way to set a fee. You will do better to refer clients you don't want to see, and let your practice contain only those clients who help you to work at your best.

6. *Identity questions*: I have witnessed new therapists, fresh out of graduate school, decide to charge a high fee as a way to validate themselves. "I have a lot of life experience. I know everything I need to about psychology. I'll charge $150 an hour," a new graduate might say. This often speaks more to an issue of professional identity than to good business sense. I have also seen this go the other way, where a therapist with 30 years of experience, who works wonders with clients and has a waiting list, seriously undercharges and suffers as a result. She feels she isn't worth more.

EXERCISE: SAYING YOUR FEE WITH A SMILE

You will know that you have set your fee well if you can state it out loud with ease, as naturally as you might say your name.

- Stand in front of a mirror, make eye contact with yourself, and state your fee as you would to a client.
- Observe your nonverbal behaviors.
- If you can't say your fee without grimacing, rolling your eyes, giving an embarrassed laugh, or looking down at the floor, go back and review the criteria to make sure you have set a fee that makes good business sense for you.
- Repeat this exercise with a friend or colleague and ask for feedback about how you look and sound.

LOWERING YOUR FEE

What do you do when a potential or existing client says that you are too expensive? Many therapists have a sliding scale. But before you jump to the conclusion that you must have one in order to retain clients who can't pay your full fee, consider these questions: How does a sliding scale fit into your business plan and business vision? What purpose will it serve? How will you determine the rates? A sliding scale presents some inherent problems for you, placing you in a role for which you have no formal training—that of a financial analyst/evaluator. If you offer a sliding scale pegged to a client's income, you assume the task of evaluating what your client earns, spends, and therefore can afford to pay for therapy. I believe that clients who ask if you have a sliding scale are really asking if they can pay you less, not to have their financial life examined. For this reason, I prefer that instead of offering a sliding scale, you consider one of the following straightforward options for discounting a fee:

Run small groups or classes. Offer ongoing groups at a rate lower than your individual fee. Groups let you leverage your time and still offer quality service. An ongoing group might start with one person; add others as you can. Group therapy (or coaching or consulting) is a great way to deliver therapy services. A group does not have to be defined by the number of people who attend, but by the type of work that takes place. A group can be eight people, but I have also seen successful groups made up of three. Think about your experience with groups and define what makes your groups different from individual sessions. For example, in my groups I use peer feedback, highlight the group psychodynamics, use psychoeducational content, set up role-plays between group members, and design community-building interactions, none of which I do in individual sessions. When you are clear that group therapy is distinct and different from what you do with a client during individual sessions, you could conceivably start a group with one client, as long as he or she understood that in time, the group would fill with others. I coached a therapist who had a group of two people that ran for a year. Both clients felt that they benefited tremendously from the experience. The work was different from an individual session, with much more time for feedback and a focus on social and group dynamics. Neither client felt that the group lacked anything; it felt "full" enough to them. Redefine your perception of a group and run more groups to offer value and simultaneously leverage your time.

Prorate your time slots. Offer hard-to-fill times at reduced rates. This gives you a way to fill your hours and have some discounted sessions. Give each session a rate. For example, early morning sessions are $80 per hour, midday are $70, evening sessions (prime time) are $90.

Offer shorter sessions at a lesser price. Some clients might prefer 30-minute sessions at half your rate instead of full-hour sessions at a full rate. This is especially helpful for clients who want frequency rather than intensity. Instead of seeing a client for 2 hour-long sessions a month, you could schedule that same person for 30 minutes twice a month. For well-motivated clients who need to pay less, this can be a helpful treatment option.

Discount prepaid packages. Prepaid packages reward those who pay up front and make a solid commitment. You save on billing time and retain serious clients who have reduced financial circumstances. If your going rate is $80 per hour for individual sessions, offer a special package: 10 sessions over a 3-month time frame for $750, prepaid. Define all your packages and discounts in writing. This is best done if you accept credit cards, to give you control over billing. See the section in this chapter on becoming a merchant account.

PACKAGING YOUR SERVICES

Sometimes the issue isn't your fee, it's how you present your services. Most of us want to feel some sense of choice and control when we purchase services. Create a menu of payment options for clients by packaging your services. Packaging creates choice and gives clients a sense of control regarding how they spend their dollars, a strong business selling point. By mixing and matching services and their price points, you can custom-design an optimum package for every client. One way to present these packages is to name them, price them, and then list them in all of your marketing materials and on your Web site. Here's an examples of how one coach packages her services:

Sandy Forster (Coachville, 2002), a money coach from Queensland, Australia, offers the following diversified services to help her clients have greater levels of prosperity: individual coaching, telephone classes, audiotapes of a money-based program, and workshops. She has packaged these services into three combinations, and named the packages Gold, Deluxe, and Elite, but you can adapt this idea and use more neutral names for your packages:

- The Gold package includes ten weeks of group coaching with daily e-mail support and is priced at $295. This package is designed for those who want the most economical coaching.
- The Deluxe package includes the services of the Gold package, plus a one-on-one prosperity coaching session with Forster and is priced at $495. This is designed for those who prefer additional focus and support.
- The Elite package adds these services plus a CD set, a workbook, and a series of six one-on-one prosperity coaching sessions with Forster, for a fee of $1,400. This package is geared to those individuals who want the added focus of private coaching sessions as well as tools to use repeatedly.

   Forster says that she finds having various pricing options and package inclusions means that she has something for everyone and is able to attract clients from both ends of the economic scale, to assist them to bring more prosperity into their lives.

Even if you offer only one service, you can create a menu and a pricing package. Let's say your only service is individual therapy sessions. The variables we will use for your menu and package of services will be time and frequency. Here are your two menu items:

- individual sessions, one hour in length, at a rate of $100/ hour

- individual sessions by phone for 30 minutes, at a rate of $50/hour

Based on these two menu items, here are four packages a client can choose from. Each one has been given a name, a description, and a price point:

Package #1: *Crisis Intervention*: Best for someone who is in a difficult situation and needs outpatient treatment with multiple sessions per week plus an additional check-in phone call once each weekend. Eight hours per month, two sessions a week. Price: $850 per month.

Package #2: *Working Through*: Recommended for those who need to slow down the pace of therapy, consolidate gains, feel supported, set new goals, and continue to build momentum. One hourly session a week. Price $400 per month.

Package #3: *Maintenance*: Supportive therapy, best for those in stable relationships and situations, good for staying on a steady track. One hour every other week and two 30-minute phone sessions on the other weeks, twice per month. Price: $300 per month.

Package #4: *Transitioning*: Helpful for those who need only minimal contact. Two 30-minute phone sessions every other week. Price: $100 per month.

EXERCISE: PACKAGING MY SERVICES

Follow the directions to package your services, by combining, naming, giving definition, and pricing the packages.

1. List your current services.
2. Combine them into several distinct packages.
3. Name each package.
4. Give each a rationale and description.
5. Price each package.

When someone questions your fee, or the fact that you don't accept managed care payments, you can let that person know that you have many options that make therapy affordable: groups, discounts on prepayment, less intensive packages that allow someone to see you fewer times but still receive high value and make progress, time-of-day slots that are discounted, and shorter sessions for a lower price.

MERCHANT ACCOUNTS

Another way to help clients pay for your services is to expand your range of payment by accepting credit cards, that is, becoming a merchant account. The fees that are collected by credit card companies are offset by the immediacy of payment. This gives clients another way to afford your services and eliminates the need for collections from unpaid bills and checks that do not clear the bank. The steps to accepting credit cards are the following:

1. Investigate the offerings of various credit card providers to become a merchant account. (I have recommendations for various providers on my Web site resource page at http://www.privatepracticesuccess.com).

2. Purchase a credit card machine to process a client's card each time *or* use a secure Internet site to bill the client after the session. You will need to determine which option fits you best prior to signing up with a company. Regardless of which option you choose, the funds will be deposited into your bank account.

3. Develop a permission form that you have a client sign (name, credit card number, and permission statement for you to bill for sessions) that you keep on file in a secure place.

4. Let clients know about this additional payment option on your business brochure, on your Web site, and in your office waiting room.

ELIMINATE CANCELLATIONS

Profit can leak out of a practice from client no-shows or cancellations. You can help to reduce this problem by addressing this in a clear, immediate fashion during the first phone contact. Help new or potential clients understand your cancellation policy prior to booking their first session and what your expectations about attendance are for new clients. If you establish rapport during the booking conversation, it may reduce no-shows, since your new clients will have already established a relationship, albeit a brief one, with you. Additional information about your policies can be part of your voice mail ("press one if you are a new client, press two to hear about the no-show or cancellation policy or to reschedule") or on a follow-up e-mail after booking, or by directing someone to your Web site that posts the information. Some therapists find that a reminder call or e-mail to a new client reduces no-shows. Collect immediately for missed sessions (another value in using credit cards, or have a bill for the missed session to give a client at the next scheduled session).

EXERCISE: CANCELLATION POLICY CHECKLIST

Use this guide to help you develop your cancellation policy and then keep it in place.

❏ My cancellation policy is clearly explained in on my policy sheet, my brochure, my Web site, e-mails from my office, and/or my voice mail.

❏ I educate all new and potential clients to the policy in my intake form and verbally at the first session.

❏ I collect for cancellations immediately by credit card or by presenting a bill at the next opportunity.

❏ I am flexible with existing client cancellations, in that I either make the policy workable (24 or 48 hours notice) or allow that the missed session be billed at a discounted fee (as long as this is clearly spelled out).

❏ I (or my staff) contact new clients a day ahead to remind them of their appointment.

❑ I am consistent with my policy, even when it makes me nervous or anxious, to let my clients understand that my practice operates with policies and boundaries.

RAISING YOUR FEE

During a bad economy, raising your fee may drive clients away. But despite a down market, you may be ready to slightly raise your rates. It's time to raise your fee, even a little, if:

- You' re impoverished. It does no good for you to be broke and sacrificing within your business. If you are in debt or facing poverty, look to see if you are undercharging.
- You increased your expenses. If you have upgraded your business with a new location, expanded phone service, bigger staff, or more services, you may need to raise your fee to cover these added values.
- You want a cost-of-living raise. Be a good boss to yourself. Give yourself a raise to cover the cost of living. Raise your prices, raise your self-esteem, and lower your resentment.
- You received additional training. Most therapists invest heavily in their ongoing training. If this is true for you, know that this investment will serve you well and benefit your clients. Raise your rates to match your level of experience and certification.
- You have a waiting list. Sometimes raising your fee can be a response to having too much business. Raising your rates may help slow down referrals a bit and ease up the pressures of a long waiting list.

When you are ready to raise your fee, you can follow these steps in order to preserve your ongoing relationship with existing clients:

EXERCISE: RAISING YOUR FEE

If you need to raise your fee, do it in the least disruptive manner, using the following points as a guide.

- I give my clients clear notice of fee changes, verbally and in writing. (Since money is so emotional, it's best to make all communication regarding money very clear).
- I give my clients ample notice of fee changes (30 to 60 days), since any change in the frame of therapy may trigger decisions to leave. This way, my clients have time to leave well.
- I anticipate a reaction. Most of us don't like change of any kind, especially about increasing prices.
- I am available to process any reaction with my clients. For that reason, I inform them in the beginning of the session, not on their way out the door at the end.
- I help them to use their reactions as part of the therapeutic process, a chance for deepening their work. I calm my anxiety and present the change cleanly.
- I don't offer an overly long explanation. A long explanation may soothe my anxiety when I tell my clients that I am raising my fee, but it doesn't necessarily help them.

MULTIPLE INCOME STREAMS

In my earlier books I have promoted the idea of diversification with your product line. Many therapists and service providers have a variety of offerings that can give them active and passive income. Active income means that you are seeing clients and your time is involved. Passive income derives from product sales that happen without your involvement or time at the point of sale. Currently, passive income is best accomplished with the help of the Internet and a Web site (see Chapter 9 for a full explanation of how to set up a Web site.) For example, Bruce, an addictions counselor and trained acupuncturist, has six separate profit centers within his sole proprietorship. The active income streams include:

- individual counseling
- addiction groups
- family counseling sessions
- educational classes about addictions

The passive income streams include:

- a membership Web site (a Web site with a monthly fee to access)
- audiotapes for sale on his Web site
- books for sale on his Web site

Bruce has lots of crossover from his passive income streams into his active ones, and vice versa.

Casey Truffo, my colleague and fellow marketing coach and author of *Be a Wealthy Therapist* (2007), sees the advent of Internet-based income streams as the new direction for therapists, to help them leverage their time and move beyond a "one-to-one" ratio of one hour equals one fee. To Truffo, quick product sales satisfy several customer needs: immediacy of information (they can download an audiotape within minutes) and price point—most Internet products offered by service professionals are substantially less expensive than a full course of therapy.

According to Truffo (2009), clinicians can leverage their income by augmenting in-person practice sessions with informational products—books, CDs, audiotapes, e-books, and e-courses—created once and then sold repeatedly via the Internet. With this additional income stream, you can add to your hourly session revenue. While the time and effort of producing Internet-based products (recording audio, developing e-books, shooting video) is substantial, it only must be done once and then, with the help of a Web site designer, the products can be placed on a "kiosk" (sales page on your Web site that is linked to your payment choice). Since the Internet never closes, consumers can purchase products for immediate download and use even while you sleep. Often these products require their own marketing plan, which is different from how you would market your traditional services, but again, you can find the help to create the exposure and platform you need from many sources, in order to sell your products over time. See Casey's Web site in the contact section of this book for more tips and ideas about multiple income strategies.

EXERCISE: INCOME STREAM CHECKLIST

Check the services you already offer or want to add to your practice to generate additional income.

❑ individual sessions in your office
❑ workshops (self-sponsored or hosted by other organizations)
❑ classes or telephone groups
❑ e-mail consultations
❑ on-site consulting for corporations and organizations
❑ organizational development (team-building, mediation, leadership training, etc.)
❑ conducting assessments or supplying testing materials
❑ publishing or self-publishing and distributing books, manuals, or pamphlets
❑ selling audiotapes or CDs you produce
❑ selling videotapes of your workshops
❑ additional complimentary product sales
❑ writing articles for publication
❑ radio or television appearances
❑ public speaking engagements
❑ other training or teaching endeavors
❑ program development for yourself or others
❑ licensing your programs to others
❑ Web site or e-mail newsletter with membership fee

Add services in a planned, not random, manner. Set aside the resources, space, and budget to finance the additional profit center. Treat it like a separate yet valuable part of your existing practice. Track the income separately and the time involved. Note the cross-referrals it gives you. When it is well established, consider adding another one.

KEEPING EXPENSES LOW

Direct and indirect expenses in a streamlined therapy practice generally run 30% to 40% (not including self-employment taxes). When your income is low, you need to look for ways to cut expenses. But remember, your practice still needs money and investment, even during a recession. The goal is a leaner practice, not one that is starving.

Best investments in a down market include the following:

- *Technology*: Software, systems, computers, pagers, voice mail systems, anything that helps you to be more productive.
- *Visibility*: A Web site, effective print advertising, Internet advertising such as Google AdWords; join communities to help you become better known; write and build your platform.
- *Leveraging*: Bring in associates to rent unused office time; share advertising campaigns or marketing ideas and assignments; use peer supervision; train with colleagues.
- *Evidence-based methods*: Measure successful outcomes and promote to existing and potential clients and referral sources.
- *Networking*: Attend meetings, continue to maintain a strong, active network.
- *Business identity*: Keep business cards, brochures up-to-date; practice your introductions and how to articulate your services to others.
- *Supervision*: Maintain professional support.
- *Self-care*: Stay in good mental and physical shape.
- *Small, meaningful touches in your office*: Provide your office with small things that heighten your enjoyment in your environment.

Worst investments in a down market include:

- *Large capital expenses*: Minimize equipment, or buy at a discount or on eBay.
- *Costly training programs*: Limit training unless you are sure it will have a satisfactory ROI (return on investment.)
- *Office decoration*: Expensive artwork or furniture, while nice, rarely gives you an ROI.
- *Expensive printing*: Don't overdesign your business materials or your Web site. You only need it to be "good enough."

Cut back on these items:

- *Your menial work*: Hire others to do menial work and free yourself for the important aspects of delivering service, marketing, or networking.
- *Print Advertising*: Advertising needs repetition to be effective and yields results sporadically. Instead, network in low-cost ways. Go to lunch with a different potential referral source every week.
- *Image*: You don't need an expensive wardrobe, flashy Web site, or luxury suite to do great work. You can serve your clients well from a professional yet modest suburban office, rather than a downtown expensive high-rise suite. Many clients prefer a "homey" touch.

HIDDEN EXPENSES

Some of the expenses you incur with a service-based business are less obvious, but still real. One is the psychic cost of working with the psychology or physiology of others. Since you need to be emotionally open and empathic with clients, you may take in some of their feelings. You need to psychically clean out from time to time. Get sufficient *positive* peer support. Consultants, psychotherapists, and coaches may contend with physical ailments based on sitting still for hours at a time. If you are a physical therapist or other type of body worker, you may find your own body aches from the efforts of massaging or manipulating others 6 hours a day. Again, make sure you budget for the self-care you need to stay in good shape. (See the self-care checklist in Chapter 2 for ideas.)

Eliminate your debt. Debt is costly, based in part on the interest you lose by not having collected monies owed to you, but also in the time you spend trying to collect unpaid fees and the psychic energy or feelings of frustration you carry in association to the debt. Avoid carrying large amounts of receivables, the payments owed to you by clients, by instituting a policy of getting paid at the time of delivering service. If you have existing receivables, contact all the people who owe you money by phone or letter. Be firm and try to clear up the accounts. If that doesn't work, consider using a collection agency to collect large amounts. If some of your accounts receivables are the result of therapy that ended poorly, and a dissatisfied client refuses to pay, a better business decision may be to simply write off the account as a "bad debt" and take the loss. Sometimes the energy you will need to expend to recover payment from a dissatisfied client is counterproductive. If the amount is under $1,000, you may find it best to walk away from the situation and put your energy toward generating new, and better, referrals. Talk with your accountant about writing off all of your bad debts at the end of the fiscal year.

THE MICROPRACTICE

In a 2006 survey, John Klein of *Psychotherapy Finances* found that only 50% of mental health clinicians own and use a computer in their private practices. "Too often, at the point of delivery, psychotherapy is basically a cottage industry," he explained. "It's someone in a room, doing paperwork, by hand, with little interest or understanding about virtual marketing, high-tech delivery methods or automated operating systems" (Grodzki, 2007, p. 27).

But for those who are tech-savvy, consider the benefits of a micropractice. Gautam Naik (2007) described a micropractice as "a Norman Rockwell practice with a 21st-century backbone." The leading proponent for this is Gordon Moore, who quit his big practice 6 years ago and wrote about starting a micropractice. In 2001, Dr. Moore borrowed $15,000 to start a solo medical practice in a tiny space with no nurse, receptionist, or waiting room. He bought computer software to help him track patients' appointments, illnesses, and medications and to process insurance claims. Patients at his "micropractice" can call or e-mail to get appointments the same day. Visits last 30 minutes. Dr. Moore can be reached day or night on his cell phone. To refill a prescription, he walks "zero feet," he says, and taps a few keys on his laptop. According to Moore (2002), his micropractice's overhead consumes about 35% of revenue, while a traditional practice's overhead can be as much as twice that.

One therapist who operates a micropractice is Charles Scot Giles (2007), a board-certified chaplain, counselor, and hypnotherapist. Scot's practice is traditional in content and services, but uniquely spare in administrative costs and staffing. Here is Scot, in his own words, explaining how this kind of practice works:

> Talking a year ago with a physician friend about how I run my practice, I was surprised when he told me there was a name for what I'm doing. "You're running a micropractice," he said. "What's more, more and more physicians are doing the same." So I decided to learn more about it and improve my game. A micropractice isn't really new at all. It's an updating of a successful old model of a doctor working out of a limited space, giving people the time they need, answering phone calls personally, and offering quick appointments to those who call.
>
> The way a contemporary micropractice differs is that it uses 21st-century technology to eliminate all or most staff, and to cut through the paperwork that caused most doctors to leave solo practice. As a result the overhead is low. This allows you to spend more time with people and less time on administration. I use technology to do things that in other practices are done with staff. Computers do my accounting, billing, record-keeping, scheduling, and keep me current on research. I use waiting lists when I must, and I'm always looking for ways to streamline (called "continuous flow processing"). I keep my practice lean and personal.
>
> It's worked for me. Because I have tight control of overhead, I've not had to raise my rates in years. I can usually get new people in within a reasonable time, and I've always got room to accommodate emergencies or special circumstances for established clients. Despite the fact that I give away a lot of what I do in free programs, my paying client schedule remains comfortable and I do fine.

Like Scot, I have also been running a micropractice for years, but my version of this pared-down model is less minimal and more integrative. I rely on technology to allow me to be a solopreneur, although I do have one regular staff person, who is a virtual assistant. She lives and works in Toronto, Ontario, Canada, which is in my time zone. She is an adult with her own business and bills me as an independent contractor. We share information over voice mail, e-mail, fax, Internet, and Intranet. She provides me with about 10 hours a month of administrative help, at a reasonably modest expense. I spend another 10 hours a week doing administration myself. It is not difficult to put policies in place to make sure an assistant is HIPAA (Health Insurance Portability and Accountability Act) compliant and can keep files and billing confidential. Because my practice is highly diversified, it must accommodate my roles as psychotherapist, business coach, teacher, trainer, and writer. To do this, I have added additional resources such as software programs and Web hosting services.

The hallmarks of a micropractice are:

- *Very low overhead.* Do as much as you can by yourself so you do not have to hire staff or pay other providers. Have better balance in your life by not having to see so many clients to cover your costs. Maximize your net earnings even though your gross earnings might be less than your competition.
- *High technology.* Use 21st-century technology to do things that are traditionally done by staff. Use voice mail, e-mail, Web sites, and computerized practice management and record-keeping software. The office is basically paperless. Anything that needs to be stored is quickly scanned and attached to the client's chart. The original document goes into the shredder. The computer backs itself up to a removable hard disk system every night. Read further to see how to use high-tech resources for your practice.
- *Unfettered access.* Make it as easy as possible for clients to get hold of you. Update voice mail messages each day telling people when to expect a return call. Allow established clients to call on your cell phone or e-mail to help cut down on telephone tag time.

HIGH-TECH RESOURCES

Every small business owner is short on time. One way to maximize your business operations, to save time and money, is to use technology. I have found that with some helpful coaching, even the most computer-shy professional can benefit from adopting some high-tech resources. Avrum Nadigel, an adolescent and family therapist from Toronto, Ontario, Canada has a background in business and consults for hospitals and other organizations about using technology such as Web 2.0, podcasts, and blogs. He is my go-to guy for all things technological, and offers a basic tool kit for small business owners.

According to Avrum, people approach technology backward. "We get excited about technology and find cool software to download to our computers, but we forget to attach the software or gadgets to a theoretical paradigm that makes sense to us," he said. "Since the Internet is endless, with this approach we could spend our lives exploring new things, instead of finding things that are relevant to help us get our work done." Avrum suggests the following tool kit that is grounded in the basic needs of the average change agent (therapist, coach, consultant, service professional).

1. *Set goals*: Select a practice management approach that helps you manage all the information, tasks, and goals of your practice. The two most popular approaches correspond to two best-selling books: Stephen Covey's *7 Habits of Highly Effective People* (2004) and David Allen's *Getting Things Done* (2002). If you want to get the essence of each approach quickly, without reading the book, http://www.wickipedia.com is the place to go. Just put in the book title and you can see an overview of the salient points. Based on the approach you like, there is software to help you implement the approach for your practice. If you like Covey, the best software is called Plan Plus (go to http://www.planplusonline.com). If you like Allen, try his software from: http://www.davidco.com.

2. *Manage information*: Avrum recommends one of two software packages to help you manage all the information flow of your practice. If you use a PC (personal computer) he suggests http://www.act.com. If you use a Mac, he likes Daylight software: http://www.daylight.com.

3. *Preview before you purchase*: Software is expensive and Avrum suggests you check things out before you purchase in one of these ways.

At the vendor Web site, look for the FAQ (frequently asked questions) to see what the software does. See if the Web site has a chat board or a bulletin board for users and read some of the posts to see what kind of support is possible for new purchasers. Go to http://www.youtube.com, type in the name of the software you are considering purchasing, and most likely you will find a video posted there to show you how to use the software.

4. *Bring in more resources*: For almost any method you like to use, there is probably some software to make it easier. Are you a family therapist who likes to create a genogram to diagram a family? Do it on your computer with software such as http://www.genopro.com. Want to let clients schedule their own sessions online? Try http://www.therapypartner.com (also does online billing) or http://www.basecamp.com. Need a calendar you can access anywhere? Try one of the free ones, found on servers such as Yahoo! or Google. Hate to take notes? Maybe http://www.evernote.com will make it more enjoyable.

5. *Work smarter.* Avrum is a self-confessed computer nerd, so he gets a lot of pleasure from high-tech gadgets. This is one that sounds helpful for our professions. It's the smart pen from http://www.livescribe.com. It works like a real pen, but one that has a an infrared camera that records what you write or draw, an audio recorder that records what you hear, and a computer embedded in the pen. Later you can replay the audio or video that coordinates with your notes. Avrum uses it during his family therapy sessions. Using the special paper that comes with the pen, he makes notes, such as: "New patient: young man, 27 years old, suicidal." When he reviews his notes, he taps on the word "suicidal" and the patient's voice is activated, speaking about his suicidal feelings. Avrum has the exact dialogue from the session to add back into his notes. He says this has taken his notes to a new level of accuracy and immediacy.

As you continue to look for ways to upgrade your practice management, trim expenses, and increase profits, this checklist may be of help.

EXERCISE: PROFIT DRAINS, PROFIT GAINS CHECKLIST

Check those that apply to you.

Profit Drains

❏ I have no business plan or a weak business plan.

❏ I don't have enough liquidity or cash on hand so I am always borrowing money.

❏ I offer the wrong services to the right people.

❏ I offer the right services to the wrong people.

❏ I am in a location not conducive to getting or retaining clients.

❏ I don't have a good accounting system for accurate tracking of finances.

❏ I have too much credit card debt.

❏ My income can't support my lifestyle.

❏ I have poor communication with my clients regarding fees and my policies.

❏ I spend too much time doing menial work and too little time earning money.

❏ I have poor self-care resulting in feeling burned out.

❏ I don't automate. I don't use or own a computer. I don't have a Web site. I do all my record keeping by hand.

❏ I spend little time thinking about practice management or ways to automate or update my existing systems so that I can spend less time in the office doing administration and more time providing service to clients.

Profit Gains

❏ Every dollar I spend on my business contributes to furthering my profitability.

❏ I have less paperwork come across my desk since I automated my systems.

❏ I only work with serious clients (those clients I consider ideal for me and my services).

❏ I reduced my debt and high interest payments.

❑ I pay attention to details of finances.

❑ I collect fees as soon as possible to eliminate accounts receivables.

❑ I put profitability ahead of comfort or appearance.

❑ I have a good accounting system in place to be able to see my finances and budget to date at a glance.

❑ I am a skilled manager of my practice.

❑ I made a list of my expenses and cut them by 20%.

❑ I leverage my time and efforts to get the most money for the least time.

❑ I surround myself with bright people dedicated to my success.

❑ I ask questions and consult regularly with my "advisory board"—those people who want me to succeed and have wisdom or skills that can help me do so (see Chapter 15).

❑ I have multiple profit centers and/or a menu of pricing and packaging.

❑ I spend 80% of my time delivering service and generating referrals, 20% of my time doing all else.

❑ I have good self-care in place, so that I am not exhausted, overwhelmed, or depressed.

❑ I am a model of my services. I walk my talk.

CHAPTER 8

Low-Cost Marketing

One problem with a private practice is just how private it can become. Many therapists who offer valuable, important services remain unknown to those who could benefit from them most. In a down market, you need to be less hidden. You will want to increase your marketing, but not your marketing expenses. In this chapter, we will explore low-cost, effective marketing strategies. In Chapter 9, I will walk you through another important marketing process: developing an Internet presence.

During a recession your potential market increases: The numbers of people in psychological, financial, spiritual, and/or physical pain grows. But do these people who need your services know you exist? If not, it is your job to help them find you. Do they understand the value of your services? Again, it is your job to articulate the benefits you offer. Once these issues have been achieved, do people feel compelled to take the final step and sign up as clients or patients? Again, it is your responsibility to "close the sale" and help potential clients get started with their therapy. In sum, the three steps to capitalizing on marketing opportunities inherent during a recession are:

- *Keep your practice visible.* Your target market needs to be able to find you.
- *Make the value of your services explicit.* Your target market may think they cannot afford your services. You have to look for ways to stay flexible—access, pricing, availability, payment options.
- *Convert effectively.* All marketing is basically a numbers

game: The conversion rate (the difference between the number of potential clients who may hear about your services and those who will follow through and become actual clients) is *at best* 5 to 1. You need to know how to enroll clients with integrity.

How do you accomplish these steps during a crisis, without accruing big expenses? Print advertising (yellow pages, direct mail, magazine and newspaper ads, etc.) is expensive. Speaking and writing is time consuming and only effective if you can enroll clients (convert members of your audience into paying clients). The best strategy for marketing in a recession is the easiest one for most therapists: creating relationships, also known as low-pressure networking. I will show you how to reach out to your community using your existing strengths so that you don't need to feel promotional, awkward, or anxious. Networking by attraction instead of promotion can help showcase you at your best.

I make a distinction between push marketing and pull marketing. Push marketing is promotional. You push yourself, your product, or even your message at a potential client or referral source. Pull marketing is about connecting. You honor the best of yourself as you build relationships within a larger community. Marketing by attraction feels like a magnetic pull, highlighting the best elements of your work and allowing the right clients to naturally gravitate toward you. It is nonlinear and carries no personal, human cost.

Generating referrals by pull marketing is similar to building an engine. The engine requires some work to build properly and put in place, and it needs continual injections of high-quality fuel, but once it begins to run, it keeps going. I want you to build a referral engine that you can depend on, fuel every now and then, and forget about the rest of the time. Once you do this properly, the engine will have a life of its own.

On the other hand, push marketing is basically selling; each sales call requires considerable effort from you. This is why so many therapists get tired even thinking about marketing—it's an exhausting process. Pull marketing or generating referrals can be energy *producing*, once the engine gets set and going. The small actions that build the engine can have steady, lasting results. Instead of getting up each day and *digging* for referrals, I am going to teach you a strategy so that you learn how to *seed* relationships in your community. Therapists who enjoy the marketing process know how to:

1. Articulate your basic message.
2. Ask for the referral with ease.
3. Give to get.
4. Enroll.

When the steps are used together, they form a more satisfying process, one that helps you feel calm because you are prepared, nonpromotional because you have a larger purpose, and focused because you have a plan. Use all four and networking will no longer seem like such a mysterious, difficult challenge.

ARTICULATING YOUR BASIC MESSAGE

Your first step is to be less of a secret. Simply get out more. Only by reaching out beyond your office door can you meet those who can refer clients. To do this, you need to have strategies that are natural for you—methods that don't make you feel awkward, nervous, or phony. I see many talented and gifted colleagues fall short in this area due to personal shyness or timidity when it comes to speaking about their work. They say:

"I feel that if I talk too much about myself it's like boasting, and I was taught not to do that. I am more comfortable listening than speaking about myself."

"I go to social and professional gatherings and wait for a chance to bring up what is new in my practice, but I can wait all night for an opening. The right moment to speak up never seems to come."

"I don't say much about my work because I am just like any other (therapist, healer, coach, consultant). There really isn't anything special about me. No one would care. I get tongue-tied when I try to sell myself."

Launching ourselves into a conversation with the intention of trying to let others know more about our services can feel risky and complicated. But business assertiveness is a learnable skill. Let's look at some ways to make it easier.

First, recognize that speaking up about your work is not an ego-driven exercise. Instead, it is a way of creating synergy, to be part of the energetic flow of business, connecting needs and services. Let people in your professional and social circles understand your services and your value in helping others. To minimize your discomfort when asserting yourself, connect to a larger purpose. The first step is to identify yourself with an upbeat, constructive narrative.

EXERCISE: SPEAKING ABOUT MY PROFESSIONAL IDENTITY

Write the answers to the following questions to develop a better perspective about your professional identity.

1. What do you love most about being a therapist, healer, coach, or consultant?
2. What are your special skills or talents?
3. What are you known for professionally within the community (reputation, connection, perceived value)?
4. What are your credentials and affiliations?
5. What are your specialties or niches?
6. Who do you consider resources (your social and professional network, all referral sources, business-related contacts, other community-related contacts)?
7. What materials do you use to support your practice and your professional identity (any written material you have developed or created including print advertisements, manuals, written policies, newsletters, brochures, business cards, books, audiotapes, videotapes, seminars, PowerPoint Presentations, etc.)?

8. In a sentence or phrase, what would you most like others to know about you and/or your practice?

VERBAL INTRODUCTION

Next, in an engaging and attractive manner, create a short, verbal introduction that sums up the essence of who you are and what you do as a therapist. The criteria for this are:

- *Have no more than three or four short sentences.* This is an introduction you are going to memorize, so keep it brief and easy to remember, and hold it in your mind at all times.
- *Use no jargon words or technical terms.* If you use a technical term in your introduction, your listener will tend to stop at that term and not hear the rest of the introduction. If you must use a technical term, anticipate that your introduction will do little more than explain the term. My advice is that you drop all jargon and let the introduction be about who you are and what you do, rather than the techniques you use.
- *Keep your language upbeat and positive.* This is an opportunity to attract others, not discourage them. I want you to project what excites you about your work, not what you find difficult.
- *Target only one aspect of your work.* You may have a diverse set of skills, but this is a short introduction. You simply can't say it all. I suggest you target the aspect of your practice that you want to build—an area where you want to generate referrals. Are you trying to fill a new group, reach a specific clientele, attract an ideal client type? You will have more impact if you let this introduction speak to just one component of what you do.
- *Learn to love to say this introduction.* The most important part of this introduction is learning to love to say it. The sole purpose of the basic message is to become a container for your passion about your craft. The words are just a vehicle to express your underlying feelings and enthusiasm. When you can speak about your work

with love, people will naturally want to move closer to you. Passion is attractive.

STYLES

I have found four styles that can help structure your basic message. Pick one to work with. Under each style I have given you several examples that come from my classes and my workbook: *12 Months to Your Ideal Private Practice* (Grodzki, 2003). Don't just borrow one of these, because it won't carry your particular essence. Do the hard work and compose your own.

All styles should begin with this first sentence:

"My name is _____ and I am a _____."

The first blank is your name. The second is your professional title. Some therapists have trouble deciding which title to use—the most generic, the most technically correct, or the title that reflects their key training? I suggest you use the title that is simplest and easiest for the public to understand. Make sure to select one you most like to say, so that you are able to smile, not frown, when speaking.

Style 1

"I specialize in _____. What I enjoy (value, appreciate, love, cherish) about my work is _____."

This is a straightforward, conversational introduction, one that you can use to highlight your niche, philosophy of service, and enthusiasm about your work.

Psychotherapist: "I specialize in working with adults who are going through difficult times in their lives—divorce, job loss, depression, maybe the loss of a family member. What I love about the work I do is that although I initially see people at a low point in their lives, as we work together they find the courage, skills, and resilience to keep going and make life worth living."

Movement therapist: "I specialize in helping people who suffer from chronic physical pain relearn how to move their bodies. In some cases, just by learning to walk, sit, and stand with better coordination, my patients are able to correct and heal old, problematic injuries that have caused them years of distress. I really enjoy watching people relearn a basic skill that sets them free."

Style 2

"I support _____ in their desire to _____ by the means of _____."

This style is very useful if you are trying to break down the process of why people come for therapy and what you have to offer.

Psychologist: "I support couples in their desire to make their marriage a success from the start. I do this by offering premarital counseling classes and weekly couples therapy sessions, both of which give couples the confidence and skills they need in order to make a new marriage really work well."

Family Therapist: "I support adolescents in their desire to become responsible and independent young men and women, and I do this by helping them identify their true potential."

Style 3

"You know how _____ ? Well, I _____ ."

This style is especially effective if you have a complex message because it sets up an analogy that speeds understanding.

Family therapist: "You know how easy it is to get lost when you are walking in a dense forest and don't have a compass or a map to use as a guide? Well, I help families who are feeling lost and confused by functioning as a guide for them, and together we develop reference points, such as how they can set house rules, talk to each other, and resolve conflicts."

Life coach: "You know how a personal trainer helps people get their bodies in better shape? Well, I work with people who want to get their lives in better shape. Instead of meeting at the gym, we meet each week by phone and have a focused coaching conversation that will help them to set their priorities, stay on task, and take the necessary steps to get their life where they want it."

Style 4

"If you _____, I'm the kind of (therapist) who can help you to _____ ."

This style lets you define the type of clients you like to work with and get more specific about the benefits you have to offer them.

Psychotherapist: "If you are a person who has been in therapy before and is ready to try it again in order to make lasting change, I am the kind of experienced therapist who can help you to understand and resolve your issues at a deeper level. Many of my clients find that by working in a deeper way, they develop the possibility of creating real transformation in their lives."

Addictions counselor: "If you are an addict and you are really serious about wanting to stop using and turn your life around, I'm the kind of addictions counselor who can lend a hand. I've been there, I've helped others, and if you'll let me, I believe I know how to help you, too."

Pick one style and write your basic message. Take your time and be prepared to do several drafts. Remember, the words you choose are important primarily as a vehicle to hold your passion and enthusiasm for your work, so pick words and phrases that you like to say. People will remember the feeling they get from hearing you long after they remember exactly what you say.

ASK FOR THE REFERRAL WITH EASE

In business, letting other people know about your business needs is considered a normal interaction. Most therapists shy away from asking for help in building their businesses. The hardest aspect of networking must be the "ask"—the way you close the conversation by asking for referrals. But therapists in private practice are business people; we need a way to communicate our legitimate business needs, such as our need for referrals (the life blood of our business), in a way that matches our sensibilities and ethics. The "ask" is similar to closing a sales call, where you ask a potential buyer to purchase your product. But in our very relational professions, we need a way to close that is also relational. The following ways of asking may work for you. I have seen therapists use one of these and put them on their Web site, in their waiting room, or on brochures, so that existing clients, potential clients, and referrals sources understand that referrals are welcome and important. The most straightforward way to ask for referrals is to add a simple declarative statement onto the end of your introduction that lets the person you are speaking with know that you are interested in seeing more clients. The sentence I like to use is:

"I have some openings in my practice that I am interested in filling."

Other statements that work well include:

"I am building my business and I would appreciate if you could become one of my referral sources."

"I welcome any potential clients who you think would be good for me to work with."

"I prefer to see only people who have been referred to me by someone I

know and trust, and would like to have that kind of referral relationship with you."

"My practice is built on referrals and I would greatly appreciate getting referrals from you."

IDEAL CLIENTS

What qualities characterize the clients who you enjoy working with most? Chances are, they will be clients who also get the most out of being in therapy with you. Notice that your ideal clients probably mirror some of your own characteristics. For example, my ideal psychotherapy clients:

- *Have a sophistication about the process of therapy.* They know the value of not missing sessions, paying on time, and following through on assignments between sessions, which makes us able to focus on the issue of their therapy more than the boundaries.
- *Are self-motivated and ready to make lasting change.* Since I have a small practice, I limit myself to working only with serious, committed clients.
- *Value direct and honest feedback from me.* Since I integrate my coaching style into my therapy sessions, I work best with clients who are strong enough to hear direct interpretations.

Create your own profile of your ideal clients. Limit it to just a few items, making the criteria inclusive, rather than exclusive. A good profile invites someone into a therapeutic relationship instead of pushing someone out. The more you can speak about your ideal clients (those with whom you do your best work) to referral sources, the easier it is for them to begin to think: *Who do I know who would be right for Lynn?* To be most effective, your profile needs to focus on clients' attributes as well as on specifics such as age, issue, and gender. My ideal client profile is flexible and changes as I change. Yours will, too. Remember, your profile says as much about who you are as it does about those you would like to attract.

At times, ideal clients are created by a process of education. Your ideal client profile can be shared conversationally with new clients. It will help new clients understand your approach and your expectations, and show them how to "get their money's worth" or increase the value they receive from their time in therapy. This one step can help you think in a more focused way about the direction of your practice.

EXERCISE: IDENTIFY YOUR IDEAL CLIENT

Fill in these sentence stems.

- My ideal client appreciates _____
- My ideal client values _____
- My ideal client understands _____
- My ideal client agrees to _____
- My ideal client lets me work at my best by _____
- My ideal client works with me in the following way (presenting problem, amount of time spent in therapy overall, how often seen, types of issues tackled, results at different time periods, gains by end of therapy): _____

SHARE SUCCESS STORIES

We all want to get value for our spending. How do you explain the results of your work when networking? Expand the conversation by giving an example of what you have to offer. Having a success story is one way of showing your work. Instead of just telling about your work, share a highly edited case example. Give your listener an example of why your services matter. When crafting a success story, make sure that you respect confidentiality, ethics, and your professional sensibilities.

In order to create a success story, do the following:

1. Use a composite of several clients or an unrecognizable, unnamed client with a generic problem. Minimize any details that would break confidentiality.

"Several years ago, I had a client come to see me who had a very difficult time with managing anger."

2. Highlight what *you* did specifically that helped.

"I put this client into one of my groups, which are a good environment for anyone who has anger issues. I helped my client learn how to identify when he felt angry, how to release his feelings safely without violence, and eventually how to see what triggered him. I encouraged the group to role-play difficult situations, so that he would find constructive ways to appropriately relate to people, even when he was triggered."

3. Include the results.

"After less than a year of being in group, my client made some important shifts in relating with others. His family deeply appreciated how well he listened and how much calmer he could be. At work he was accepted into a fast-track management training program because he could stay calm under pressure and communicate well with others."

GIVE TO GET

How do referrals happen? What motivates other people to refer their friends, colleagues, and relatives to you? Sometimes it is based on word of mouth—people feel appreciative about who you are and what you have done for them, and it is natural for them to want to tell others about you. If you consistently do good work as a therapist, your clients will tell others and, over time, you will build a practice of referrals. But building a client base of referrals from your existing clients takes time. You may want to speed up the process or reach out to a wider pool of people than your existing or previous clients. If so, you need a way to share who you are with others on a wider scale, and you need a way to do it that evokes a positive emotional response from the public. You will need others to carry your message for you, to expand your reach. To put it simply: You need to be connected with groups of people. Creating enthusiasm and appreciation is an art that is based on giving more than getting.

Cathy Lange, owner of BusinessWorks of America, Inc., a leadership and executive coaching company, has developed the "give to get" strategy into a way of life. Cathy has a huge network of professionals in her local area who call her "friend." Her business is built on word of mouth. Cathy seeds many of her professional relationships with the idea of giving. "When I meet someone, I think about how I can be of help, long before I ask for anything," she explained. What does she have to give? "Well, I love to take people out for lunch. I offer resources and referrals. I open my Rolodex. I can spend time, give free advice, sometimes have some expertise that makes a difference. I often mentor others. I feel that when I meet someone I like, it's easy for me to have their best interest at heart. I might send someone an article, invite them to a networking event, send them a book, connect them to other resources, make introductions, listen to what they are saying, or just demonstrate added value to the relationship."

Cathy does not "give away the store"—her professional services are highly valued by the organizations she works with—but when she networks she is open and generous. "I offer what I can in a sincere way, without expecting anything in return. But often in business, it is understood that there is a quid pro quo, and the generosity is usually mutual." Because Cathy is articulate and has a strong professional identity, basic message, and many success stories, her networking yields results.

EXERCISE: BUILDING COMMUNITY

Use this exercise to create a give-to-get community.

- Create a diagram of concentric circles and place your practice at the center.
- Name each circle to reflect the links to existing communities that surround your practice now. One may be your geographic community (neighborhood), another may be your professional community (clini-

cal societies, business associations), others may be related to shared interests (sports, arts, volunteering, religious or social interests). These do not need to be communities that you currently take part in, only communities that exist that you could join, if you desire. Add as many circles as you need to represent the position of your practice.

- Pick one circle. Think how to add value to that circle. Don't contribute money. Instead, get personally involved and give something of yourself to this community for the purpose of improving your world. Feeding the circle will enrich your immediate environment—one form of reciprocation.
- Create a plan of action to begin the process of adding value to this community.

Circular positioning builds relationships because you have directly contributed to bettering people's lives. It's these relationships that are the basis for reciprocation, which may take many forms, including forms that benefit your practice. What comes back is often in the form of deeper relationships with the people in the community to whom you have chosen to add value. As you connect to people and let them know about your passion for your work (by articulating your basic message), referrals and opportunities often circulate back to you. Here's the catch: The reciprocal nature of circular positioning only works if you contribute from a desire to really enrich a particular community. It's a natural phenomena; as you build a base of stronger relationships based on adding value to a community, the community naturally reciprocates to add value back to your life (and often to your business). I call this "karmic marketing" because, with this strategy, what goes around, comes around. One 20-year veteran social worker has a strong connection to her local community, since she has children at home. She volunteers time at their schools and the neighborhood swimming pool. She gets known through these channels and develops relationships with other parents and teachers, but these are close relationships and, as a result, not appropriate for her practice. Instead, she makes dozens of referrals each year to other therapists. Those therapists she refers to then reciprocate in kind because she knows how to ask for the referral back, to make it reciprocal.

MAKE VALUE EXPLICIT

It's hard for colleagues to refer to you unless they have direct experience of your skills and results. Invite a small group of colleagues to join you for a chance to learn something new and teach them something that you do well. What do you know that you could teach to your colleagues? How can you talk with them about your successes?

One licensed counselor had good skills helping teenagers to manage their anger. To build a peer referral network, he invited a circle of colleagues for coffee and bagels on a Saturday morning and taught them two effective techniques that help angry teens calm themselves. The group discussed the techniques, brainstormed about ways to adapt them for broader clinical use, and socialized. This boosted his reputation and referrals from those who attended. A body therapist taught colleagues a lovely, gentle meditation. A social worker facilitated a formal book club with a reading list of clinical texts. A massage therapist showed his peers how he combined deep breathing exercises with muscle relaxation.

You don't have to be brilliant or have a revolutionary new method to make this strategy effective—just be willing to give away your best ideas for free. Some therapists think they need to fiercely guard their hard-won knowledge. I find that creativity works best when it's free flowing. The more good ideas you give away, the more good ideas will occur to you to replace them.

EXERCISE: COLLEGIAL REFERRALS

Use this exercise to help you identify colleagues and specify skills to share.

- List three specific skills you would like to demonstrate to others.
- Make a list of colleagues to share the skills with.
- How will you set this up logistically; when and where will it take place?
- What is your budget for this project (time, money, energy)?

- How will you make this gathering highly enjoyable for everyone?
- How will you further collegiality in the room, the sharing of ideas, and new relationships?
- How will you stay open to new opportunities that can arise from this experience?

EXERCISE: MY NETWORKING STRATEGY CHECKLIST

Check those that are true for you now and try to check them all as soon as possible.

❑ When networking, I focus first on creating relationships, not selling myself.

❑ If I join an existing group, I plan to attend meetings regularly. If asked to volunteer to be on a committee, I select one that allows me to get to know the whole membership personally, face-to-face.

❑ I know how to work a room. Working a room means that I can come into a room alone, if need be, go up to one person or a group of people, wait for a break in the conversation, put out my hand, smile, say hello, and use my basic message as an introduction.

❑ I follow up appropriately with new contacts. I don't flood new contacts with my materials (that's push marketing). Instead, I find ways to further a real relationship and make new friends.

❑ I opt for mutuality. I try to refer back to my referring sources whenever I can.

❑ I double the number of people I know each year.

CONVERT CLIENTS BY ENROLLING

Enrolling is a sales term that means getting people to sign up to buy your product. For therapists, coaches, consultants, and healing professionals, enrolling means persuading potential clients (such as people in your audiences) to become paying clients. This topic is rarely discussed in the professional literature because it is considered to be too coarse, too business-y, much too promotional. But many therapists wonder how this is done and despair when they do the hard work of planning and giving a talk, and get good evaluations, but don't get any new paying clients.

I got very interested in the enrolling techniques that are taught to salespeople and wondered if I could adapt them to work within our profession. I developed a method of enrolling that borrowed important elements of enrolling from a sales perspective, but modified them to reflect the ethics and sensibilities I adhere to and believe in as a therapist and coach.

I informally tested the method by asking those I coach to try it when giving a talk or presentation. Based on several years of their results (new clients signing up after talks, significantly better responses at all presentations where this was used), I now think that enrolling can and does work well within our helping and healing professions.

The method of enrolling I offer is a much more subtle process than salespeople use and it requires a very different positioning or posture for the therapist. Your positioning is to show up as a therapist, in your professional role, from the start of the talk. In your role as a therapist, focus on forming a "real" or authentic relationship with members of the audience. Be experiential and show—don't just say—what you do. Experience is much more powerful than explanation.

Next, build a bridge from the experience to the services you offer. Your audience will feel connected to you, understand that you have something important to offer them that matches their needs and wants, and clearly comprehend how to engage your services.

Sound simple? It is, but not all simple things are straightforward. Let me break this skill down for you and explain it with a real-life example.

The three steps are:

- Stay in role.
- Show don't tell.
- Build a bridge.

Stay in Role

To enroll successfully, you have to be willing and able to work deeply and authentically right from the point of contact. This is where most therapists go awry in public speaking. They are comfortable in the role of therapist with a client in their office, but the moment they get in front of an audience they take on a new role of a teacher, trainer, information provider, or facilitator, which is valid but less authentic for the purposes of marketing. Think about it this way: The primary motivation for people to hire a therapist is because they are in pain or discomfort; something is wrong in their lives. If you approach your presentation as a quick-fix, you remove their primary motivation for hiring you and undermine your role in the process. But this is what many therapists do when they get in front of a room. They become anxiety-dispellers with a lot of suggestions and ideas to immediately fix a serious or compelling problem.

Show, Don't Tell

As you may have experienced in your life, the best therapists, coaches, and healers don't see it as their job to necessarily remove or reduce anxiety or fix anything in the first contact. That would be disrespectful to the client, the situation, the issue, and the relationship. Often, great therapists need to heighten anxiety, because they must open up important, tough issues or frame old issues using a new perspective, or try to get to really know the person who is sitting in front of them. Great therapists offer the potential of something bigger than anxiety reduction for potential clients. They offer transformation, vision, healing, or change.

Can you handle showing up in your role as a therapist when you are a speaker, perhaps heightening the anxiety in the room as you stay in that role, and not trying to just fix the problem or give solutions right away? Since the first step of enrolling requires you to quickly form a real, deep relationship with audience members, you will need to practice starting and staying in that role.

Build a Bridge

You need to be explicit with your audience about how they go from the experience you are offering to working with you as a client. You can't expect them to walk over the bridge to you until you build it (taking them step-by-step through the process) of hiring you. Don't be vague. Help people in the audience understand how specifically to take the next step in working with you. You might say: "Some of you may be filled with more questions than answers at this point. That is expected because we are exploring this topic on a deep level, which is the way I am trained to work. So if you are one of those people who want to continue the conversation with me, here is how to take the next step. Come up after the talk and get my brochure and let me know that you want to schedule a session. I will get some contact information from you so that I can reach you to find a time for us to meet. I will make a quick note of what aspect of this talk was most important to you, and then when we next meet, we can continue from this point."

Enrolling in Action

Jill, a therapist in practice for 10 years, gives talks on stress reduction for people who are battling chronic, serious illness. She gives these talks as a way to market her services, hoping for new clients. She speaks to associations, hospitals, clinics, and nonprofit volunteer groups. She gives four to six talks a year. She gets great evaluations. She does a long guided imagery during the talk and people leave the hour feeling better and much calmer. Even though Jill assumes that the audience will automatically make a connection from their experience of feeling better to eventually calling for a session when they feel bad again, she does not expressly make that link and they do not follow through. The talks rarely yield her new clients.

I asked Jill how much time she normally spends hearing why people have come to the talk. "About five minutes," she said. I asked her to spend 20 minutes, one third of her time, on that section.

"That means we would be doing nothing but talking about their chronic aches and pains. I want to get to what will help them, not dwell on the pain," Jill said.

"What if someone comes into your office?" I asked her. "Do you rush over their initial complaints?"

She said no, that she spends a lot of time hearing all the depth and details of presenting symptoms and issues. Jill's first error was being afraid to show up at a talk as a therapist.

"Show up at the talk in your role as a therapist and behave more like you do in the office," I said. "Let people hear you being a therapist and a healer, not just a teacher."

Jill said she normally spent 45 minutes demonstrating a long guided imagery. I asked her to do no more than 15 minutes of that this time, and take 20 minutes to process the results with the group. She was to pick a small piece of imagery to show the group, in effect giving them a "taste" of stress reduction instead of the whole meal. She was to take 20 minutes to process the experience, again standing in her therapist (not facilitator) role.

Then I asked Jill to take the last 5 minutes to bridge the experience to her services, by explaining that there was much more she could offer with more time, and all that people needed to do was to come up to the front of the room at the end of the talk to get more information about how she might help them in their specific situation. Jill tried this method of enrolling at her next talk. She reported back that the opening 20 minutes were a very special, touching experience. Not everyone shared, but those who did voiced the fears, worries, and concerns of all. Jill encouraged them to speak fully, and she mirrored back and enhanced what they said. The atmosphere in the room quickly became compelling and deep. After the "taste" of stress reduction, Jill reported that the group seemed hungry for more. This is the right response for an hour-long talk, as opposed to hearing that people are satiated. Then she processed with the group and more emotional, touching sharing occurred. She bridged her services, articulating her basic message and letting her words convey her passion for her work.

After the talk five people came up to get her card. Jill had her calendar with her and four people booked introductory sessions. Another dozen wanted to chat further, but Jill, having been coached, did another bridging technique. She listened carefully to each one and then said, "I think a problem of this nature deserves the respect of more time and attention. I have methods and skills that can really help with the problems you describe. If you want to schedule a session with me, I would be happy to work with you." Two of these people called her the next week. Not all of the introductory sessions became paying clients, but Jill found this technique much more successful than any she had used before. Ultimately, she got three new paying, ideal clients from this one talk.

Enrolling as a coach or consultant is a similar process. Stan, a psychologist in a well-known university town, has an opportunity to enhance one aspect of his practice—peak performance coaching. The university track team coach invites him to spend a morning with the team each semester. Stan gives the runners tips on staying mentally alert and focused. He would like to enroll some college runners in his private practice for peak performance coaching, but so far this has not happened as a result of his talks. Stan told me that he considers the morning with the team as a class; he becomes their teacher. He prepares a lecture with handouts and diagrams. He lectures students about the brain, neurology, and their physical performance. His experience is that the students are interested in what he has to say, but his efforts do not translate into any new coaching clients.

I asked Stan to stop being a teacher and become a peak performance coach. At his next session with the runners, he was to put away his handouts and diagrams and, instead, coach the runners to peak performance. Stan was understandably nervous about this shift in roles, but willing to try something new. The next college semester started. Stan spent a morning with the running team and then reported back to me.

"In the past, I spent the morning with the runners in a classroom. This time I asked the runners to meet me on the track. I explained briefly who I was and why I was there. Then I asked each student to think about how he most commonly got mentally distracted during a race. Each one shared a small anecdote about distraction. There was a lot of head-nodding as the students commiserated with each other over common distractions, and some laughter at the more absurd anecdotes. It felt good to do this: more like I was leading a coaching group instead of teaching a class.

"I had them line up and timed a short run, during which I asked them to be distracted by thoughts of an upcoming exam. Their times were not good, as I had expected. Then I taught a focusing exercise and the students repeated the run and vastly improved their times. They could see exactly what I was talking about, in terms of focus. They got excited." I validated how well Stan had handled the second, experiential step in the enrolling process and then I asked how he concluded the session.

"Well, then I kind of blew it. They were excited and really ready to know more, but we were out of time and I got nervous. I just thanked them for their time and put my cards out on one of the bleachers in a nonassuming way. I didn't explain how I could take students further, or that I have so many other techniques for them to use, or let out any of the passion I really feel about my coaching practice. I've got to work on that part." I agreed that Stan needed to rehearse the final stage, making a bridge from the experience to his services. Stan needs to feel at ease with asking for the referral, by letting the students specifically know how and why to hire him as a coach. This final step of enrolling is essential in order to see the ultimate results of having new clients.

Part III: Rebrand

Survival is not the goal, transformative success is.

—*Seth Godin*

CHAPTER 9

Having a Strong Internet Presence

The number of U.S. adults using the Internet to find health-related information surpassed 100 million this year. Mental health sites are among the five most popular types of health sites on the Web. If you are not part of this give-and-take about mental health, you are missing out on an easy and natural way to reach those people who actively seek your services. In stark contrast to the medical model, where patients expect their doctors to tell them what they need to know, today consumers research their problem, possible treatment, and potential practitioners, all online.

Therapists, coaches, and consultants who rely on the Internet for marketing recognize its primary benefit: It is relatively low cost and it works while you sleep. For Generations X and Y (those born between 1970 and 2000), the Internet is the new yellow pages. These generations are more comfortable with the Internet than with any other type of research tool when finding services. For those who use the Internet as a research tool, searching for professionals' credentials prior to hiring them is part of the process of due diligence. These potential clients will want to look you up, see pictures, read your bio, or visit your Web site. You need a Web site to be part of this communication loop.

WEB SITE DEVELOPMENT

Here's how Deborah Gallant of WebPowerTools.com, who has been my helpful adviser for all things Internet-related, suggests you get started:

1. *Register a domain name.* This is your address in cyberspace (like http://www.privatepracticesuccess.com). You can register it at any of the domain registration sites (like GoDaddy.com or Register.com), since they all link to the same database. Register your own name definitely, and if your practice has a catchy name, try to get that, too. They can all point to the single Web site. Some quick guidelines:

- Shorter is better.
- Dot-com is better than dot anything else (.net or .biz).
- Make it easy to spell.
- Go for something unique and distinctive so there is no confusion with anyone else.

2. *Set up a professional e-mail address at that domain, even if you aren't ready to build a site yet.* This is a mark of a professional. Rather than using AOL or Yahoo! for your e-mail, promote your business and set up a signature file for your e-mails formatted as below:

Joan W. Therapist
Marriage and Family Therapist
999-999-9999
joan@joanwtherapist.com
www.joanwtherapist.com

3. *Then comes the Web site.* It should contain the following content elements:

- Your contact information: name, address, telephone number
- Your biography and photo
- Your services
- A map to your office
- A form to fill out to contact you
- Legal terms of service and privacy policy
- Many more things can be added, like articles, resources, links, workshops, and so on

The site needs to be built (written, designed, pictures added) and hosted (a firm must place it and maintain it on the Internet). You can build a Web site yourself, even if you don't know anything technical, with a number of different systems. Or you can hire a designer or developer to do it for you. Doing it yourself is cheaper and you maintain control of your Web site so you can change, update, and evolve it over time. A designer can make your site slicker and more graphically pleasing, but you will pay anywhere from $500 to thousands of dollars and you may have to pay every time you want to update or change it.

WEB SITE DEVELOPMENT DOS AND DON'TS

- *Don't wait too long to get your Web site up and running.* You needed to do this yesterday. It can be simple and imperfect. It will evolve over time
- *Don't overspend on a fabulous logo or design.* While good graphics are nice, they are not what determine conversion (turning Web site viewers into paying clients).
- *Do make it information rich.* Add content to your Web site—articles, assessments, book reviews, anything that would be of value to readers and help you talk about it: "There is a great article about this on my Web site. Why don't you take a look at it?"
- *Do figure out the objective of the Web site.* What do you want readers to do when visiting your Web site? Phone you? E-mail? Subscribe to your newsletter? Determine the overall objective and make sure that each page leads the viewer clearly in that direction. Each Web site also needs a "call to action"—a clear invitation to take the step.

GETTING FOUND

A Web site functions like a brochure floating in space. It exists, but no one may see it unless you help direct them to it. You can direct people to your Web site in one of four ways:

- *Advertise in print*: You can and should promote your Web site via a brochure, business card, print ad, or other piece of marketing material that contains your domain name.
- *Promote online*: Some therapists find that paying for advertising, such as pay-per-click advertising, helps drive traffic to their Web site.
- *Link*: Linking, also called off-page optimization, makes your Web site more competitive by having other sites refer back to your site. The more competitive your market, the more it helps to have good links.
- *Optimize*: If you want to boost your chance of having people find your Web site when they search the Internet for certain terms, you can follow the steps below to position your site via a SERP (search engine results page, such as Google or Yahoo!).

The first method of Web site advertising—advertising in print—is self-explanatory, so let me explain the other three: promoting online, links, and optimizing. After reading this, you may decide that the suggestions are too time-consuming or difficult, and you may hire a company to help you achieve these goals. But even if you hire someone to effect a Web site advertising package, I still want you to understand what it all means. This chapter may be too technical for those readers who know little about Web sites and the Internet, but remember, this is part of your future entrepreneurial skill set. So stick with this and read on!

GLOSSARY FOR WEB SITES

First, here is a short list of definitions to help you understand this section.

Conversion: This refers to any Web site viewer who becomes an actual client by taking your preferred action step: contacting you, making an appointment, purchasing a product. You can have microconversions (you want a visitor to go to the next page on your site, or sign up for a newsletter) and macroconversions (you want a visitor to book a session, make a purchase, or contact you for more information).

Keyword: A keyword or phrase of words determined by you. Keywords are those key terms (depression, couples counseling, therapy, treatment, etc.) that need to show up frequently and in the right way on your site, so that those doing searches for your services, and the search engines themselves, can quickly locate you.

Since keywords are so important, you need to do some research to determine the best target keywords and key phrases. There are three core tools out there that can help you determine good keywords/ phrases.

- WordTracker: For a fee, http://www.wordtracker.com will suggest hundreds of related phrases based on the number of users searching for it and the number of Web sites targeting it.
- Overture: By going to the free Overture keyword service at: http://inventory.overture.com/d/searchinventory/suggestion/, you will find a service that some find easier to use than WordTracker. It works in much the same way as WordTracker but doesn't tell you how many Web sites are targeting each keyword phrase. For example, Overture shows that the word *psychotherapy* got 35,000 individual searches in January 2007, while the word *counseling* got 69,000. Which word will you use on your site?
- Google: Go to https://adwords.google.com/select/KeywordTool External to use the Google free service that tells you which keyword phrases are being targeted by other Web sites.

Search engine: Software that searches for information and returns sites that provide that information. Examples of search engines are Google, Yahoo!, and MSN.

SERP: This is the list of Web sites that users see after typing their search query into an engine. For example, typing "couples counseling" into Google gives you a page with a list of Web sites, known as a SERP. Marketing advice says that conversion (from Web site visitor to paying client) starts at the SERP.

Search engine ranking: This refers to the position at which a particular site appears in the results of a search engine query. A site is said to have a high ranking when it appears at or near the top of the list of results. Results are typically numbered starting at 1; thus ranking at 1 is ideal.

PAY-PER-CLICK ADVERTISING

If you can't get people to see your Web site, you can't find new clients. One way to find more viewers is via Internet advertising. Pay per click (PPC) is a form of search engine advertising where you pay an agreed-upon, set amount every time your keywords are searched so that your site shows up as 1, 2, or 3 on the search engine. For example: Imagine I live in Columbus, Ohio and need a couples counselor. I go to Google and in the search box I write: "Couples counseling, Columbus, Ohio." Will your Web site show up on the first page? This is not random. Those Web sites that show up with a high ranking are either optimized by the use of text, links (read on to the next sections), or advertising that gives you top placement on the page known as "PPC" advertising.

The PPC advertising is based on a system of bidding for the right to "own" keywords. First, research your keywords using the sites I suggested in the glossary section of this chapter. Then pick your keywords and bid (agree to a fee with the search engine). For example, you can open an account with Overture.com, a search engine advertising site that is part of the Yahoo! search engine. Let's say you decide to bid on the keyword phrase of the following four words: "Couples counseling Columbus Ohio." Overture will show you who else is bidding on the keywords you want, and what it will cost you to get the results you want. Some keywords cost as much as $4.00 each time the word or phrase is searched by a visitor; others go for as little as 10 cents.

Or, you can use the popular Google AdWords PPC site by going to Google and clicking on the link to AdWords. The Google service will allow your Web site listing to appear in a special section at the top of the page in a box, above the regular listings, each time the keyword phrase is searched. Internet marketer Joe Bavonese (2007) worked with a therapist to help the therapist better utilize Google AdWords. Although the therapist's results were initially disappointing with the advertising click per pay (CPP), Bavonese helped him refine his keywords. Using the Google keyword locator, they found that "adolescent depression" would cost the therapist $0.90 to "own" (each time the phrase was searched); that phrase got searched often—an average of 1,200 times a month. In contrast, the keyword phrase "adolescent counseling" got searched only 475 times each month, but bidding on that phrase would cost $1.30 each time. The therapist was able to save money by purchasing the advertising for "adolescent depression" and, over time, found that it yielded clients and an amazing return on his advertising investment of 700%. It pays to do some research.

LINKING

Another way to increase traffic to your site is to have it linked from other Web sites. A link is a mention of your site, including your site domain name, on someone else's Web site. Search engines will often increase your ranking if your site has what they consider "good links"—nonpromotional listings of your site on other sites that have similar content and/or relevance. Getting good links is, on the whole, something that doesn't happen overnight, but it is part of optimizing your Web site to make it work well as a marketing tool.

EXERCISE: LINKING YOUR WEB SITE TO OTHERS

Here are ways you can increase links to your Web site over time.

- *Do get a listing in a popular directory.* Open Directory Project, Google, and Yahoo! keep lists of links to various businesses.
- *Do submit your site to online directories for similar services.* Try to link to professional associations, forums, and other colleagues' Web sites. You can link for free to some sites, and others for pay, such as Psychology Today or Find-a-Therapist.com.
- *Don't be fooled into signing on to promotional sites that promise to increase your links.* Web sites abound that promise

help with linking schemes. Many of these schemes are detected by Google and other search engines and will hurt your ranking.

- *Do submit online press releases.* You can promote your practice with a press release (notice of what is new and relevant) to the public, and can include your domain name in the press release. An example of a site where you can do this is http://www.prweb.com.

- *Do write articles about the areas you specialize in.* Submit the article to article directories. Many of the article directories will keep a link of your site in the biography portion of the article you write or toward the bottom of the article. An example of article directories are http://www.goarticles.com or http://www.findarticles.com.

- *Do link with local business associations.* Your local chamber of commerce, women's business associations, and service organizations may keep lists of resources on their Web sites.

- *Do create good content.* If your Web site is filled with good information, articles, or assessments, you will naturally want to share these with your clients, colleagues, friends, and family, and they will help spread the word.

- *Do be patient.* Linking is a process that evolves over time. You can't rush this.

- *Don't link to a page you have reservations about your visitors seeing.* The last thing you want your Web site to appear as is indiscriminate or cheap. Linking to sites of poor quality will only lessen your link popularity, if not completely destroy it.

LINKING PARTNERS

Finding partners with whom to link is a reciprocal process, similar to finding colleagues with whom you might share referrals. You may link to large locator sites such as PsychologyToday.com or GoodTherapy.com or any of the other sites that, for a monthly fee, host your profile information and link to your Web site. But some linking partners are more informal and free. Each year, I get approached by people who want to link with my various Web sites, and I approach others with whom I feel a connection. This is a win-win process. It grows your community and your outreach, and it drives business to your site.

EXERCISE: INTERNET CONNECTIONS

Take these steps to find additional linking partners.

- *Determine your criteria.* Just like making referrals, you want to link with partners and sites with whom you feel some connection. Your criteria might include relevant, quality, highly ranked, noncompeting Web sites that have a links or resources page. Do a search. Go to sites and objectively assess them. Look at the quality of the product, the graphics, and the ease of use.
- *When you decide you have found good partners, approach them with respect.* Add links on your own links page to their sites to show good faith. After you have added the links, take the next step in good Internet etiquette and contact their Webmasters by e-mail to let them know you have linked to their sites and why.
- *Then ask for a mutual link.* Make sure you emphasize that you have actually visited their sites and why you chose them. Give them the address of your links page, and ask them to check out the link for themselves. It's a good idea to mention that they will not only benefit from the increased traffic your Web site will direct their way. Finally, tell them you would greatly appreciate it if they would reciprocally add a link on their own links pages to your Web site.

OPTIMIZATION

The term *Web site optimization* means "improving the ranking of your Web site on the SERP." Using our earlier example, if a potential client is looking for couples counseling in your city and goes to a search engine such as Google and types in: "couples counseling Columbus Ohio," a highly optimized Web site would be first on the list.

We examined how to make this happen by PPC advertising, but you can also improve your ranking with attention to other factors regarding the design and content of your site. Optimization takes some work and some time to achieve, but it is critical because Internet users are impatient. Data show that 80% of users will start a new search if they can't find what they're looking for in the first page of Google. If your Web site isn't mentioned within the first or second page, you may not be found. And there are 300 million searches carried out every day. So you want your Web site to be easy to spot, and that means you need to optimize it.

EXERCISE: WEB SITE OPTIMIZATION

Take these steps to help your Web site get noticed by search engines.

- *Do have sufficient content* and keep it fresh and up-to-date. Search engines like Google love content—the more content there is on a page, the easier it is for search engines to work out what the page is actually about. Your pages should not be too short; it should have at least 250 words to the page.
- *Do focus on good and unique content that will be useful for your clients.* The best criterion for a Web site to attain and retain top search engine ranks for a long period of time is for it to have a great content. In the world of search engine optimization, content is king! Add significant value to your Web site by creating first rate content and give related Web sites a reason to link to your site directly.
- *Don't copy and paste from another Web site.* The major search engines will often discount Web pages that seem to be similar to another site. The important thing to remember is that copying and pasting from another Web site infringes on intellectual property and can hurt your search engine ranking results. Don't do it!

- *Do put keywords and phrases in both the first and last paragraphs of your home page.* (Example: If you offer counseling for depression in Los Angeles, then you want some of your keywords—"counseling," "depression," "Los Angeles"—to be in the text in both the beginning and the ending paragraph on the home page of your Web site.)
- *Don't put too many different keywords or topics and ideas on the same page.* Make your key phrases appear more concentrated and relevant so the search engines can find them. You can always add more pages.
- *Do give keywords emphasis by using bold type.* Highlight your various key phrases. This makes them jump out to the search engines.
- *Do use your keywords in the page titles.* Each Web page has what is known as a page title (the address bar at the top of your Web browser for each page). Don't pick the page titles randomly. This is another chance to use your keywords and help the search engines find you. Different pages should have different tags; don't use the same ones throughout your site.
- *Don't use a lot of flash graphics in your Web site.* Flash is often what is responsible for the cool moving graphics you see at various Web sites. Flash, when used sparingly, can be nice, but search engines often have a hard time reading flash pages. Less is more.

CONVERSION

In the end, results matter most. The bottom-line question about Web sites is whether Web site visitors convert to paying clients. The principles of enrolling (see Chapter 8) are one way to enhance Internet conversion by making sure that viewers get an experience of you in your role (have content, audio, or video that features you in your role) and then bridging from the experience to your services, showing viewers how to take the next step.

Conversion rates are low overall. Internet industry surveys rate the overall Web site conversion rate at 2%. But even with a low conversion rate, because your Web site is a form of passive marketing, a 2% return can mean a resilient practice over time. Online conversion works like a funnel: Imagine that over 2 years you have 1,000 (100%) visitors to your Web site. Perhaps 600 of these (60%) view your services page; of those, 300 (30%) read an additional article; of those, 50 (5%) take the next step and call to set up an appointment; of those, 20 (2%) become paying clients.

If those 20 paying clients stay for 6 months and see you weekly at your fee of $100 an hour, they might provide you with additional income over 2 years of $48,000. What would you spend for that extra income? If you consider that Web site design and development, optimization, and even PPC advertising could cost as little as $1,500 during those 2 years, you end up with a very good return on investment (ROI) for Internet expense.

Enhancing conversion can take several forms: Joe Bavonese (2009) suggested a three-step process of conversion: content, the call to action, and the ease of contacting you. The content of your site needs to focus on the needs of the potential clients. Eliminate all extraneous text so that a quick read of your home page underlines your services and your unique selling point. According to Bavonese, the call to action, an advertising concept, directs visitors to what you want them to do. This is similar to the Web site objective in the Web site dos and don'ts mentioned earlier in this chapter. Finally, common sense will help you see the importance of easy contact. Is your phone number too small to read without eyeglasses? Do you hide your contact information on a back page? Some people will only glance at your home page for seconds before moving on. Make sure that you message is clear, directive, and explicit.

Remember, your Web site serves three purposes: (a) It credentials you to those who want more information; (b) It helps people find your specific services; and (c) It is a vehicle for opportunities, by giving you a platform to spread not just word about your practice, but your thoughts and ideas, into the greater community.

SOCIAL NETWORKING

Just as with regular networking, you can build community by Internet "social networking"—using Internet communities for marketing. As with traditional networking, prepare for this by developing your professional identity: Make sure your Web site is clear and articulates your message and services. Have an e-mail address that is based on your Web site domain name (e.g., joan@joanwtherapist.com instead of joan@aol.com). Next, find those existing business Internet communities, social Internet communities, and hobby or special interest Internet communities that appeal to you and join a few of them.

Some of the personal Internet communities include Facebook and MySpace. While these two communities originally appealed to young adults and teens, today communities that try to connect professionals and business owners are on the rise, such as LinkedIn, Twitter, and Gather. You can join these sites for free and develop a profile (your picture, contact information, and introduction to your services), which gives you exposure. Being a part of the social network on the Internet can help you find contacts in your line of business, spot opportunities, and drive people to your Web site. For example, on Twitter a "targeted chat" group of working moms helped therapist Susan Epstein advertise her telephone seminars, her Web site, and her speaking services (Klein, 2008).

Deborah Gallant suggested the use of a "social marketing guerrilla strategy." She has had success with suggesting to therapists and others that they go online and find online groups and communities. For example, one therapist who specialized in infertility found several communities that catered to women struggling with this topic. She became a member and used the "give to get" strategy from the previous chapter. On the chat boards when women were asking for information, she offered resources, advice, and ideas. She used a signature line with her professional status and contact information at the end of each posting, and was pleasantly surprised when potential clients e-mailed her, referencing her postings as the way they found her services. Gallant cautioned those who use this strategy to remember to

(a) participate as a helpful voice; (b) get recognition; and (c) follow the rules of the group. With a great signature line, you will get known in your niche.

Can't find the communities you want online? Start your own. Host telephone seminars, create a Web site chat room for others to post on, have a blog and place for comments. Bring in the phone to help. Special interest groups meet regularly using bridge lines—low-cost telephone conference lines that can accommodate hundreds on each call. Professional groups organize Internet chats to open up networking and topics to their membership. Connecting to existing Internet communities or developing your own communities is a good way to gain visibility with little cost but your time. Remember, there is much that can be done, but just as with any marketing concepts, you need a plan to decide what is the right strategy for this time given your energy, effort, and finances. Just because you could do it doesn't mean you should. I continually explain that every practice needs a marketing plan so that you know what you will take on this year for the short term and what you will delay until the long term.

SOCIAL MEDIA

Social media refers to Internet broadcasting. Whereas traditional broadcast media (newspapers, television, radio) are often out of reach for the small business owner for purposes of advertising or publishing, social media makes it possible for you to reach out to a large market for little money. Writing for others' Web sites, creating a blog (your own collection of articles), posting video to a site like YouTube, having audio that others can access and download, or sending out a regular e-mail newsletter is one way to become better known.

My first newsletters were typed, printed, and mailed to a small group of referral sources and existing clients. It cost me $400 each mailing. Today my list of readers tops 7,000 people, in 10 countries. I pay a total of $35 per month (to my Web host) to send out as many copies as I desire. The time lag between communications is frustratingly slow with traditional media. This book will require almost 9 months of production time from start to finish, which is difficult when I have a timely topic. An e-book can be produced within a month and accessed by readers immediately. You need familiarity with software and just a few skills to publish via social media: multimedia projects—a videotape, or an audiotape, podcasts, broad-casting live with your own Internet radio show, sharing pictures—are easily achieved with brief software training and relatively little cost. Producing the same via traditional media is prohibitive for the small business owner.

But ease creates its own problems, especially regarding quality. Traditional media have standards, licensing, and oversight. The book you are reading was edited by several professionals; an editorial board had to approve the initial proposal. The cover and catalog entry had their own approval processes. If I produce an e-book, e-mail newsletter, audiotape, or videotape on social Internet media, I account to no one but myself. While I may feel the rush of immediacy and freedom, I can't match the quality control, corporate knowledge, careful vetting, and even the ethical stance that working with traditional media brings.

TRACKING RESULTS

I know that many readers will find that this chapter is overwhelming and too technological. Surveys show that psychotherapists, more so than coaches or consultants, tend to be technologically reluctant: 50% do not use a computer in their homes or businesses (Klein, 2006.) But even though you may not be ready for Internet marketing yet, according to most business prognosticators, increased Internet use will be a part of your future.

In terms of how to prioritize an Internet campaign, there is no way to know for sure what strategy will best work for you until you try it. Internet marketing works better for some than others, depending on the competition of Web sites, density of therapists offering the same services, and whether or not the local population of your target market uses the Internet to find services. For every small business, part of what happens while you are marketing is that you are conducting marketing research. You need a way of tracking your efforts. You will learn quickly what produces results (referrals, new clients, opportunities that translate to income) and what doesn't.

Tracking your Web site effectiveness may be best done by Google, for free, at their section on analytics. By applying a "tag" of numbers to your Web site, Google will chart the frequency of how your site is accessed. Other linking partners such as PsychologyToday.com offer an overview of how effective your profile is on their site, how many viewers you had, and how many followed through. But you can track each and every contact as well, the old-fashioned way, by asking potential clients how they found you. Then you can keep a chart of how many clients a year were referred by the Internet, as you determine the return on investment of both time and money in terms of your Internet strategy.

CHAPTER 10

Best Business Models, Part 1

Most small business owners focus on the details of their business instead of the bigger picture of their business model. But during a crisis, using the wrong business model can break your practice. Your *business model*, or the way you structure your private practice, may be an unfamiliar term. You may have adopted or adapted the model of others. For years, I borrowed the business model of my first therapist who later became my supervisor: It was the only way I knew to run a private practice and it worked so well for her that, without much thought, I copied what she did. After several years I realized that her model was not working as well for me because I was a different person with my own business methods, goals, and finances. As I began to determine how to make my practice reflect more of who I was and what was important to me, I shifted my business model and began to notice how many possible models were being used in the profession.

In my work as a business coach and author during the past decade, I continued to notice the myriad of business models. During the past few years of a difficult economy, I could see from observation, reading, and meeting with many therapists, coaches, and consultants that four distinct models were most consistently profitable. These models, which I will explain and help you understand in this chapter and the next, seem to work best in a crisis, yet they are resilient during good economic times as well. Some or even all of them may be familiar to you because they are already used within the marketplace. But if you have never fully considered your own model and whether it is best for your purposes, Chapters 10 and 11 will be essential reading.

As I compiled my research and thoughts about these four models, I noticed that each related to a matrix of four business development strategies developed by Igor Ansoff (1957), considered the father of strategic development (1957). I use Ansoff's growth matrix (see Figure 10.1) as a jumping-off point to help my clients understand why and how these four models of private practice work so well. Within my adaptations of the Ansoff matrix, you can decide which of the four is your best business model, one that reflects your comfort level with purpose, risk, expansion, and long-term profitability.

Please read and explore each model of private practice. Note the case examples and do the exercises. Then determine the model that best fits your situation and your goals. Resist the desire to mix and match the models. They are best adopted as is—so that, just as Ansoff interpreted, the model can make best use of the factors that spell success or failure for a practice. The models presuppose a practice that is entirely, or at least partly, free of managed care or other unhealthy financial dependencies. They are scalable (can expand to accommodate group practices or multiple centers of operation). They are profitable and can be operated with moderate expense. They are easy for

Figure 10.1. Ansoff growth matrix

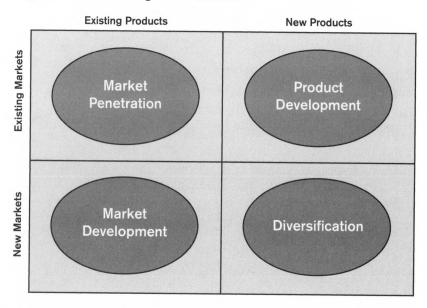

your clients to access. They are ethical and protect the values of professional licensure. But each one represents a distinct business vision and/or practice philosophy. Curious to see which one works best for you? First, take a look at the Ansoff growth matrix.

The Ansoff matrix is set up along the lines of markets and products (or services), existing and new. Existing markets and services are the least risky to own and operate. As you approach the business models that require new markets and services, your investment and your practice's financial risk increases. But so may your outreach and profits. Here is my adaptation of the first quadrant. This is a low-risk, familiar, and desirable model of private practice that Ansoff terms "market penetration." My adapted business model based on this quadrant is the boutique practice (see Figure 10.2).

THE BOUTIQUE PRACTICE

Figure 10.2. Boutique practice

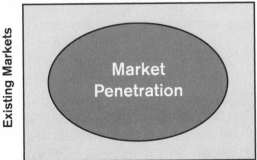

Ansoff matrix quadrant:	Market penetration
Expansion criteria:	Existing markets, existing products
Private practice application:	Boutique practice
Focus on:	The "who" of the practice (the therapist)
Target market:	Those who can afford quality services and want you
Degree of business risk:	Low

Overview: The boutique practice is the opposite of a generic practice. It connotes the ultimate in specialty, customer service, and expertise. We see this model frequently within the professions of private practice—for good reason. It is profitable, low risk (does not require high expense to maintain, relies on your existing services and existing market), and promotes the aspects most therapists enjoy: finding those people who come to your practice to work with *you*, not just with any therapist. Therapists who operate a boutique practice build a reputation and may have spent considerable time and money over the course of their career on training. But most often they describe their approach as "eclectic"; they are not attached or branded by any one particular method. In a boutique practice, the clients come by referral, seeking out that particular therapist. Boutique practices charge fees for services within the moderate to high range when compared to other similar practices in their locale. The boutique practice is a growing trend within the medical model of health care. Some physicians use this model to build a "premium" or "concierge" medical practice: For an additional fee in the form of a yearly retainer, you get a physician who will guarantee immediate access, longer appointments, and, since the physician limits the caseload, hopefully a greater degree of care. For therapists, the idea of a yearly retainer in addition to session fees challenges professional ethics. But the concept of specialized services for a specialized clientele is still viable and sound.

Strength: Why do clients seek out a boutique practice, even in a down market? For these clients, when purchasing services as important as health care or personal growth, finding the right therapist, coach, or consultant is more important than the cost of the service. Price is not the primary consideration: These clients want to be treated by the best. To develop a boutique practice, you as the owner need to offer good skills and confidence and build visibility. You must be seen as the "go-to" practice for the population, topic, or services you offer. (Reminder: To see the services that sell best in a crisis, see Chapter 6. To identify the strategies that build name recognition, see Chapter 8.)

Value: Although a boutique practice needs to grow, it relies on slow growth: Your target expansion rate is a slow, steady stream of clients referred from existing clients or solid external referral sources. Your clients want to trust you; most will prefer to stay with you until their treatment is complete. To build trust, your seniority, skills, and the overall solidity of your practice (how long it has been open) are some of the factors that confer safety. Therapists in a boutique practice strive to be their best, one step ahead of client needs. You will need to be an educator about your services to define the value your practice offers, so clients understand from the outset why your fees and policies may be more inflexible than other practices.

Many therapists already operate a boutique practice, but few make this explicit by highlighting the aspects that mark them as a boutique (the value clients receive, the therapist's standing in the professional community, the high degree of accessibility, the specialized service). If this is your chosen business model, you must let others know about your philosophy of business and that you are a specialized practice for discriminating clients. Let clients and referral sources read or hear that you are continually engaged in training to maintain your specialized skills, or that you limit your caseload to provide customer care, or that you customize treatment plans, or you include unbilled services (phone calls, reports, etc.) on the client's behalf. If this is not explained clearly, a client or a referral source may not appreciate your practice or understand why your fees are higher than in a generic practice.

BUZZ MARKETING

Boutique practices use the "buzz factor"—word-of-mouth marketing from existing satisfied clients and referral sources to carry the practice message. Buzz just happens, but you can encourage the buzz factor in the following way.

As we observe marketing phenomena, we see ordinary citizens who voluntarily, for no direct pay or other monetary rewards, enthusiastically offer their time and energy to market products for businesses, via word of mouth, writing reviews of their favorite products, or delight in telling others what they enjoy, according to an article in the *New York Times Magazine* (Walker, 2004). Sometimes this type of marketing is directly solicited. For example, marketing companies such as BzzAgent harness volunteer, unpaid citizens and monitor the buzz factor of products it represents by making sure that the volunteers who sign up to be word-of-mouth marketers have a list of talking points about the products they so actively promote to friends, families, and even strangers. BzzAgent can dramatically increase the sales of a newly published book, or the number of people who get interested in eating at a chain restaurant. The volunteers willingly and devotedly spread the word about products not for financial rewards, but for complex social reasons. Influencing others feels good and often gives purpose to one's everyday life, especially if that everyday life lacks sufficient meaning or excitement. And the volunteers, when polled, say that they get a thrill out of being first, knowing about a product that they like before others in their social circles do, and becoming trendsetters. The social science researchers who studied this phenomenon admit that most people engage in this kind of voluntary word-of-mouth buzz about books, movies, products, restaurants, and so on, as a part of normal social discourse. We call it making small talk, telling others about something we did or bought or saw that we liked.

ENGINEERING YOUR BUZZ

What is unique to BzzAgent and other such marketing companies is recognizing that this voluntary buzz can be structured and advanced as part of a formal marketing campaign. BzzAgent makes sure that every product's talking points are clearly articulated to their volunteer army. How might a therapist, coach, or healing professional adapt this research for increasing word-of-mouth marketing about a private practice? As marketing guru Seth Godin wrote in his book *Purple Cow* (Godin, 2003), services or products that have the buzz factor don't just get lucky. They are engineered for buzz, first by being of high-enough value to matter to others. Services that are worth talking about get talked about, with the right marketing help. First, consider what services you offer that are "buzz-able." What do you offer that provides tangible benefits? What is the best of what you do for your clients? Where is your primary value?

Not sure of your value? Ask existing clients to tell you what they are getting out of your work with them. Or get feedback in writing using evaluation forms. Next, create talking points. Talking points are the articulated benefits of your services. Craft and abbreviate the feedback into short statements, and use them as bullet points in all your materials. Post some of your talking points on your Web site and in your printed materials. Spell out specifically how clients improve and what they accomplish by working with you. Your talking points are the messages you want others to carry for you. Craft your talking points carefully and then make sure they are visible and can be understood by others. Use them yourself in conversation about your business, via success stories (see Chapter 8).

You can also engineer buzz via an Internet process. If you have a video, article, audiotape, or something specific of value to promote, one buzz strategy is to let others know about it via social media marketing (see Chapter 9). Place a mention about what you have developed or are working on in your profile in a site such as LinkedIn. If you have video, place it on YouTube. Submit your product for review on one of the sites that compiles new and interesting postings such as Digg, Delicious, or StumbleUpon. You can have people talking (and purchasing). Best bets for this type of buzz are products that are amusing, inspiring, or timely.

EXERCISE: DEFINE YOUR TALKING POINTS

Complete these items to let existing and new clients and referral sources understand what you have to offer that they can buzz to others.

- What are the benefits of working with you versus another therapist?
- Why is your caseload small and select?
- What do you offer that is different or unique?
- What do clients value about your practice and services?

- What can clients expect in terms of accessibility, and outcome?
- Who is your current competition in this niche and what makes your practice different?
- What successes have you had and why?
- What products for disbursement (business cards, brochure, white papers, article reprints, Web site, videos, audiotapes, books, handbooks, etc.) do you have that further your talking points?

BOUTIQUE PRACTICE IN ACTION

The majority of the clients I coach (therapists, consultants, coaches, service-oriented professionals) want to develop boutique practices because, as we explored, the clients are open to paying full fee, even in a down market, and the trust level is established early on. Here is a case example based on a composite of several clients, so that you understand the strategies that can enhance a boutique practice during a crisis economy.

Kathleen is a psychologist in a small, solo boutique practice who does testing and treatment of children with learning disabilities. Within this specialty, she has niched even further to offer services primarily to those children who suffer from sensory integration disorder, a mild to severe cluster of symptoms on the autism spectrum. Kathleen treats children and refers their parents for family therapy elsewhere. Her practice is full, since she has honed in on a very viable and needed service during a down economy (see Chapter 6 for services that sell).

But her practice stays full because of her results. Her clients come from a large geographic area because she has built name recognition. When she created her practice a dozen years ago, she also offered her services to a national charity for learning-disabled children. This gave her a platform for writing papers for their conferences and speaking about her topic. She developed a national reputation as an expert in her field, even though she was new to the field when first volunteered to be on their advisory board.

She set up meetings with principals of 10 area private schools and offered to visit the schools once a year to offer free at-service talks for faculty, as well as to observe and identify helpful strategies for any at-risk children within the classroom. This act of giving (see Chapter 8 and the exercise on building community) gave her credibility with the principals, and referrals followed. Early on, she decided that she would create a team approach with parents and use a transparent process. Rather than hide behind the medical persona of an expert, she takes the role as the educator, helping parents to learn about their child and to see her as part of a team of support. She is explicit about this approach and mentions it in her brochure, her Web site, and even on her voice mail ("Hi. This is Kathleen, here to support you and your child in health and healing. If you are a new client, press one to hear about my team approach to your child's testing and counseling.")

Each parent fills out a monthly rating chart about their child's progress, which Kathleen's part-time secretary/receptionist puts into a spreadsheet for each child. The parents and Kathleen review this spreadsheet and it gives parents a sense that their child is moving forward and that Kathleen is again the captain of the team. This builds satisfaction and enthusiasm and, when money is tight, it helps parents see the value of their therapy dollars. In exit interviews (when the treatment is over there is a final session for review), the use of the spreadsheets is always mentioned by parents as one of the helpful elements of the overall treatment. Kathleen has a list of talking points that are posted on the wall in her waiting room, on her Web site, and in her brochures. These speak to her rate of success, what parents can expect in terms of time and treatment, and her flexibility with what she knows are busy parents and sometimes overwhelmed children.

Part of her flexibility is her use of packaging services and fees. Kathleen uses a menu of services (see Chapter 7 for this strategy to package your services). Based on her recommendations, parents select the course of treatment they can afford given their budget and time. Kathleen's fees are high, but since she uses a packaging plan, she takes credit card payment and offers a 5% discount for prepaying 12 sessions at once. She has no collections and is able to keep a full practice going, even during this recession.

CONCEPTS FOR A BOUTIQUE PRACTICE

- *Be a big fish in a small pond.* You want to target a narrow-enough market so that you can be well known. It's better to be a big fish in a small pond than an average fish in the wide sea. Kathleen keeps her specialty narrow enough that she can "own" her target market. When the keywords "sensory integration" and the city she lives in are entered into Google, her Web site comes up first or second.
- *Educate the market.* You want your marketing time to be educating others about your specialty and treatment. You need to position yourself as an expert. Writing, speaking, and teaching will play a large part in your marketing plan. And remember: Your focus is on your existing market, so much of this education will be for your existing clientele. Kathleen educates her market with her team approach, so that her clients can speak with clarity about what she does for their children, the success that it has, and how professional and accessible they find her as a person.
- *Affiliate for leveraging market share.* Your best referral sources will be those who also serve your target market in other capacities. You want to become known to the "trusted advisers" for your target market (those on whom they rely for good referrals). Kathleen built her affiliations with the schools and the nonprofits at the same time that she built her practice.

Next, moving along the Ansoff matrix to the quadrant he calls "Product Development," which I adapt for another desirable practice model with just a bit more financial risk: the brand recognition practice (see Figure 10.3).

THE BRAND RECOGNITION PRACTICE

Figure 10.3. Brand recognition practice

New Products

Existing Markets

Product Development

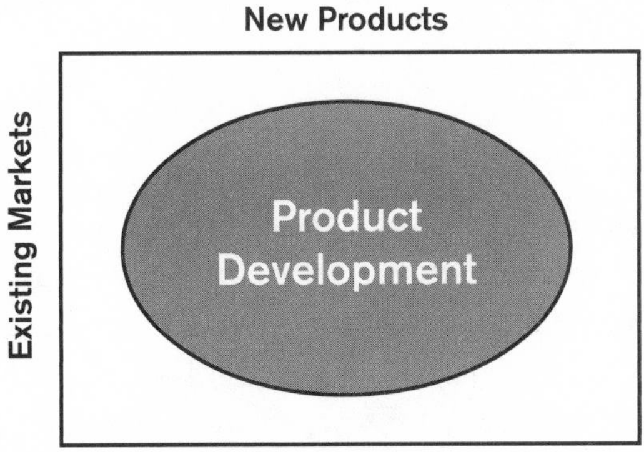

Ansoff matrix quadrant:	Product development
Expansion criteria:	Existing markets, new products
Private practice application:	Brand recognition practice
Focus on:	The "what" of the practice (the method)
Target market:	Educated consumers who prefer the brand
Degree of business risk:	Moderate

Overview: In this model, another popular model of private practice, your method of working becomes your calling card or brand. With a brand recognition business model, you sell the "what" (the method) of the practice instead of the "who" (the person/therapist). The method may be one you create or one you have trained to use. Either way, this method-based practice requires a significant investment in training and development—hence the higher risk based on financial investment. If you are working within your own method, your investment will reflect your time: development, research, measurement, articulation, public education, and of course its promotion. If you adopt an existing method, the investment will be in terms of time and money: training, supervision, practice, and certification, or may include material or licensing fees and affiliation with one or more organizations that represent the method. You stay with your existing target market of clients, while promoting the brand. The fees for a successful brand recognition practice are often similar to those of a boutique practice, within the moderate to high range.

Strength: How does a brand recognition practice fare in a down market? It may be vulnerable to the market, but it has resilience in that it can be leveraged by bringing in associates who work at a lower rate. In a group practice based on brand recognition, hiring associates makes sense: The practitioners become more interchangeable if the method is king. It is also an easier business to sell—a practice centered on a brand or method is a better transferable asset than a boutique practice, whose draw is the therapist. (To see more about building a business to sell, read Chapter 13). If you have enthusiasm about the brand and are a true believer in your method, your task is to educate and generate a similar belief and enthusiasm in others (clients and staff). Marketers call this developing brand loyalty. Therapists who do well with a brand recognition practice invest heavily in their training, attend brand-related conferences to keep up their credentials, and, when asked what they do, mention the brand (method) within the first sentence.

Value: If the method has "legs," that is, gets media attention, has a charismatic spokesperson, has a well-regarded book, has an organization that spends time and money on public relations, is well regarded with other professionals, etc., than you as the practice owner will get referrals by brand association. Your best clients will be those educated consumers who search out the method via the Internet and find your Web site, or ask other professionals for a referral to the method.

This practice is obviously not for the therapist who sees herself as eclectic; a better choice would be the boutique practice. Years ago, I attended a professional training with a therapist who was promoting his method. "Don't integrate this method into your eclectic practice and expect to see results," he cautioned those of us who worked eclectically. "Either use this method unadulterated, or let it go." He was making a strong case for his brand recognition practice.

DUE DILIGENCE

Often, a therapist hears about a method from a colleague or reads a book promoting a method. She takes some training to try it out. Impressed, she makes a decision (sometimes an expensive decision) to invest in further training. At a recent seminar, I asked the 100 therapists in the room how much they had invested in training post–graduate school. The average answer from therapists in practice for 10 years or less? $50,000. Then I asked if the training lived up to its potential, in terms of both clinical results and business results. Only 40% of those who had invested so heavily felt it had met their expectations in both areas. We therapists and other service professionals become attracted to a method and invest heavily, without having investigated its efficacy and its business worth. Due diligence means "thorough investigation." As a professional, you have hundreds of choices regarding what methods to use, but it may be hard to do due diligence, especially when you want to explore not only the clinical efficacy of the method, but also its business advantage. You can change that for yourself. Here are factors to consider from a business perspective:

- *Check for brand acceptance*: Did you ever give a party only to have no one show up? You can invest heavily in a brand or method of training, but if it is unfamiliar, or has negative research attached to it or just bad press, you may not have anyone seek out your services. If you choose an unknown method, your investment will be more risky. Rather than gravitating to something untried, or the "next new thing," select a brand or method that has recognition in the marketplace. Is this method important when your referral sources want to refer? Ask your market. Have any of your colleagues or clients complained about this method? Find out.

- *Ask for research*: Know the efficacy of the method or training in which you will invest. Is there research? For example, a report issued by a panel of the U.S. government's top scientists found that the majority of treatments for posttraumatic stress disorder (PTSD), which are used to treat hundreds of thousands of veterans, lack rigorous scientific evidence for their efficacy (Verdantum, 2007). Some of the treatments researched are popular among therapists. But if you decide to build your treatment of PTSD around one of these less-than-effective treatments, your brand may face rejection by educated potential clients. Ask the method vendor (organization that sells the training or certification) for research results.

- *Request brand support*: If you add a new product or method, talk to the vendors and ask about how they promote the method to the public. Do they provide referrals to the practitioners they train? If not, be wary of a large investment. Go with those vendors who care about your success. For example, the Academy of Cognitive Therapy supports research studies and places articles about CBT (cognitive behavioral therapy) in the media and hosts a Web site that lists certified CBT practitioners. EEG Spectrum International, a vendor that trains practitioners in neurofeedback, promotes journal articles and case studies, advertises the method in print ads in magazines, and has a Web site referral list. Building market share for a method should be the responsibility of both the vendor and the practitioner.

BEING FIRST

When you invest in a brand, you want to be ahead of the competition. Will you be first with the method in your local community, and for how long? One therapist (let's call her Sue) became certified in a popular method of couples counseling as an Imago Relationship Therapist. The method's spokesperson, Harville Hendrix, had a best-selling book coupled with appearances on *Oprah*. Sue was literally the only therapist certified at an advanced level of training and the majority of her referrals came from the Imago Relationship International Web site or word of mouth, as people searched for Imago therapy. Sue's clients wanted a therapist using the Imago method because they had seen Hendrix on *Oprah*. Sue had a waiting list, and her practice flourished for many years. But then Sue's story changed. With the popularity of the method, more therapists got trained and Sue's practice referral base dropped sharply. Eventually Sue found that her method was no longer such a draw—so many other therapists could offer the same type of sessions.

If you are first with your brand in your area, see if you can more aggressively mark your territory. You have made a big investment: Lead with method in your business card, brochures, print advertising, and Web site domain name (see if you can use the brand in your domain name along with your city, such as "brandname"city.com). Even when other practitioners begin to come into your area, try to differentiate your practice based on longevity. Sue found referrals picked up when she used an explicit tag line: "Experience with helping couples learn to find love again using Imago Therapy for over 20 years."

This business model is at a higher risk because you need to market the brand continually. Brand marketing includes print advertising, a yellow pages ad, a Web site, business brochures, and networking. You will need to spend time and energy on building and maintaining the association between your practice and your brand. Try to be a leader by being first in your geographic area or position yourself as a senior practitioner by giving back to the professional community.

DEVELOPING DATA AND MEASURES

When you use a brand recognition model, you want data and measures to encourage new clients to purchase your services. Create your own data and track your results, suggests Scott Miller, cofounder of the Institute for Therapeutic Change. In his workshop, "Improve your clinical effectiveness 65% without hardly trying" (2005), he suggests that we need less "evidence-based therapy" and more "therapy-based evidence." Whether you are a consultant, coach, healer, or other service-oriented or helping professional, you need evidence of results to help potential clients understand the value of your offerings. This is not a difficult process to start and can yield big results. Here's how to proceed.

EXERCISE: TRACKING EVIDENCE

Use this exercise to develop measures for your client population and referral sources, to validate your effectiveness.

- *Measure subjective results*: Offer a pre- and post-test to your clients to help them and you track the outcomes after each session. This can be as complex as having clients fill out a form on a computer in the waiting room with a code to keep their pre- and post-answers in their own file, or a handwritten sheet that is filled out, or a few verbal questions you ask at the beginning and at the end of each session and note.
On the front end of a session, ask:

What are your 10 goals for the next 3 months?

What would you like to accomplish in today's session?

How will you know if we succeeded in addressing that goal today?

At the end of the session ask:

How did we do in accomplishing your stated goal for today's session?

What will you take away from today's meeting?

How would you rate the effectiveness of the work together today on a scale of 1 to 10?

- *Track results over time*: Now you can start to create a graph, spreadsheet, or other tracking mechanism to capture the data.

This provides great feedback and important information about what your clients find satisfying. Researchers Scott Miller and Barry Duncan (1997) offer a program for counselors called ASIST (Administration, scoring, interpretation, and data storage tool) (see http://www.talkingcure.com), an end-user software program that provides therapists with real-time feedback regarding their client's experience of the alliance and progress in treatment. But you can create your own pre- and post-feedback tracking survey, asking questions of each client at a regular rate, and then determining any markers that seem critical for your practice, such as:

What does an average client accomplish over the course of 1 session, 5 sessions, 10 sessions?

What are the most common stated client goals?

How often are they accomplished with the first 30 days? 60 days?

What is the most commonly stated "take-away"?

How long does the average client stay?

What is the average client rating for effectiveness of a single session?

- *Promote the client-based results*: Now that you have data, it is important to be able to display this as part of your marketing and educating. Imagine being able to state (on your Web site, to insurance panels, to referrals sources) that:

"Ninety-five percent of our clients say that they met their stated goals in each session during a 6-month period" or

"Eighty-five percent of our clients are repeat clients, and surveys show that they rated their treatment at 9.5 on a scale of 0 to 10"

or other outcomes based on surveys or data that you control and maintain.

SOLIDIFY YOUR BRAND

You can build a solid connection with clients if you help them own the gains they make. Using the above data and measures, you can bring the topic of results into the process of the therapy session. Too often therapists don't have this kind of discussion with clients until the termination process, as a way of evaluating the course of treatment. But this kind of discussion is needed earlier, to solidify the changes that the client achieves. Make the process of therapy less mysterious. Help your clients to articulate their gains and understand why the process is working on an ongoing basis, so that they really understand the effectiveness of your services and talk about your brand with others:

- *At the end of sessions, leave time to debrief.* Too often we work right up until the last minute of the session. Leave time to debrief and assess. "What was most important in our work today? How specifically might you make it count in your life this week? Was there anything that happened that you don't understand?"
- *Have a 3-month verbal progress update.* Give clients a chance to evaluate results and gains from that time period. Celebrate with them. This is not wasted time. This helps clients feel hopeful and see that they have accomplished steps in the process.
- *Find a process of measuring that fits your therapeutic style.* Make this normal and natural. Help clients both articulate ongoing gains and better understand the therapeutic process that they are in.

THE BRAND RECOGNITION PRACTICE IN ACTION

Ned is a composite of clients I coach who have successfully developed a brand recognition practice. He is a licensed counselor working with men and has a practice using one of the most recognizable brands in psychotherapy: cognitive-behavior therapy (CBT). CBT is well researched and tested by a number of studies and often mentioned in the media. Ned purchased his training from a for-profit company. He asked the vendor who offered the training what he could expect in return to help him build his practice. The vendor was reluctant at first to offer much beyond a certificate of completion, but at Ned's insistence, the vendor agreed to allow Ned to copy some of the company's marketing texts and written materials for his own use.

Ned collects mentions of CBT research in online media and provides links to the articles on his Web site. He joined the Academy of Cognitive Therapy, which lists certified CBT practitioners on its savvy Web site that also features a long list of media-placed articles. Since Ned's population—"men"—is broad, he brands his practice with CBT to set him apart from others in his locale. Ned promotes his brand via his Web site, incorporates it into his business name, and uses CBT research as a talking point for his networking. When he visits a corporate headquarters (many of Ned's clients are stressed-out executives), he tells them that his therapy won't waste their time because it is focused, specific, on task, and best for business executives who want change now. When he speaks to physicians, he again stresses that he only uses CBT, which is well researched and tested, so that they can feel secure that the referrals they make are going to satisfy the needs of their patients for a science-based treatment. Ned keeps measures of his client's progress and talks about these with his clients and his referral sources.

Ned uses the yellow pages for advertising and runs a print ad in a local attorney-based publication (another good source of referrals). He has optimized his Web site using Google AdWords (see Chapter 9) and when someone Googles CBT and the name of his town, his site is ranked high. Ned keeps track of all referrals and where they come from. Fifty percent of his referrals come through the Internet and his yellow pages ad. His brand is ubiquitous: He writes a brief CBT blog for his Web site and sends a compilation of the brief articles to his referral sources once every 6 months as a professional newsletter. His car's vanity license plate spells CBT. He has pens that he gives away in his waiting room with CBT on them.

CONCEPTS FOR BRAND RECOGNITION

- *Promote the brand, not the man.* Make sure that your brand suits your personality and your purpose. Ned is a booster of CBT and modest about himself. This makes it easier for him to market, he says, because he can comfortably "sell" the method, but is shy about selling himself. It's important to note that Ned is a true believer and would use CBT even if it were not a popular method. He believes, and his enthusiasm helps him attract new clients.

- *Measure often.* Track your results so you can promote your brand. Ned's brand lends itself to frequent measuring of outcomes and success, and this helps Ned with his marketing and keeping his faith high in the brand.

- *Set aside an advertising budget.* To keep your brand visible, you need to advertise via the yellow pages, print media, Internet advertising, and Web site optimization. Ned uses all of these to keep his practice full, even though his work is often short-term given his methods.

CHAPTER 11

Best Business Models, Part 2

In chapter 10 we examined two popular crisis-proof models that relate to the lowest-risk quadrants of the Ansoff matrix. The next model is less common in private practice, but may fit your needs and your practice philosophy. This model is set up to serve people at a lower cost, which makes it attractive for a crisis economy if your mission is to help a broader market. Ansoff calls this model of reaching new markets with existing products (or services) Market Development; I see it in use primarily within the medical community. This model of practice is best known as the retail clinic (see Figure 11.1).

RETAIL CLINIC

Figure 11.1. Retail clinic

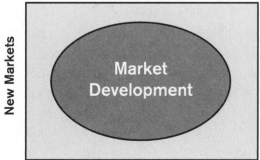

Ansoff matrix quadrant: Market development
Expansion criteria: New markets, existing
                               products

Private practice application: Retail clinic

Focus on: The "where" of the practice
(accessibility)

Target market: Anyone who needs services
right now

Degree of business risk: Moderate to high

Overview: A retail clinic is a bare-bones operation whose focus is reaching those people who need less costly services. This is still a fee for service practice, and your target market is people who need services quickly. But a retail clinic makes it easy for people to find services and treats them as consumers, not patients. A retail clinic thrives on volume; you work with a less affluent client and set up a clinic-like environment where people can be seen for generic conditions: anxiety, depression, couples therapy, or family therapy. The team approach works well in this model and it is used successfully by group practices. If you like working with colleagues and prefer short-term methods that yield measurable results, a retail clinic may be a good option. Your fees will be in the low to moderate range.

Strength: A retail clinic combines affordability with access (you open early and stay open late and operate with a staff of therapists). In a single day at a retail clinic, you may treat depression, anxiety, couples problems, parenting issues, and/or addiction concerns. If you are a coach in a retail clinic practice model, you will be offering a mix of life coaching, career coaching, and basic business coaching at a reasonable price, perhaps on a contract basis, to employees within a large corporation. Volume keeps the retail clinic afloat. Retail clinics operate without lots of amenities—you don't need or want a fancy office, but you do need staff. This is a successful model for a group practice, as long as the group is trained in short-term methods. Since volume is the name of the game, you must keep your clientele turnover rate to a determined number of sessions. Having a constant flow of new clients and hours open to see them means that the methods will be goal oriented and brief. This is a good model for a practice that works with small groups and you can find this model used by outpatient addiction clinics, eating disorder clinics, and clinics that specialize in behavioral change or symptom cessation (e.g., stop smoking clinics). Unlike a boutique or brand recognition practice, which may have no formal staff, a retail clinic operates best when the clinic employs a capable office manager.

Value: You need to stay visible, using advertising and marketing in order to attract new clients. Given that marketing budget, you want to run a lean operation in terms of management. You will need office management and a receptionist to book appointments, although some forward-thinking clinics rely on software to do a lot of this, including setting appointments (see Chapter 7 to review the systems and software for a micropractice and a high-tech practice). The retail clinic first gained popularity in the medical field. QuickHealth has opened retail medical clinics in northern California, offering primary care, pay-as-you-go clinics for working families. While the clinics vary by company, most treat 25 to 40 medical conditions and charge $45 to $75 a visit. MinuteClinic, which pioneered the retail clinic industry in 2000, operates 87 clinics and is being bought by CVS. They advertise short waits and 15-minute exams, and some give out pagers so clients can shop while waiting. If the presenting problem requires a physician, patients are referred to their primary care physicians. If they do not have one, the nurse-practitioner refers them to one from the clinic's referral list. "I'm seeing kind of a newfound energy from patients around choice," said Tom Charland, past MinuteClinic senior vice president. "I'm reluctant to call it power; I don't think it's quite there yet. But in the United States, apart from the health care industry, consumers exhibit a fair amount of power as purchasers, as consumers. I think that is starting to happen in health care with the trend toward cost shifting" (2006, p. 1).

ATTRIBUTES

The American Academy of Family Physicians suggests that these features are important to consider in a retail clinic:

- *Narrow your scope of service*: Retail clinics should have a basic system for diagnosis first, and then a well-defined and limited scope of clinical services. A retail law clinic would need attorneys who can do a generalized practice of family and civil law. A retail consulting clinic needs management consultants who can handle diversity training, conflict resolution, and strategic planning, all in a week's work. A retail therapy clinic needs therapists who can counsel families and individuals for a range of generic mental health care issues quickly.
- *Utilize evidence-based medicine*: Clinical services and treatment should be short-term, solution-focused, cognitive, skill- and/or evidence-based.
- *Promote a team-based approach*: The clinic should have a formal connection with local psychiatrists and other specialists for referrals as needed. This clinic is best for general counseling issues that can have a psychoeducational component.
- *Rely on electronic records*: An important aspect of this model is having easy, computerized methods of record keeping, payment, and outcomes of service.

EXERCISE: IS A RETAIL CLINIC RIGHT FOR ME? CHECKLIST

Check the following statements to see if a retail clinic matches your philosophy of service.

- ❑ My goal is to see those clients who really need services and have less disposable income.
- ❑ I am very comfortable with brief, solution-oriented methods.
- ❑ I like a lot of variety to my clinical day.
- ❑ My preference is to work with others collegially, in a clinic setting.
- ❑ I have an outgoing personality and really like people.
- ❑ I am happy to see someone a few times if I know that I really made a difference.
- ❑ I want to be free of managed care but still see a broad population of clients.

❑ I do my best work when my client count is full and my day is busy.

❑ I am very well organized and can manage a lot of data and appointments.

PRINT ADVERTISING

In a retail clinic, 25% of your total expenses may be spent on advertising. Unlike the first two business models presented, this type of practice does carry more financial risk—and usually requires a small business loan of $10,000–$25,000 to launch for rent in a well-trafficked area, phone book and print advertising, and 3 to 6 months of cash flow to help cushion the inevitable start-up time. Advertising is essential. Focus on visibility. You want your practice to be located in a storefront in a retail shopping area, with easy parking and heavy foot traffic. You need staff and associates so that you can be accessible to clients on weekends and evenings. Pick a practice name that is easy to understand and remember; make sure the services are presented without jargon, in ways that clients can quickly identify and purchase. You need to price your fees in an attractive way, so that clients pay without feeling a need to use their insurance. Keep sessions short and time-limited. Package services in a menu listing, so that clients can have some control over what they buy.

According to industry surveys, yellow pages ads are still important for psychotherapists across the country. Forty-seven percent of therapists rely on yellow pages print ads for marketing efforts. Because these ads are expensive, you want to make sure that you get the most from it. For a retail clinic, a yellow pages ad is a must. Here are tips regarding your ad:

• *Keep it short and sweet.* With a yellow pages ad, you pay for space and the real estate is expensive. Stress the essentials. You can't say it all. Graphics, pictures, or words in quotations get attention (example: "Fighting with your family? I can help!").

- *Refer readers to your Web site.* Web sites have more space and function like a brochure. Make sure you mention your Web site along with other contact information.
- *Use the three-item rule.* Graphic designers suggest that any ad have only three items for the eye to focus on. (An item may be a block of text, a graphic, a headline.) Group text together to make one item. Less is more. Have some white space for the eye to rest on.
- *Focus on benefits, not features.* For a quick read, you want the reader to find hope in your ad. Don't list all your degrees or experience or methods. Instead, bullet a few hopeful outcomes. "Resolve worries," "Stop smoking," or "Become a loving family" can be more powerful than telling readers that you are an adjunct professor at a local university or what your society memberships are. Save those for your intake packet.
- *Post up.* The best positioning for an ad is the closest to the beginning of the category. Have your practice name start with the letters A-C to achieve the best positioning. One therapist uses "A Relationship Center" instead of "The Relationship Center" for this reason.
- *Eliminate jargon.* Readers of the yellow pages are less likely to respond to vague words or professional jargon. Eliminate what my colleague Wendy Allen calls "glaze-over" words—words that we professionals like but may be confusing or without specificity for the public (such as *blocked, closure, metamodel, congruence, envision, synergy,* and *self-actualization*). Better to use ordinary, clear language for these ads.
- *Repeat often.* Statistics say that a yellow pages ad and print ads need to be seen at least six times before a reader is motivated to call. Budget for the long-term posting of your ad.

RETAIL CLINIC IN ACTION

An addictions clinic in a city in the Midwest transformed itself from a traditional counseling center into a retail clinic. The clinic is a partnership and the owners had a vision of low-cost services and quick program turnover to serve an urban community. The partners purchased a building to house the clinic—a large investment up front, but one that has paid off in the long term since they have less overhead and a reasonable mortgage instead of a lease. They are located in the center of their city with a large parking lot behind the building (easy access for clients). They employ 25 part-time therapists and have numerous groups that run each week. The center has several strong referral sources: area hospitals, employee assistance programs (EAPs), the court system, and area schools.

The addictions clinic operates as a strict cash-only, fee-for-service clinic. New clients pay by the program (a monthly flat fee per person for outpatient group and individual check-ins), not by the session. This keeps billing costs at a minimum and ensures that the therapists can have more stability around their schedules.

The biggest practice expense (beyond staffing and salaries for therapists) is the yellow pages ad, which costs tens of thousands of dollars each year and shows up in several different phone books. The office environment is clean but very bare-bones. The clinic is open 7 days a week, around the clock, and does walk-in business.

The clinic hosts 12-step AA groups in its group rooms on the weekends, which further promote their services. New clients are scheduled for a first evaluation session within 72 hours of contact. Last year the clinic grossed just under $1 million, but the profit margin was a low 5%. The partners keep careful track of the operations and expenses and work within the practice themselves, running groups and seeing clients. They hope to sell the practice within 10 years and, as a result, they spend considerable marketing time securing contracts for services and making good connections with their referral sources.

CONCEPTS FOR A RETAIL CLINIC

- *Run a bare-bones operation*, set up to cast a wider net than a boutique practice and serve less affluent clients. Keep an eye on expenses and management.
- *Pick a location that is accessible*, say a retail shopping mall. Staff up so that the clinic is open when clients can come (evenings and weekends).

- *Offer shorter sessions with an attractive fee-for-service price point.* Short-term methods, small groups, and quick treatment turn-around allow for ease of scheduling.

CAREER COMPONENTS

The final Ansoff model, which he calls Diversification, is the highest risk model in terms of financial investment, since it relies on bringing new products (or services) to new markets, always an expensive proposition. But this can also be a very resilient model because it offers varied and wide-ranging services to multiple markets. I see this popular model, which I call career components (see Figure 11.2), as a lego-like set of services that fit together. This model works best when the components have some shared connection or common theme, so that the parts of the diversification are not too dissimilar. A diversified practice of providing individual therapy and dog walking is less robust than one providing individual therapy and teaching the fundamentals of therapy at a local university. The career component model attracts therapists, coaches, and consultants who prefer a mixture of work. Since some services have a limited appeal or narrow markets, multiple services and additional markets can buffer a practice in an uncertain economy and boost earnings in a strong market.

Figure 11.2. Career components

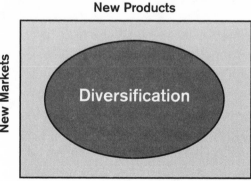

Ansoff growth model:	Diversification
Expansion criteria:	New markets, new products
Private practice application:	Career components
Focus on:	The "how" of the practice (multiple roles)
Target market:	Various and distinct markets for each separate service
Degree of business risk:	High

Overview: Those who operate highly diversified practices liken it to juggling, but instead of balls, they are juggling components of their careers, trying to keep all aspects of their professional roles in play at the same time. Roles might be: clinician, teacher, speaker, writer, coach, consultant, expert witness, researcher. The business risk (or investment) in this model is due to the fact that each role or service may require additional training or certification and may require its own marketing effort. The most profitable way to operate a diversified practice is to separate your multiple roles into income streams; imagine each stream as a train, on its own track, running in and out of one station (your practice) but kept separate enough on paper so that you can track its profitability. For example, clinical services might be on one track with their own budget, marketing plan, and client base. Consulting services would be on another, with expenses of a separate consulting Web site and networking budget. Combined fees for a career component practice can be the highest of the four models, since some of the career components will be in product sales, coaching, or consulting arenas.

Strength: Diversifying your business into a career component model can even out the ups and downs of a small business. When one service is not selling well, your other services may be in demand, leveling the profit picture. You develop additional "business muscles." Years ago, health fitness experts realized the value in "cross-training"—incorporating more than one form of exercise into a workout to keep an athlete in peak condition. Just like an athlete, it's good for therapists to become cross-trainers and diversify, to become more flexible, versatile, and profitable.

Value: The most profitable diversification strategy involves finding at least one component or income stream that is highly independent. For example, if you are a psychotherapist and take managed care, have another component that does not rely on insurance or the medical model, such as executive coaching, leadership training, or teaching. Some consultants, reliant on corporate dollars, find success by diversifying into softer services such as personal training, meditation instruction, or life coaching. Writing and speaking can offer further diversification to a practice, as can a foray into legal venues as expert witnesses and mediators.

EXERCISE: HOW TO DIVERSIFY

When you identify with one established role, it can be confusing to think about adding another. To help you think this through, consider the following categories. (Adapted from *The Business and Practice of Coaching,* Grodzki and Allen, 2005.)

1. *What is the previous work and/or life experience that you want your new service to feature?* When did you feel best appreciated by others? Who did you help and how? Look at your past life experience. What roles have you taken on in life? What challenges have you faced and overcome? What have you learned that informs how you help others? What have you achieved in your relationships and your personal life that are part of the values you have to offer others?

- What do you love to do with your spare time?
- In what capacity do you volunteer your time?
- What have you always wanted to do in your life or work that you don't get a chance to do now?
- At the end of your life, what is the legacy you hope to leave?
- What needs do you see in your local community or society at large that go unfilled?

2. *Where have you achieved excellence in your life?* What have you learned to transform? What handicap or limitation have you overcome?

Where do you shine in your life or work? Your accomplishment can be a signal of the gifts you have to offer to others. Incorporated into your business, it can make your practice stand apart from the crowd.

- Where have you achieved excellence in your life?
- Where do you stand out from others in the work you do?
- What limitations or problems have you overcome in your life that inform your work today?
- What are you best known for among your friends and colleagues?
- What accomplishments or achievements come easiest to you in your life or work?
- What challenges do you enjoy the most?

3. *What skills and strengths do you possess that you want to use more often?* Your list of personal and professional skills and talents may be broad or specific but just because you are competent in an area, doesn't mean you have to build a business around it. One therapist noted her long prior career working as an addictions counselor within a prison setting. She was very skilled at anger management. She could calm an explosive situation, teach anger management skills, and show an inmate how to redirect anger in a more constructive way. But she decided she didn't want to use that skill in any diversification. "I have helped enough people to calm down for one lifetime," she said. Instead, for this question, she listed those skills and strengths that she had but did not use often, untapped talents that she said she would love to bring into play.

- What skills and strengths do you possess that you want to use every day?
- What positive traits about yourself do you observe that keep repeating in various situations over time?
- What skills and strengths do you value, in their own right, regardless of recognition by others?
- As you rethink a recent goal that you accomplished, what natural skills and strengths did you use to achieve it?

- What social or intellectual skills have helped you to develop into the person you are today?

MAKING IT REAL

Now you need to apply a business planning approach to your thinking. Any diversified service must be one for which there is a target market and you need to give yourself time to test out your market prior to committing a large expense. Good questions to consider include:

- What would be my first steps in implementation?
- What help or resources do I need to make this happen?
- Who else do I know who are using this approach? How does it work for them?
- What are others charging who offer similar services?
- What will I charge?
- What contacts do I need to develop to find new markets?
- What is my timeline for this endeavor?

ENHANCING SELF-PRESENTATION

Can your current role (say, that of healer) translate into another (that of teacher)? It depends on what the new situation and setting require. One therapist in California taught systems family therapy at a local community college in addition to seeing families in her private practice. When a member of her class asked her about the infighting within her family's business, she made some suggestions based on her Bowenian training, and soon found herself with a new role: family business coach, hired at a substantial hourly rate to sort out the dynamics interfering with the founder and his family during their board retreats.

But after the first business retreat, her feedback from the founder was that while her content was interesting, it was not totally relevant.

She needed to upgrade her language to match a business perspective. She started to do some reading on executive coaching and subscribed to a family business journal to educate herself about business goals and terminology. She bought a new wardrobe of business suits: no more unstructured long skirts and flowing blouses. She learned to use PowerPoint for presentations and developed new business materials for this aspect of her work. Now, along with her teaching and therapy private practice, she specializes in family business consulting. Her services include structuring family governance, developing succession plans, and one-on-one "shadow coaching," where she spends a day in the life of a founder of a family business, to get a better sense of what is happening on the ground. She charges $2,500 per day, a standard management consulting fee, and says that one third of her practice time is spent with these business clients. When added to her more traditional psychotherapy services, it has allowed her to gross upward of six figures each year.

Building market in venues outside of your clinical population requires a new set of skills, including:

- Networking with advisers who make referrals
- Establishing a reputation within a different clientele
- Learning to contract, sell services, and bill for services in new ways
- Refining your language, materials, and methods
- Changing your image
- Enhancing self-presentation.

EXERCISE: SELF-PRESENTATION CHECKLIST

Check the items that will help you enhance your image for new roles and new settings.

❑ My clothing fits well and is a professional style.
❑ My hair, makeup, and wardrobe are in harmony with my professional role.

❑ I have good posture and stand straight.

❑ I wear shoes that allow me to stand comfortably and walk easily.

❑ I am in control of any and all nervous habits (nail biting, coughing, hair twisting, gum chewing).

❑ I have heard myself on audio and I have a pleasant, clear, assertive speaking voice.

❑ I have seen myself on video and I have a direct, friendly, professional demeanor.

❑ I make eye contact when I meet someone.

❑ My business card and business materials display confidence.

❑ I have learned to translate my clinical ideas and concepts into language that fits other settings.

❑ I have asked for feedback from others regarding my self-presentation.

❑ I project the image that my role requires.

❑ I have started a library of resource materials and books to support my new ventures.

❑ I have a budget for equipment upgrades to make sure that my work can be received well.

CAREER COMPONENTS IN ACTION

As described, many therapists, coaches, healers, and consultants combine a variety of roles or services to create uniquely diversified practices. Here are a few examples: Susan Shevlin (2002) developed a condition at age 16 that progressed to blindness. She became a counselor and used her blindness to help her connect with the illness or disabilities of her patients and then added life coaching to her practice. "I transformed my physical blindness into insight. Today I practice what I call 'vision coaching.' In dealing with my blindness, I went through many shifts and changes during which I discovered my strengths and limitations. That passion later turned to a vision for assisting others to use and maximize their own strengths which, in turn, led me into the field of therapy and coaching."

Olivia Mellan is a psychotherapist working with couples in Washington, D.C., who privately struggled with her own shopaholic tendencies. As she began to confront her money attitudes, she developed a second specialty to help others deal with their money issues. She added several income streams: writing (she is author of *Money Harmony: Resolving Money Conflicts in Your Life and Relationships* and four other books), journalism (she is a columnist for Investment Advisor), speaking (Mellan gives keynote speeches to corporations, and she has appeared on *Oprah*, the *Today* Show, and ABC's *20/20*), and other nationwide media (she hosts her own radio show).

Some professionals diversify based on their prior experience: C. J. Hayden, business coach from San Francisco, said "My business background is very eclectic. I had over fifty jobs before I turned thirty and changed careers six times. I find that having experience in many different industries and environments has contributed greatly to my value as a business coach." Diversification is part of her business plan. She cautions other coaches not to expect to earn a big income from coaching sessions alone. Most successful coaches she knows teach, consult, train, write, speak, conduct group programs, develop products, or license intellectual property, in addition to individual sessions. CJ writes, speaks, and has taught coaching skills for Marriott International, Wells Fargo Bank, and BP Amoco. She has a variety of passive and active incomes from her coaching services, classes, books, tapes, and affiliations with multiple Web sites. According to CJ, coaching is just a springboard for a larger, diversified business.

Like these other examples, my personal practice is also highly diversified. I have worked as a psychotherapist in private practice since 1988 and continue to see therapy clients 50% of my working time. My various business coaching services have been ongoing for about a decade (seeing clients, teaching teleclasses, giving seminars and workshops, writing, and speaking) and take up the remainder of my time. Tracking my expenses, income, and time for all of these different endeavors was essential. For example, for the first 2 years as a business coach, I earned money but not a profit—my expenses in creating a new market were huge. Writing my first book (which took 9 months) netted me about 10 cents per hour! All along, my psychotherapy practice funded these new endeavors until I was able to create a sufficient market for my business coaching services. Now the business coaching aspect of my practice is more profitable than the psychotherapy end, but I still love being a therapist and would not want to stop seeing individual clients.

CONCEPTS FOR THE DIVERSIFIED PRACTICE

- *Track each service or income stream separately.* Don't make the mistake of blurring your areas of diversification when it comes to your profit and loss statement. Track each service or income stream so that you can analyze its profitability and the time and energy each one takes to maintain. Because each added service or product may require time to become profitable, you need to monitor its progress, and that requires costing out expenses as well as income separately.
- *Develop different but complementary services that can multiply referrals.* Remember the concept of cross-training I suggested. Add services that can complement each other but are different enough to reach separate markets.
- *Find independent markets.* If you are a therapist, make sure that at least one service is not dependent on insurance or health care. Since your goal is autonomy, try to balance your diversification so that additional services don't rely on the same markets, especially if those are markets that make you dependent (such as insurance payments, EAPs, or other discounted contractual arrangements).

CHAPTER 12

Your Crisis-Proof Turnaround Plan

This brief chapter is a summary of what you have read and learned so far. All the preceding chapters contribute to formulating this plan. If you are coping with a crisis, complete this plan quickly and begin to take action immediately. If you are not in crisis, use this as a preventative exercise in improving or enhancing your current practice. Either way, think through the following questions and fill in the chart provided to develop a plan for today and for the future. Each aspect of this plan references a previous chapter. As you go through the plan, I give you chapter references and point you to my earlier books in the event that you need to do more reading or research in order to fill in a section of your plan.

The goals of your turnaround plan, after you review your situation and define your business model, include the following:

- Boost profits
- Protect the practice
- Improve management and systems
- Grow your client base
- Monitor progress
- Measure results
- Stay in action.

The plan is set up in several steps. First you will recognize any symptoms of crisis, which you can review by going back through the integrity repair exercise in Chapter 1. Then you will list the sources of your challenges, based on the review in Chapter 3. Next you will select your business model (Chapters 9 and 10) and write a simple vision statement. Then you will specify the services of your redesigned practice (see services that sell in Chapter 6) and articulate your unique selling point (Chapter 8).

The next step on the plan is identifying your goals: financial (Chapter 7), marketing (Chapters 8 and 9), risk protection (Chapter 6), and business operations (Chapter 4). Each of these categories has space for five goals, the bread and butter of your plan. The goals section has a timeline for completion and a designation of who will be responsible for achieving each step. The final section helps you define "your people"—your support system—those who can help you stay motivated and on track (Chapter 6), and your extreme self-care actions (Chapter 2) to keep you in good shape. That's it. If you have been doing the exercises in the preceding chapters, the plan will be a compilation of the thinking and writing you have already completed.

PRACTICE TURNAROUND PLAN

The symptoms of my current practice crisis include:

1.
2.
3.
4.
5.

The sources of the crisis as best as I can determine include:
1.
2.
3.
4.
5.

My model of practice and my vision for the next year, in a sentence, is: _____

The needed services that I offer are: _____

The strengths and selling points of my practice are: _____

Goal Chart

Start date	Financial goal or action	Intended benefit $$	Whose job?	Timeline to complete
	1.			
	2.			
	3.			
	4.			
	5.			
Start date	Marketing goal or action	Intended benefit $$	Whose job?	Timeline to complete
	1.			
	2.			
	3.			
	4.			
	5.			
Start date	Risk protection goal or action	Intended benefit $$	Whose job?	Timeline to complete
	1.			
	2.			
	3.			
	4.			
	5.			
Start date	Business operations goal or action	Intended benefit $$	Whose job?	Timeline to complete
	1.			
	2.			

Start date	Management upgrade goals or actions	Intended benefit $$	Whose job?	Timeline to complete
	3.			
	4.			
	5.			
	1.			
	2.			
	3.			
	4.			
	5.			

Start date	Additional goals or actions in any category	Intended benefit $$	Whose job?	Timeline to complete

My support system to help me accomplish this plan includes:

1.

2.

3.

4.

5.

My daily and weekly self-care includes these actions:

1.

2.

3.

4.

5.

TURNAROUND TIPS

This plan needs to be visible at all times. Keep it in a file you can readily access, or posted on a bulletin board, or on a series of index cards on your desk. Look at it each day. Work your plan. Here are some additional tips to help you implement it:

- Stay calm—any crisis gets better over time. Wait it out. Take the next step. One day at a time.
- Avoid excessive doomsayers, those who remind you how awful your situation is right now. Stay focused on what you can control.
- Remember the serenity prayer: "God grant me the serenity to accept the things I cannot change; courage to change the things I can; and wisdom to know the difference" (Niebuhr, 1934, p. 250).
- Even if you are scared, don't procrastinate. This is a time for action. Don't wait and worry. Improve those things you can.
- Commit to taking one daily action for your practice. What does your practice need you to do today? What will you give to your practice for its health and well-being? Be a good parent to your business.
- Don't be afraid to reinvent your practice. Remember to welcome change during a crisis. What can you simplify, improve, or enhance?
- Start to save, even before you think you can. Put some money in the bank.
- Double your efforts for existing clients. Make sure that they are satisfied with your services.
- Don't isolate. Connect with peers. Network. Affiliate. Small businesses still need to grow, even during a crisis.
- Keep a gratitude journal. What is going well each day? What opportunities can you spot (even if you are not ready to move forward)? Have a business affirmation (see Chapter 16) to use each day—a mantra that promotes your goals and keeps you focused on your task at hand.

Part IV: Reinvest

The only safe ship in a storm is leadership.

—*Faye Wattleton*

CHAPTER 13

Build a Practice to Sell

During an economic or personal crisis, you may need to consider selling your practice. Not every practice can or should be sold. A good time to try to sell a practice is when you have worked hard to develop a method, program, or reputation for specialized services that can be transferred to others, and you want your efforts to continue within the community. A bad time to sell is when you are desperate for cash. Trying to sell a practice quickly, under pressure, will not yield good results for the buyer or the seller. This is a process that takes time to achieve. Let me explain.

In order for your practice to be attractive to buyers, it needs these areas of preparation:

- Documentation
- Transferable assets
- Valuation
- Positioning for sale.

This process may seem daunting, so let me walk you through the nuts and bolts of selling your practice. Is it possible to sell a small therapy (or coaching or consulting) business when you are the primary asset? Yes, but you will need to start positioning it *today*.

First, you may wonder who would buy your practice? Why would someone want to buy your practice rather than starting a new one? For some buyers, a functioning, existing practice is an important shortcut. Sometimes buying an existing practice is more profitable than the cost, time, and energy of starting from scratch. Your buyer may be new to the area or new to the profession and wants to benefit from your groundwork. A buyer may find it hard to break into a specialized market; if you have built a strong reputation, the buyer benefits from your visibility. Buying your practice (and your business name and corresponding reputation) can be a reasonable way to become quickly competitive in a tough market. Or you may have developed an important method that a buyer wants to promote beyond your interest or energy.

DOCUMENTATION

The first, most important step you can take now to make your practice salable in the future is to document your income history. Keep good records, year by year, to document not only profit, but measures such as rate of new client calls or contacts; how long the average clients stays; what the average client yields in terms of income; all of your expenses; return on investment when possible (e.g., how many clients come via the Web site, offset against the expense of the Web site or any Web site advertising); and the mix of payments or fees that your practice earns.

If you have staff, keep records on their productivity and their expense. How many hours do you or other partners work? If you have purchased equipment or software to operate the business, how much did the equipment cost and what does it produce? If your bookkeeper can create charts or graphs to compare the documentation year by year, and if it shows growth or resilience, this is a strong selling point.

Also document your effectiveness with clients using measures (see the section in Chapter 10, "Developing Data and Measures") What are the average demographics of your clients (population, age, reasons for seeking your services)? Can you document the results clients achieve during the first 6 months? What are the results over longer periods of time? Do you have endorsements in writing from referrals or letters of appreciation from satisfied clients? If so, this is also a powerful selling point for a practice, especially if the methods are transferable. This type of documentation is only possible if you start long enough before sale to capture and code this information.

TRANSFERRABLE ASSETS

The biggest impediment for a buyer is how to replace you, if you are the primary asset of the practice. Even in a solo practice, you can create assets that are transferable. The more you quantify how you do what you do, and why, the more a buyer could replicate your success. Think about educating a potential buyer. What would the potential buyer need to know to get your results, both clinically and operationally? Start now by establishing your methods: in writing, by audiotape, or in video. Create as much product as possible. Write, research, and publish (or self-publish).

Here's a list of additional tangible assets that can add to the selling price of your business, and how to accomplish each one:

- *Brand name*: If you can name your type of services in a recognizable way as separate from your identity, you have a salable asset. You can more easily sell your methods than sell yourself. Look at your professional field for examples of this. You will find programs and methods that are trademarked. Read Tom Peters's classic article "The Brand Called You" (Peters, 1997). Go to the United States Post Office Trademark Office Web site (http://www.uspto.gov) for complete information on how to trademark a brand name. Brand names carry value, since they have a separate identity, apart from their developers.
- *Business identity*: Your successful advertising, Web site, brochures, business card, logo, yellow pages ads, newsletter, and so on can all be transferable assets for a buyer who is willing to continue the look of your practice.
- *Mailing list*: Build a large, opt-in direct-mail or e-mail list for your practice of clients and referral sources. A practice with a direct-mail list of 5,000 current names can significantly add to the value of a business. Use your advertising and speaking engagements to build your mailing list, not only to generate referrals. Keep a good database. Rent direct-mail lists from colleagues or other organizations who support your work. Get permission from those on your list to transfer their names to the new ownership; be ethically correct by transferring the names only of those who have given their permis-

sion. See Seth Godin's book, *Permission Marketing* (Godin, 1999), for an fuller explanation of the steps that help to achieve this goal.

- *Promotional materials*: Develop brand-name recognition via your promotional materials now, with brochures that highlight the method or the program name more than your name. Take the time and effort to create a good package of materials. Keep a portfolio of your winning advertisements, brochures, and marketing materials that have generated good results for your business, along with the details of those results. This is part of the package you can offer someone who wants to reproduce your success. One consultant has a wonderful packet of materials she takes to every marketing call. The packet is a custom-printed large folder and contains her business identity (business card and brochure) and a 10-minute CD of her giving a keynote talk, a white paper about her method, a reprint of an article about her from a major magazine, and a clear explanation of her process and her prices. The packet took several years to develop and refine. It is colorful, well organized, and embossed with her business name. She tells me that even when she is not feeling "on" for a marketing call, the packet "makes the pitch for me."

- *Ancillary products*: Develop a product line of materials to sell—programs, assessments, pamphlets, manuals, audio- or videotapes, training materials, books. If you have not promoted your product line sufficiently while owning the business, it doesn't lessen its potential value to another buyer. Get legal advice regarding licensing agreements for all written and recorded products. Keep thorough records and originals of all scripts, tapes, videos, and manuscripts. Make sure the packaging reflects your quality and matches your brand.

- *Business management*: If you have created a thriving business with easy-to-understand administrative systems in place, you have an additional asset. Find systems to put in place that are easy to explain and transfer to others. Document your systems in a written manual—staffing procedures, outside contractors, maintenance services, written agreements, marketing, networking, and the program development process you use. Present a potential buyer with a clear, complete business management program.

- *Goodwill*: If you have developed a reputation or strong community ties, this is an asset that can be transferred to the new owner with your help. Offer to make introductions within the community, or share referrals and resources to help the new owner assimilate into the community you have built around your practice. One therapist who was selling her practice had a distinctive way of working with addictions; the bulk of her clientele came from the 12-step community. When she decided to sell her practice, she carefully screened buyers so that she found a therapist she liked and respected. She defined the methods she used and prepared a manual for the potential buyer, developed a procedure for training the potential buyer, set aside 5 months to make a good transfer with the buyer (for example, she had the buyer sit in on a month's worth of sessions with every client), and in the end the majority of her clients stayed with the new owner.
- *Real estate*: If you have selected a prime location that helps to attract clients or is located near an important referral source (hospital, corporate headquarters, shopping district that invites walk-in traffic, etc.) and have a long-term lease, this may be an important asset to highlight. Likewise, the state of the facility and any equipment or furniture that are included in the sale of the office can be strong selling points.

VALUATION

Valuation is a business process that often involves a professional who assesses the assets and determines an asking price for your practice. But there is a distinction between value and price that is important to remember. Just as in any other sales situation, value is in the mind of the beholder. You might value your house at the top of the real estate market because it sits on a large lot and you value the space this offers, but a potential buyer might see the lot as a liability because of the expense of maintaining it. There will be a difference between value and actual sales price. Regardless of how you value your practice, the actual sale will be a negotiation.

One executive coach had a long career as a senior manager in an information technology firm. After retirement from that firm, he developed a coaching company consisting of one person, himself, to do as a coach/consultant what he had done as a manager: coach senior managers in the IT field in areas of business management and leadership. Even though his was a tiny firm, he conducted business and set up procedures to mirror those of a larger company. He developed a professional, glossy packet of printed materials for marketing that clearly outlined his services. He kept a file of endorsements of past and existing clients. He maintained an active mailing list for both direct and e-mail communication. He kept exacting written records of all outcomes and processes of each coaching contract, including financial transactions and billing.

The executive coach wrote two handbooks for a new owner, one describing his marketing approach and the other a "train-the-trainer" manual for delivering his programs and services. The marketing handbook succinctly explained how he made the first contact with a potential client, the formulas he used for pricing, three possible formats for proposals, written examples of signed client agreements, and all his business policies. The second one gave a new owner the ability to match his coaching results. He kept profit and loss records for each year he was in business. After 5 years in business, he could show a total revenue of $430,000, with the bulk of revenue coming from the last 2 years and with an average 20% profit for those years. He used a business valuation company to provide him with an estimate of selling price. Based on the systems in place, the transferable nature of his services, his careful documentation, solid client reputation, and the strong balance sheet, he was able to sell the practice for $185,000 (equal to his current gross annual earnings) with an agreement to take 6 months at a small salary to help hand off clients to the new buyer.

What would your practice sell for? Different practice brokers use different formulas, but one often-used formula for a medical practice is to price it at one to four times the annual net earnings. In my experience, I have seen therapy and coaching practices sell for less than this, at best one to two times earnings. This will vary based on your:

- business assets
- history of earnings
- level of debt
- cash flow
- market for similar businesses
- projected future earnings.

POSITIONING FOR SALE

How would you describe your practice to make it most attractive for sale? Similar to creating a listing for a real estate sale, you want to articulate these factors:

- summary about practice
- length practice has been established
- revenue for the past few years
- why you are selling (bankruptcy vs. owner retiring)
- if owner is willing to help train/assist new buyer
- if property is owned or leased
- unique selling factors about practice (competition, expansion potential, special niche)
- asking price.

Here is a sample listing similar to those you can find at various online business broker sites. Note the features that a broker would highlight to enhance the asking price:

Summary: This particular practice specializes in child and adolescent psychology as well as evaluating adults. The practicing doctor did psychological evaluations and therapy with parents and children and charged an average of $150 per hour. In the many years that this doctor did research, was a professor, and practiced psychology, he built an outstanding referral base. The current leased office houses all the needed equipment to continue on with the research and development. The owner is willing to contact all the referrals and make introductions, to help ensure that goodwill and prosperous business continues for the new owner. Centrally located, this practice has built an outstanding reputation and has come to be recognized locally, statewide, and beyond!

Property: Available for lease to new owner; centrally located.

Year established: 1985.

Support/training: Owner is willing to stay for a negotiable period of time to facilitate a smooth transition. Key employees will also remain.

Reason for selling: Owner is pursuing other interests.

Location: Doctor's office is centrally located, and has become well known and recognized at this location. Five years remain on lease.

Competition: Minimal.

Expansion: This business can be further expanded by continuing on the established reputation and continuing to build and maintain contacts.

Asking price: $250,000.

One caveat: Selling a practice can be emotional. This is your creation and you may find it difficult to negotiate with potential buyers. Hiring an intermediary, such as a broker, certified public accountant, professional valuator, or attorney can be important to keep the sale on track and to complete the needed documentation. Prior to any sale agreements there should be a signed confidentiality agreement with prospective buyers to ensure the seller's goodwill and business are protected. David Greene, president and founder of Medical Practice Brokers, Inc., said that one mistake that sellers make is waiting too long to sell. It may take 2 or 3 years to prepare the practice for sale in order to achieve your retirement goals. Then it might take another year or more to find a buyer. Plan ahead. Don't let income/profit decline in the years prior to sale.

CHAPTER 14

Fearless Change

In Chapter 1, I offered you a crisis-proofing mantra specific to change: "Don't resist, assist." Any crisis speeds the rate of change as it exposes vulnerable or unresolved professional and personal issues. In this chapter we explore how to respond to change brought on by a crisis. Because crisis-based change feels outside our control or volition, we often react with fear and anxiety. We didn't see this coming; we are not prepared; we don't want to change our familiar and preferred way of being in the world. But when change of some magnitude is upon us, we have only one of two choices: resist or assist. We feel better if we can assist ourselves and our practices to move forward and accept the reality of change. In this way, as a business owner poised to succeed, change becomes our new normal.

It's ironic that we change agents find it so difficult to change our own practices, but we know from research in the field of brain science that this resistance to change is universal for a reason. The human brain hates change. "The brain is always trying to automate things and to create habits, which it imbues with feelings of pleasure. Holding to the tried and true gives us a feeling of security, safety, and competence while at the same time reducing our fear of the future and of failure," explained brain researcher Gerhard Roth of the University of Bremen in Germany in his book whose title translates as *Personality, Decision, and Behavior* (Westerhoff, 2008). During a real or perceived crisis, our brains want to focus exclusively on potential threats. This is a time when we need to focus forward, be proactive, plan, and keep building our businesses, even while our survival instincts are often unyielding. In other words, we often need to work against our innate survival strategies to succeed in business.

FEAR IN PERSPECTIVE

It can help to remember what fear is and what it is not. Fear has a biological basis and is an emotion we share with most animals on this planet. Birds, mammals, and humans display a common fear behavior: paralysis or freezing in place, increased respiration and heart rate, release of stress hormones, and increased tendency to startle. Our human brain devotes a lot of space to fear because it helps us survive. We fear heights because it is dangerous to get too close to the edge of the cliff. The brain's fear circuitry (the amygdala) is so complex and necessary for survival that over the course of evolution, it has become more powerful than the brain's reasoning faculties. As a result, while at times you can use logic to overcome fear by thinking your way out ("I can stay safe and inch closer to the edge of the cliff to look down without falling"), many times the brain bypasses logic or reason and floods our system with fear hormones. Then we feel the fear intensely. Fear is "far, far more powerful than reason," said neurobiologist Michael Fanselow (Begley, 2007), of the University of California–Los Angeles. "It evolved as a mechanism to protect us from life-threatening situations, and from an evolutionary standpoint there's nothing more important than that."

To be a leader during a crisis, you must understand and respect your feelings of fear as part of the brain's attempt to keep you safe and whole. But fear is primarily a feeling and, at best, a reminder or warning system of potential danger. As Jay Uhler, organizational and clinical psychologist, explained, fear does not predict the future; it only tells you that you are afraid.

This is why the strategy of "feel the fear and do it anyway" is so powerful. When you can overcome the feeling by taking action and replacing the paralysis with an immediate experience of something other than danger, calm returns. "Slowly, when what we have feared does not come to pass, our logic turns back on," explained neuroscientist Joseph LeDoux of New York University. "The prefrontal cortex tells the amygdala to stand down" (Begley, 2007).

Review your crisis-proofing turnaround plan (Chapter 12) to help your prefrontal cortex get back in control as you appeal to reason and logic. Minimize fear-based triggers temporarily to support your focus. One client does this by limiting her exposure to TV, newspapers, and radio during those days when she is attending to her marketing plan. "I can't have my head filled with the stories of the deepening recession when I am trying to stay calm and make a cold call to set up a networking meeting."

We may also need to cope with the fear and anxiety in our professional organizations. Ecological, biological, and social systems are homeostatic and prefer the status quo. Sam, a management consultant, attended a professional meeting and mentioned the practice-building strategies he was considering for his small consulting agency, only to be loudly told by others, "Forget it. You are wasting your time. That won't work." He decided he would continue with his plans but not mention them to colleagues anymore.

I spoke at a conference of social workers in a northern state recently and asked how many relied on managed care. Ninety percent of the therapists in the room raised their hands and explained. "Lynn, our population is low income and it is not possible to have a fee-for-service practice in this area." One therapist stood up and said, "I disagree. I started my practice two years ago. I read Lynn's books and decided to follow her advice. Today, in only two years, I have a thriving, full-fee practice, even during this recession. I have a waiting list. I have a Web site that brings in good referrals. I diversified my services, have automated my systems, and am ready to hire an associate. Everyone I knew told me that I couldn't operate a practice unless I was willing to accept managed care. I am here to tell you it *is* possible." I meet people at my workshops throughout the country and hear this refrain over and over again—it *is* possible to build and maintain an ideal practice, one that is both profitable and purposeful, even during a personal or global crisis.

See the strategies in this chapter that can calm your brain so that you can pay attention to the big picture and possibility. Focus on the possible: Where are the gaps in the marketplace? What services do others need most? How could you help more people? What is the value of the help you have to offer? What has worked for others? How might you adapt these strategies for your practice? What will you need to do differently to proceed? If you are consumed by fear and anxiety, you will not be able to see the answers to these and many other questions. Let's bring your prefrontal cortex into the discussion as we explore more about the nature of making change during difficult times.

DEGREES OF CHANGE

Change is not one vague totality; change has structure and stages. Let's imagine that even though you are scared about viability, you want to make your practice less dependent on a financial contract that limits profitability (managed care, employee assistance programs [EAPs], other discounted-fee arrangements). To let go of a safe but limiting financial contract might be unwise during a crisis, but in order to evaluate it properly, you need to be rational, especially about how change operates. Do you even know how you usually make a change and why you prefer one style of change over another? Marilyn Ferguson (1980), behavioral scientist, classified change into four types.

1. *Change by exception*: If this is your pattern of change, you are a person with set beliefs. On occasion, you will allow an exception to your belief, but even with this exception, you do not change your set belief. To make a change, you have to allow for a onetime exception to the rule.

2. *Incremental change*: If this type of change is your pattern, you change, but only gradually and unconsciously. You change slowly over time, until it seems to you that you have always been this way.

3. *Pendulum change*: If this is your pattern, you swing wildly and completely from one belief to its opposite. The new belief is zealously held, with no middle ground.

4. *Paradigm change*: This pattern of change allows you to think outside the box. Discordant information is considered and integrated and new ways of thinking emerge. As Ferguson pointed out, it is only paradigm change that promotes transformation, and for transformation.

YOUR STYLE OF CHANGE IN A CRISIS

During a time of crisis, a paradigm change is the best strategy. It is fast and complete, and it can help take your practice in a new direction. Recall the story of the addict and the pothole in Chapter 6, where the paradigm shift in recovery occurs when the addict decides to walk down a different street. Can you help your practice (or yourself) walk down a different street? Here is how one therapist made the shift.

Rachel, a psychologist in practice for 15 years in an economically hard-hit state, has watched her practice fall from 25 to fewer than 8 sessions booked each week. She is desperate to rebuild, but her only ideas about finding new clients are halfway measures. She will take a bigger ad in the yellow pages a year from now and, until then, attend a few association meetings to chat with colleagues and hopefully get some new referral sources. When I tell Rachel that desperate times call for desperate measures and that she will need to do more, she resists, saying, "But I have never had to market or advertise much or network before. My clients came from word of mouth. I am not used to doing anything differently. None of my colleagues do any marketing and I don't see why I should need to, either."

I hold firm to my coaching request. I ask her for a quick list of the biggest, boldest actions she could take to fill her practice within the next month. I promise she will have the ultimate control over which, if any, of these strategies she will actually adopt. I just want her thinking right now.

Rachel comes to the next session with a list that includes many good ideas: creating a Web site, linking it to several other association sites, networking with family law attorneys in her city (she specializes in working with parenting issues), calling several organizations—hospitals, agencies, nonprofits—to see if she can affiliate or contract services to them. I then ask her to create a plan, again with the caveat that I just want her thinking; she has ultimate control over whether she will take action on the plan.

She creates a plan that involves meeting with attorneys and querying nonprofit agencies, by first making cold calls. She tells me that she is proud of her plan and thinks it would work, but then with a frown she tells me that my coaching is not done. "I only agreed to these steps because you said I have ultimate control. I agree this might work, but I am not going to be able to do this. I hate cold calls. It's not me. I just can't."

Time for a paradigm change. To Rachel's surprise, I concur. "You are right. You would make a mess of your plan if you were to take it on. Thank goodness you said no," I agree.

Rachel laughs with immediate relief. "So what was the point?"

The point, I tell her, is that as the owner of her small business, she must come up with plans. "What is the average client worth to you?" I push on. We do some calculating and Rachel tells me that the average client stays with her for 5 months, sees her weekly, and, with expenses figured in, yields her practice $1,600 per month.

"For example, with each new client bringing in sixteen hundred dollars per month, you could add a line item to your budget for cold calling and hire someone very part-time, say an intern or an office assistant, to make the cold calls. She could phone the attorneys, agencies, and other organizations to introduce your practice briefly and set an appointment for a meeting. She can even go with you to assist your presentation if you don't want to go alone." Rachel is silent and we end the session, scheduling the next time we will talk.

One month later, Rachel tells me she has implemented her marketing plan. "Did you hire an intern?" I ask.

"No, I am doing it myself." Rachel laughs. "After you talked to me as the boss and gave me permission to find some staff, it really changed my outlook. I got that this was a business and it was serious. I had to commit to growing the practice."

"So why didn't you hire it out?" I wonder.

"One of my core values kicked in. I am cheap. I hate to spend money. I decided I would try it myself and if I couldn't do it well, then I would bite the bullet and hire it out. But I did find some help. I reworked the plan a bit. I asked a more experienced colleague to partner with me on developing proposals for business with outside organizations. Together we make calls, with us both in the same room, rotating whose turn it is to call. We debrief after each call so that we get better at our scripts. Some interesting opportunities have emerged. We have a new contract with an outside company to do some training in their offices about working with difficult employees. Things are turning around on many levels."

I could hear the paradigm change in Rachel's voice, as she shifted from therapist to boss. She was learning to take charge of the future direction of her practice.

EXERCISE: WELCOMING CHANGE

Fill out the following questions to determine how to proceed with modifying or transforming your practice.

- *Change by exception*: What are you willing to try once, as an experiment, to see if it will help your practice? How can you practice be the exception instead of the rule?
- *Incremental change*: What small steps will you make over time to improve your practice operations or profitability? What can you do in a routine way so that it becomes the new normal?
- *Pendulum change*: What action will you take in direct opposition to something you are currently doing? How can you embrace even a very contradictory strategy in the spirit of experimentation?
- *Paradigm change*: What can you do to radically shift direction in your practice? Look at your situation in a macro (big picture) or

micro (detail-oriented) way to help you shift your framework. What one attitude can you turn inside out to move forward right now in a bold, new way?

GOING BEYOND YOUR COMFORT ZONE

One of the mantras in Chapter 1 was the idea of "stretch instead of stress." As you stretch your business abilities, you stay within your general comfort zone but push the edges a bit to give you more range of motion. Elaine Aron, author of *The Highly Sensitive Person* (Aron, 1999), suggested a method of regulation between overstimulation and underperforming as people find the edges of their comfort zone. Too little stretch is a way to indulge a need for safety at the expense of recognizing a need to keep growing and experiencing in the world. Too much stress and we become overwhelmed and too far outside our comfort zone. For extroverts, sales and marketing activities are easily achieved. For introverts, the thought of attending a networking meeting will cause sleepless nights.

If you are too passive, no new clients or opportunities may emerge. Head toward the outer edges of your comfort zone to stretch into new behaviors. If you are overwhelmed with too much novelty and too many projects, shift back in the other direction. Finding the balance between stress and stretch, comfort and novelty, or passivity and activation is key to sustaining an entrepreneurial approach.

Wendy Allen, psychotherapist and coach, my coauthor of an earlier book, and, most pleasingly, my sister, lives in Santa Barbara, California. Santa Barbara is a highly competitive town for therapists; there are several graduate programs for therapists there that result in a "therapist on every corner" density. Wendy has had to learn to stretch a lot, far outside her comfort zone, to keep her practice active in this environment, especially during the current recession. "I realized that despite my fantasies of retirement on a tropical island, I prefer working to not working. So I am trying many strategies to make sure I stay busy," she told me one afternoon. "I accept new clients regularly and don't turn down work. I keep my fees flexible. I offer new services."

I asked what specifically was outside her comfort zone. "The most optimistic thing I am doing is making a big investment in getting new skills. I have been in practice for over 20 years, but decided to learn a new, expensive method of marital therapy. It's a risk, but I am betting on the fact that there will be many couples who will want to see me and pay my fee as long as I produce results. I intend to use this training to brand myself with the trainer's web site and to be on their referral list."

She continued with another strategy. "Another new direction for my formerly fiercely profit-oriented, independent practice? Pro-bono service. I contacted the Vet Center to see couples as a volunteer. I need to work with a lot of couples to practice my new skills and believe that offering service to those in great need is going to be a big part of my business plan for several years to come. Finally, I am talking to everyone—my Pilates teacher, my friends, professionals, colleagues, and have come clean and told them directly that my practice has taken a hit and I am wide-open for referrals. My stretching outside my comfort zone is broadening my sense of community and enhancing my connections."

ANTICIPATING BUSINESS DEVELOPMENT

One way to stay calm is to know what is going to happen next. Is it possible to anticipate change in your practice? Businesses and organizations, large and small, change continually and in predictable ways. Your practice is part of this evolutionary spiral, even if you are blind to its patterns. As we busily focus on the daily tasks that are necessary to help our practices succeed, we miss the pattern of change that develops in similar ways for all businesses. For example, certain themes consistently emerge at different stages of small business development—a focus on survival, dealing with competition, a shift toward stability, the drive to expand, a longing to affiliate, and on and on. These themes tend to occur across the board in all businesses in a regular sequence, stage after stage, and follow a similar progression. As such, they are the evolutionary markers of a business. Although the markers are not strictly linear and don't arise in identical ways, if you are familiar with them and know where to look, it's possible to see the developmental path of any business.

When you learn to spot which stage is currently occurring, and understand the ramifications of the particular stage, you will know what tasks you, the business owner, need to attend to in order to master the challenges of that stage. You can even predict what to watch for next and how to lubricate instead of obstruct your inevitable business evolution. Business becomes less mysterious and much easier.

I find that many clients welcome having a developmental perspective on business because the actual experience of transitioning through a developmental phase is often not a conscious or especially desired event. Like most change, it just happens and it can be scary and unsettling. As a business coach who understands the stages of business, I can listen beyond my clients' presenting complaints and concerns to hear the subtle, underlying expressions that signal these developmental markers. Phrases that clients use when describing the state of their business or issues that they mention let me know where they are in their evolutionary path and whether a shift is about to transpire or is getting blocked. When I am able to explain these signals to clients, they can gain a new perspective on the situation. I can alert clients to the stage they are approaching, help them identify the challenges of that stage, and emphasize the tasks and objectives they will need to accomplish in order to do well at that stage.

Business evolves by moving through spirals of lower-order action to newer, higher-order ways of being—early survival phases; midlife stages where matters of organization, achievement, and affiliation dominate; and mature phases where the matters of integrating core values, defining legacy, and reinvention take over. I rely on the evolutionary approach of Don Beck and Chris Cowan, whose book, *Spiral Dynamics* (Beck & Cowan, 1996), defines the current thinking about the hidden codes that shape human nature and drive organizational change. Their work is an extension of the biopsychosocial systems concept of Clare Graves, an early student of Maslow. Graves, professor emeritus at Union College, proposed an eight-stage, value-based system of evolution that he applied to human beings, societies, business, and government. Beck and Cowan refined his work, giving each stage a color, clarifying the principles of the model, and then testing it worldwide—most notably to help Nelson Mandela take South Africa out of apartheid.

To make this model more applicable to the small business owners I coach, I narrowed and applied the model to the specific objectives and tasks that small business owners need to accomplish to successfully transition from stage to stage, filling in with the many strategies and exercises I have developed over time. You can see my full adaptation in my earlier book, *12 Months to Your Ideal Private Practice* (Grodzki, 2003). Here is the model in a brief form, to help you anticipate the way your practice may be responding to events and changes right now.

SPIRAL DYNAMICS

Beck and Cowan assigned eight colors to represent the eight progressive stages of human development: Beige, Purple, Red, Blue, Orange, Green, Yellow, and Turquoise. Every stage is important to examine, because you need to go through and master the values of each stage in order to evolve to the next. Ken Wilber (2001), who further defines Spiral Dynamics in his book, *A Theory of Everything,* calls this progression the need to "transcend and include." The first level of Spiral Dynamics, called Beige, represents the Stone Age human society, when our ancestors relied on base instincts to exist. As Beige human societies band together, they grow and evolve to the animistic Purple stage, which is marked by ethnic bonding, a reliance on ritual, magical thinking, and adherence to myths to counter the realities of a harsh environment. Red, the stage of power, tribalism, and emergence of a separate sense of self, evolves next; territorialism becomes primary. The rigors of these early stages lead toward Blue, the stage that places a high value on order, control, protection, and stability. Over time, the lack of personal freedom inherent in Blue leads a society to shift to Orange, a stage of independence, free-market capitalism, and entrepreneurial energy. The intense materialism of Orange creates the evolutionary shift to Green, where sharing, mutuality, and environmental sensitivity are valued. Next comes Yellow, a stage that intentionally provokes chaos, invites newness, and values flexibility and synchronicity. Ken Wilber said that a shift to Yellow represents "second tier" thinking, whereby one can grasp the entire spectrum of development and see that each level is crucially important for the health of the overall spiral. Turquoise, the final conceptual stage, values harmony and holistic principles. In Turquoise, a business could see all the many levels of interaction possible and utilize the state of "flow" for the best, easiest performance from individuals. (See Table 14.1.)

Table 14.1. Spiral Dynamics.

Color	Thinking	Value Systems—Bottom Lines
Beige	Automatic	Basic survival
Purple	Animistic	Myths, traditions, and rituals
Red	Egocentric	Power, glory, and exploitation
Blue	Absolutist	Authority and stability
Orange	Materialistic	Success and material gain
Green	Humanistic	Equality and humanism
Yellow	Systemic	Choice and change
Turquoise	Holistic	Harmony and holism

ADAPTING THE MODEL FOR PRIVATE PRACTICE

As fascinating as this evolutionary model is, I found it needed some adaptation for use in small businesses. Small businesses often develop through all the stages of the model and because business evolution is rarely linear, your practice may go through stages repeatedly. For example, some senior therapists in today's recession find themselves back at Beige (survival), with a sense that they are starting over. But if they mastered the values and objectives of this stage once, rebuilding from this stage the second (or third) time is not nearly so difficult. They have the feeling of "been there, done that" and know the steps it takes to rebuild.

My adapted model shows those in private practice how to accomplish four goals:

- Understand the signals that alert you to the stage you are in or approaching.
- Address the challenges of each stage.
- Highlight the values and most positive aspects inherent in each stage.
- Identify the tasks and objectives that help you evolve to the next stage.

To find your evolutionary stage, use Table 14.2 to determine your bottom line and see your objective. Then look to the next stage to see what to anticipate.

Table 14.2. Spiral Dynamics, Revised.

Color	Bottom line	Objective
Beige	Survival—it's a jungle out there	Counter instinct to go beyond survival by having a clear, written plan
Purple	Surviving but clueless as to why	Remove the mystery from business by getting informed
Red	Territorial and worried about competition and visibility	Claim power and deal with competition by defining your practice, not defending it
Blue	Wanting security and ease of operations	Optimize systems to promote stability; use best business practices and good practice management

Orange	Entrepreneurial and ambitious	Pursue opportunity and achievement, become highly profitable, spot and sort new opportunities
Green	Reclaiming humanistic values	Temper entrepreneurial zeal with humanism
Yellow	Bored, want to increase choices and invite newness	Break out of existing practice and reinvent self
Turquoise	Holistic; everything works	Keep the ideal practice sustained over time

EXERCISE: THE DYNAMIC PRACTICE

Use Table 14.2 to help answer these questions and determine the stage of your practice or anticipate what is to come.

1. What is the bottom line of your practice today?
2. How does this bottom line affect you as the business owner?
3. What objective do you need to attend to or take steps to achieve in order to master the challenges of this stage?
4. What will signal you that you have met this goal?
5. What can you anticipate from the next stage?
6. How do you want to prepare your practice and yourself for this inevitable shift?

CONTROL DURING TIMES OF CRISIS

Sometimes the worst part of a crisis is feeling helpless against the forces of uncontrollable change. Here are two strategies from my earlier book with coauthor Wendy Allen, *The Business and Practice of Coaching* (2005), that can help you stay calm in the midst of a crisis. They are based on the advice of a friend of mine who sails frequently and has developed simple steps to stay in control and captain her small boat.

1. *Become seaworthy*: When sailing in rough waters, my friend the sailor checks that gear is simple and uncluttered onboard. When you hit rough water, it's best to have less to attend to. Getting uncluttered mentally and physically in the face of business turmoil makes good common sense. Especially when you are under business stress, make space daily for mental downtime. Clear your brain. Relax with a hot bath. Take a walk. Schedule time for physical uncluttering, even in face of deadlines. Get as organized and efficient as possible, to help you feel some internal degree of control. Review your files; clear out old e-mail; do your errands; make sure your office and workspace are uncluttered; clear your mind with meditation or long walks each day. Then you can attend to the important goals of each week and not be concerned with the additional clutter or disorganization of mind, body, and space that can be so distracting.

2. *Heave to*: When my friend is sailing in very rough waters and the ride is getting uncomfortably bumpy, sometimes she sets the sailboat to a "heave to" position. This slows her boat down considerably but keeps it moving forward. In this way, she holds a set course but allows for some natural drift to occur. The drift creates some turbulence on the water, and that disturbance counters the aggressiveness of the waves. The pounding felt when going upwind in strong seas almost miraculously disappears.

I love this idea for those in small business. When you are in rough seas in business (or life), you heave to by slowing down, focusing tightly on your goals, and then prepare for and tolerate some drift. You will go off course and it may feel like you are wandering about, but as long as this drift is expected and you are still focused on your goals, you will be safely moving forward. Tracking this process is going to be key to knowing when you are moving forward, versus when you are dangerously off course.

Beth, an organizational trainer with several demanding clients, faced a personal crisis when her husband developed stage 4 cancer, stopped working, and began treatment. Beth's schedule suddenly filled with doctor's appointments and much worry and concern as her husband's condition progressed. Each scan he had scheduled caused her to feel terribly anxious. She and her husband would stay up half the night, worried about the results. Beth's energy level took a downturn and she canceled important client meetings. Her work was lackluster. Even though her clients understood, she was in danger of losing business. As the breadwinner of the family now that her husband was not working, she had to stay on course. She complained of feeling overwhelmed and out of control of the situation. "I can't control my husband's illness. When he is ill after chemo or up at night pacing, I have to attend to him."

I listened to the enormous challenge and stress she was under, then asked Beth to write a short summary statement that would help her set course in this storm and give her more control, to the degree possible. Her statement said: "My priorities are keeping both my husband and my business intact. Both will get my equal attention. During business hours, I will focus and be as productive as possible." She then listed weekly goals in line with her summary statement.

I also asked her to note the ways she drifted off course each week, as well as what progress she made toward completing her weekly goals. I reminded her that "small steps count" when she would get frustrated about the slowness of her accomplishments. Week after week, I checked the integrity with which she held her statement as truth, brainstormed with her about her immediate goals, listened and commiserated about the inevitable drift, and validated her slow but steady progress. We tracked her progress carefully. She did not gain clients, but she did not lose any. She met her deadlines but did not exceed them. Her husband got to his appointments, but sometimes other family members took him. Because progress was slow and drift and distraction were unavoidable, without tracking her progress this closely she would have been discouraged and would have felt like giving up. With careful tracking, she could see where she was at any given time, and with support she could begin to feel in charge of her life, despite those things that she could not control.

EXERCISE: DEVELOPING CONTROL

Fill in the following sentence stems to help develop more control during a crisis.

- To become more mentally seaworthy and clear my mind, I will take the following actions each day: _____.
- To become more physically seaworthy and clear my space, I will take the following steps: _____.
- To set course and hold my position despite rough waters, my statement of direction is: _____.
- My tracking mechanism to make sure I am on course will be: _____.

CHAPTER 15

Learned Resilience

Do you collapse or bounce back from hardship? Do you look forward or backward during times of adversity? Resilience means that in the face of crisis, you respond, not just react. You fail fast and correct fast. "Eyes on the prize," one of my clients repeats to herself during the day, to remind herself to stay focused on her goals despite the multiple stressors she faces in her business. A resilient mind-set is elegantly described in this nine-word poem by Masahide, a Japanese poet who lived two centuries ago (from Lucien Styrk's [1995] translation of Zen poetry).

> *Barn's burnt down—*
> *now*
> *I can see the moon.*

Just as with learned optimism, a resilient mind-set can be taught. I have watched hundreds of small business owners go from feeling overwhelmed, exhausted, or fearful—due to a myriad of business and personal challenges—to developing resilience and gumption. Start by noticing how you think about your business. Are you a worrier—dwelling on worst-case scenarios, feeling down about your lack of success, rejecting possible ideas because you assume they won't work? Are you a planner—making mental lists of what to do next, staying focused and motivated? Are you overly optimistic—seeing many opportunities, not able to prioritize, needing direction? Are you a procrastinator—coming up with good ideas but never feeling ready to start?

Negative beliefs and critical self-talk cause enterprenuers to collapse. Constructive, optimistic, yet pragmatic thinking helps them stay in the game, taking the next steps. Successful entrepreneurs stay resilient by adopting the following six qualities into their thinking:

1. *Given a set of challenges, they see opportunities*: Successful small business owners face continual challenges and problems. To stay resilient and upbeat, you need to see the opportunities inside each challenge, the silver lining. If staff leaves, a client terminates, a contract is not awarded, a therapist with your same skills moves in down the hall from your office, do you retreat or advance? What opportunities do you see? When staff leaves, you can hire better staff or automate with upgraded systems. If a client terminates, it is a reminder that you need to keep marketing, a given for every small business owner. Lost or unrenewed contracts push you to broaden and diversify. As a change agent, you probably use this skill of seeing opportunities within challenges for your clients to help them stay hopeful. Adopt this same mind-set for yourself as a business owner.

2. *Given a problem, they are both optimistic and pragmatic*: Successful entrepreneurs are hopeful but realistic. Can you walk with your head in the clouds seeing what's possible while keeping your feet on the ground noting what's probable? You need to balance expectations with pragmatism. Which side of the seesaw needs more weight? Do you need more practicality in your business thinking or more optimism? The best entrepreneurial equilibrium helps you see both sides of every challenge or opportunity—the risk and the reward—at the same time.

3. *They expect a lot from themselves and others. They want a lot for themselves and others*: Expecting a lot from others—those who work with you, be they staff or clients—means having clearer boundaries around your requests with clients or staff. Express your needs and wants more cleanly and directly. Expect those around you to come from the best in themselves, and hold yourself to this expectation as well. Wanting for others means that you can hold a big vision and goals for those around you. When one of my clients sets a goal, I will support the achievement of the goal by staying interested, by brainstorming, and by celebrating

when it is met, but I don't demean the client by reminding or nagging about the goal. I may hold a strong vision of success for my clients, even when they can't see how things will ever work out. I am amazed at how just holding this vision, week after week, month after month, even in the face of setbacks and challenges, can result in my clients being brave and persistent, taking difficult steps, and accomplishing great things for themselves. "I see that it's possible for you to fill your practice with the types of clients you want to work with and charge a fair fee, if you are willing to take your practice seriously." Or "I see that it's possible for you to make six figures and still have a balanced life. I'd be happy to support you to see you reach that goal."

4. *Persistence is their middle name*: This skill is necessary in business: Successful entrepreneurs have the ability to stay with a goal for a long time. Persistence is critical because business results take time to achieve. I can be relentless when I have a goal in mind and feel (and act) like a dog with a bone. I simply can't let go of a project, idea, action, or desire. I try to temper this with patience and compassion for myself and others, but I still hold on. I will adjust my behavior (if the goal doesn't work) and just try again. And again. I accept my failure as feedback and tweak my approach with curiosity each time until I get it right.

5. *They enjoy making a profit*: The definition of a business is an entity that makes a profit. This quality means that you enjoy business for business's sake. As you become more mature in your approach to money and reconcile profit and service, making money can feel congruent with providing good service. (See Chapter 7 for more about reconciliation.)

6. *They operate from a state of abundance*: Abundance means that there is enough—enough clients, opportunities, time, energy, money, ideas, and so on, for you to have what you need in your business. When you believe there is enough out there, you don't mind being persistent in your actions to get your share. When you believe there is enough, you can think strategically—the question isn't *if* but *when* and *how*. This belief makes business more fun. It's the difference between

standing on the beach watching others swim and getting your feet wet and jumping the waves. You only feel the abundance when you find the courage and will to get into the swim of things.

EXERCISE: MY ENTREPRENEURIAL QUALITIES

Look at the above list of six qualities and reflect on which are natural for you and which are not. Answer the following questions.

1. Which of these six qualities do you currently possess?
2. How specifically do you demonstrate these qualities in your life and your business?
3. Which of these six qualities do you need to develop?
4. What are the consequences for you, in your life or your business, of not having these qualities yet developed?
5. Who or what can support you in developing the qualities you need?

OPPORTUNITY SPOTTING

I have talked a lot about opportunity being the silver lining in a crisis. But how do you spot the opportunities that may exist? The first step is to train yourself to see them. My coaching clients fill out the following prep form prior to every coaching session as a way to claim their progress, set their goals, and learn to spot opportunities.

Weekly Prep Form
1. What have I accomplished since last month that I feel positive about? What are my wins?
2. What challenges am I facing this month?
3. What existing opportunities are available right now?
4. What blocks me from taking advantage of these opportunities?
5. How could I make life or work easier or better for myself right now?

Question 3 asks you to spot existing opportunities, which can occur in many forms. Here is a brief checklist to spur your ability to notice opportunity.

EXERCISE: EXISTING OPPORTUNITIES CHECKLIST

Check the existing opportunities you see for yourself, and circle those that you are not ready to move toward now, but will consider in the future.

- ❑ Areas of the market that are unserved or underserved
- ❑ Finding novel ways to reach out to people in need of services
- ❑ Identifying carve-outs (unmet areas of service that are not covered by existing contracts)
- ❑ Leveraging or sharing networking, presenting, or delivering services
- ❑ Sharing the cost, time, or energy involved with an existing project
- ❑ Finding services within potential professional trends (review Chapter 4).
- ❑ Partnering with others in new ways
- ❑ Brainstorming with colleagues about practice development
- ❑ Joining more business associations
- ❑ Introducing myself and my practice to new referral sources
- ❑ Networking with those I don't yet know
- ❑ Thinking bigger and bolder
- ❑ Redoing my brochure, Web site, social marketing profile, or other listing
- ❑ Reorganizing my office; going through old files and business cards to open up ideas of what to do next
- ❑ Meeting a dozen more colleagues, in and out of my profession, within my local area
- ❑ Recontacting old referral sources to reconnect
- ❑ Modeling a successful strategy of someone else and following through to make it my own
- ❑ Trying something brand-new in my business to experiment

❑ Taking a bold risk that resonates with my vision
❑ Doing something that no one else I know has tried
❑ Doing something that everyone else I know has tried
❑ Taking a class or a workshop that stretches my skills and getting each person's business card
❑ Expanding my Rolodex to meet 50 professionals in my community that I can refer to
❑ Completing everything on my to-do list within 1 week
❑ Saying yes to things I would normally reject
❑ Doubling my goals in my prep form for the month and accomplishing them all
❑ Doubling the amount of people I know, personally and professionally, each year
❑ Creating a project, budgeting for the project, and carrying it out to completion quickly

FILTERING OPPORTUNITIES

As you begin to tap into the abundant flow of possible opportunities, you may feel overwhelmed and in need of direction. This is a hallmark of an entrepreneur—the feeling that there is *too* much opportunity at your doorstep. In a crisis, you may feel: "There is so much I would like to do. It all has potential. What do I tackle first?" Entrepreneurial types are known for having too many irons in the fire, saying yes more than they say no, needing to sort and prioritize on a regular basis. Even if you are not yet highly entrepreneurial, you still need a way to evaluate opportunities you spot. To select the best opportunities for yourself, develop a filter. A filter is a screen of questions you look through, similar to a photographer's lens, to bring certain objects into sharp focus and blur the rest.

George is both a massage therapist and an acupuncturist who loves to diversify by learning new healing methods. His wife complains that he signs up for too many courses and plans endless projects, leaving little time for the family. George feels pressure to stay diversified and to offer a full range of services to keep his business viable during a recession. He asked me to help him prioritize. It was time for a filter. Prior to committing to any new class, project, or work-related opportunity, George first asks himself three filtering questions:

1. Does this opportunity fit into my vision of my existing practice?
2. Will it bring in money immediately?
3. Can I do this without interfering with my family time?

Unless he can answer yes to all questions, he does not move forward on the project. The path to a well-lived life is not always defined by what we add into to our already busy lives; sometimes a great life is achieved by what we let go of.

EXERCISE: FILTERING OPPORTUNITIES

Select up to three the following set of questions to create a filter for evaluating new opportunities.

1. Is it profitable? If so, what is the timeline for profitability?
2. Do the immediate rewards outweigh the risks?
3. Will this take me closer to or further from my business vision or plan?
4. Will this significantly improve my skills in a way that builds my business?
5. Will this be fun, an adventure, uplifting, good for my soul?
6. Will this help me create more community in my life or isolate me?
7. What other paths could this lead to?
8. What does my head say about this? What is my gut feeling?
9. What will I lose if I say no? What will this cost me if I say yes?
10. What must I let go of or delegate in order to take this on?

RESILIENCE AND SUPPORT

James Thomas Neill is a researcher from Perth, Western Australia ("the most isolated city in the world") working on outdoor education (see his Web site at http://wilderdom.com). He created a simple formula to foster resilience while he worked as an instructor of Outward Bound Australia:

$$Growth = Challenge + Support$$

What is your personal formula to help you to stay resilient? Don't overlook the importance of support. During times of great stress, you can enhance your body and mind resilience with an increased level of support. Support means different things to different people. For you, support may be internal (that which you provide yourself, such as how you manage your time or reregulate your mood and emotions) or external (time spent with others that includes coaching, mentoring, and collegial or peer relationships).

Let's start with internal support. What helps you to stay energized as a business owner? The fastest way to fail is to exhaust yourself. Basic self-care such as getting enough sleep is key. For most entrepreneurs, time is always in short supply. Time may be more valuable to you than money. How do you manage it? One way is to rely on a calendar to devote concentrated blocks of time to each activity instead of doing things piecemeal. Surveys suggest that you need 1 administrative hour for every 5 client hours. For many therapists, the ratio is even higher. Instead of trying to fit in 5 minutes here or there, schedule your administrative time consistently. With so many demands on your time, you can't be cavalier or casual about your scheduling and expect to feel in control. My calendar is carefully scheduled with time each week that include seeing clients, writing, exercising, spending time with friends and family, and blocks of downtime for relaxation and reading.

A system taught to me years ago by coach and entrepreneur Jeff Raim helped me think about time management in blocks. His calendar had three types of time blocked out each day: "work," "buffer," and "spirit."

Work means activity that brings you both joy and money.

Spirit means time that replenishes your soul and increases your energy.

Buffer is a catchall phrase meaning everything else.

When Jeff showed me this system, I blocked out my calendar and realized that my days were mostly work and buffer time; no spirit blocks showed up. This has changed and my time feels better managed and I am much more energized. Here is how this process worked for another small business owner.

Mary, a busy owner of a group practice, complained about exhaustion. Her mother had recently become ill, and she said she was torn between the office and the hospital. I suggested that she look at her calendar in terms of work, spirit, and buffer time. Using these categories, she had nothing but buffer. Her work did not bring her joy, she said, so she counted the time spent at the office as buffer. This became part of our coaching goal; to help her find more satisfaction in her work. But a larger problem, as I saw it, was that she had no activities scheduled on a regular basis that would fit the "spirit" definition. This was a formula for burnout and overwhelm; when so much energy and effort goes out, and so little joy or nourishment comes back, the business owner can break down.

I gave Mary some tough love coaching. "Mary, you are the primary asset of your practice. So much rests on your shoulders. As much as you need to do to keep the practice running and take care of your mother, this can't last. Your homework is to put an hour a day of spirit time into your calendar. It must be put in at the same time each day. It is sacrosanct and nothing can interfere."

Mary hated this assignment and we negotiated and talked about it for weeks. But I was clear that without spirit time, she would not achieve any of her other coaching goals. She finally found a way to carve out an hour a day—from 4:30 A.M. to 5:30 A.M. each morning! She got up and, in the quiet of the morning, had a cup of tea, turned on soothing meditative music, and did some yoga poses. This spirit time became her lifeline during the coming months as her mother got more ill and her practice took a dip from the economy. "My spirit time is essential to my well-being," she told me one day. "It's mine. All the rest of my time is spent giving to others, my staff, my clients, my mother. But that hour in the morning, that is when I give to myself."

Find a system that helps you manage your time. Schedule blocks of concentrated time in your calendar. See if you can use the categories of work, buffer, and spirit. If those are not right for you, create your own. Notice the degree of internal support you feel when you are taking care of yourself in this way.

You can combine purposes when it comes to time. During your spirit time, you can learn to tap into your inner wisdom for business purposes. Learn to use your intuition to help you feel relaxed and calmer about your practice development.

INNER WISDOM

As a change agent, you may be using your intuition in your life and in your practice, but do you use it as a business owner? Many successful entrepreneurs credit their intuition, their gut-level sensations of "just knowing" when taking steps to build their business. Tapping into your intuition can become an important sense of business support for daily decisions as well as long-term planning. I rely on this inner wisdom to help me stay calm in the midst of business challenges and as a way to analyze options, by seeing what my intuition has to say about an opportunity. I rarely act based on intuition alone; instead, I take the information, insights, and impressions that come from checking in intuitively and I add them to other more rational business strategies. Using *all* these tools, the external data and analysis I have already compiled, as well as my inner knowing, lets me make fully informed decisions.

Listening to your body or deeper self for business purposes can add to your sense of internal support: It's as though you have an "inner business coach" who helps to soothe anxieties by adding one more aspect of insight. William Duggan, author of *Strategic Intuition* (Duggan, 2007), formulates that there are three types of intuition useful in business:

1. Ordinary intuition is what most mean when speaking about intuition. Duggan says it is intuitive feeling rather than intuitive thinking

and it appears through body senses as unconscious, vague, or gut hunches. Ordinary intuition has been well defined by researcher Daniel Cappon (1993). Cappon defines ordinary intuition as a natural, normal skill that helped us survive as early humans and was relegated, as were so many of our basic human survival functions, to our unconscious mind during our evolution as a species. He details 20 qualities of intuition, the Cappon intuitive characteristics (CIC), to test and develop intuitive capacity. Using a few of the CIC, you can evaluate a business situation by asking:

"What am I not seeing about this problem?" (CIC: negative perceptual discrimination)

"How does this detail fit into the big picture?" (CIC: synthesis)

"What do I need to be open to or watch out for? Is there anything else I should consider?" (CIC: foresight)

"What will I learn from this experience if I take this action? What will I learn if I don't?" (CIC: seeing the meaning of things)

2. *Expert intuition* is a flash of insight, a way to connect what you know on unconscious levels within a familiar situation. Duggan (2007) explained that whereas ordinary intuition usually occurs with a somatic (body-based) gut-level, sensory, or emotional signal, expert intuition is primarily cognitive. The best examples are defined in the book *Blink* by Malcolm Gladwell (2007). Galdwell gives multiple case examples showing how professionals intuitively know what they know.

I use expert intuition when I am trying to evaluate a familiar business pattern. For example, I teach coaching classes by phone each spring and fall. Three weeks before a class was to start, I had only one person signed up. I thought about canceling since it was not financially viable with just one person. I was sorry to cancel because I like teaching, but I rationalized that I had other projects going on and could use the time. But as it became closer to the time for the class to start, I hesitated. I saw the data: The class wasn't filling. But at the same time, I didn't think I should call it off. One week prior to the class, I was still in a state of ambivalence. But now I had a stronger sense that I should keep the class on my calendar. I argued with myself about this: "I can't afford to teach this with one person. I need to give the student advance notice of cancellation. That's only fair." But part of me, what I would call my expert intuition, calmly countered: It will fill with enough people.

The day prior to the class five people registered. The hour prior to the class two more people signed up. After the first class started, one more person registered. How did my expert intuition know this when my conscious mind had no clue? I later went back to my records of the past 10 years of classes and checked registration dates with start times (a measure I could access from my data). Sixty percent of those attending my classes registered during the week prior to the class starting. Consciously, I had not remembered this. But my expert intuition was observing and noting this pattern. It surfaced to help me to stay calm and make a better decision.

3. *Strategic intuition* is a flash of creative insight that works only in *new* situations. Similar to a paradigm shift, an aha moment, or out-of-the-box thinking, Duggan explained how we can develop strategic intuition using the "what works matrix," a strategic process used by General Electric Corporation in the 1990s. By following the trail of what works for yourself and others, you focus on finding the elements of an idea that succeed instead of focusing on the ones that don't. Here's how:

- Set up a chart based on a stated goal (e.g., finding new clients).
- Have a vertical column listing possible solutions—all the ideas you can think of that have worked for others at other times to achieve this goal.
- Have a horizontal column listing actual evidence of what has worked for others based on observation or research.
- Compare and consider your possible solutions against actual evidence. Immerse yourself in the matrix of what works. Notice the themes and similarities between the columns. Allow your strategic

intuition, your aha moment, to spark as you begin to create new possible solutions.

This process is akin to the very best kind of brainstorming, when all judgment is suspended in lieu of inventiveness. Suzi Pomerantz, coach and author of *Seal the Deal* (2006), tells me that she uses strategic intuition regularly in a creative way. She calls herself "the gatherer" because she is always asking others: What have you done that works? What have you seen that might help me? What next step would point me in the right direction? In her process, she polls others first, and finds that this interviewing often creates a flash of insight about a thorny problem.

EXTERNAL SUPPORT

Most of those who are successful in small business ownership have had the support of others. The support may have come in various forms: a mentor, coach, family member, partner, colleague, staff, team, or peer group. To fast-track your progress, let others help. Surround yourself with people who will encourage your professional growth and success. For example, I look for support that energizes me. To help me tap into my inner wisdom, I belong to a monthly intuition study group composed of doctors, therapists, and other health providers. We meet to practice our use of clinical intuition, discuss cases, and improve our inner knowing. Many therapists use their intuition; this study group helps me make it a conscious process. Remember to bring in support to enhance your areas of personal and professional growth.

Many therapists I meet are hungry for inspiring and uplifting professional connections. When I conduct weekend workshops, I design the workshop to show therapists how to build professional support for themselves in the room, all day long during the weekend. It's normal to see therapists form alliances and collaborative partnerships by the end of the first day. Phone numbers are exchanged. There is laughter and lightness in the room, as people share and normalize their business experience. Participants have brainstorming sessions during the breaks, discover business opportunities and forming professional support groups that last for years.

When facing a serious downturn in your practice, having solid professional support can make the difference between resilience and collapse. Anne, a social worker, has been in solo practice for 15 years. She is bright, competent, and hardworking. She is also quiet, reserved, and shy; she works in relative isolation from her peers and her community. Last year, Anne's practice took an unexpected drop from 23 clients a week to 12. The drop-off in clients was the convergence of several factors—moving her office unexpectedly, losing her two main referral sources who both retired, and attrition: a number of clients just happened to finish up their treatment at the same time. Summer came and went, Anne took her usual weeks of vacation, and no new clients called for appointments.

Anne was frightened; a loss of 50% of one's income and workload is hard to handle. She did what was natural for her: She retreated inside herself, tried to think through what was wrong, and tried to calm down. She began to feel depressed. She called a few close friends and told them what was going on and they listened and commiserated. She went to a professional meeting, but no one else was complaining of a drop-off of clients, and Anne felt embarrassed to talk about her problem. When November came with no change in client count, and with a growing credit card debt, she found herself doing something she hadn't done for 20 years: She looked through the want ads for an agency job.

Contrast Anne's story to that of Jane, also a social worker, whose practice also took a sharp drop last year. Jane belongs to four professional support groups. Two of the support groups are made up of therapists who meet weekly for case consultations. The other two are made up of business owners—one is a group of women's business owners, the other an entrepreneurial club sponsored by her chamber of commerce. When Jane's practice fell off, she talked about her concerns in all of her support groups. "Right away I got professional support. My therapist colleagues assured me that they had gone through this from time to time, so I didn't feel like a pariah. They offered some good ideas, and they wanted to know each week how I was doing. The business groups took it as a personal mission to keep me motivated. Some asked me to call them each week and just let them know how I was doing with my marketing. They became a cheerleading squad for me. No one could fix the situation—that was up to me to do. But I found the support invaluable to help me stay upbeat. The women's business group also turned out to be a source of some referrals. Two women in the business group began to send several clients to me. I had never really tapped into the groups for marketing because I had been full previously. Who knew?"

Jane's practice bounced back quickly because she had so much energy to put toward her practice and she did not suffer any loss of self-esteem or financial crisis. The support acted like fuel and kept her business engine running. Being a small business owner means that you carry the emotional weight of your practice on your shoulders. Having support can make the burden lighter.

During the last few years with all of the economic downturn, a top survival strategy for all types of businesses was connection—finding ways to link, affiliate, collaborate, partner, share, network, or merge with like-minded concerns. Avoid support that discourages you. One therapist told me recently that a peer group he started to provide business support degenerated each week into a complaint session about the difficulties of private practice, which only served to further his feelings of victimization.

YOUR PROFESSIONAL SUPPORT SYSTEMS

Your professional support system will tend to fall into three areas:

1. *People you hire—staff, consultants, supervisors, or coaches who help you to reach outcomes or accomplish specific tasks*: Hiring others

is an easy way to feel supported when you feel overwhelmed, over-worked, or under pressure. Sometimes you need to hire staff—a full- or part-time bookkeeper, secretary, receptionist, or others to delegate work to and ease the pressure. Most therapists in suc-cessful practices delegate some aspects of billing, administration, public relations, Web site design, accounting, or promotion. Some also hire outside consultants—business coaches, financial plan-ners, marketing experts—to assist with operational planning, goal setting, or future development. I love hiring people who know more than I do, or can do simple tasks more easily than I can. Whatever business problem you have, chances are you can find staff, con-sultants, or experts to help you resolve it. You will need to manage your staff, but it may be a workable trade-off for having additional support.

2. *People you attract—peers, colleagues, friends, or family members with whom you may or may not actually do business, but who offer support, advice, coaching, and brainstorming:* Attracting people to your practice for collaboration can generate new opportunities and referrals for a practice. Years ago I joined two professional support groups to increase my connections in my community, since I am naturally an introvert and tend to keep to myself outside of working hours. These groups have provided a lot of emotional support for me, as well as new business opportunities that I would never have expected. As you attract others based on a similarity of goals or shared enthusiasm, you build a circle of encouragement for your-self. You may decide to pursue business endeavors with this circle of peers, or just use the time with them to mutually share support and ideas.

3. *People you are attracted to—those mentors and models of excellence who you seek out so you can shift to a higher level of accomplishment or awareness:* When you connect with mentors or those whom you admire, you can shift to a higher level of accomplishment or increased awareness. This might mean giving yourself permission to "hang

out" with others who are much farther along the path than you are. There are many ways to do this: going to workshops, conferences, or seminars; getting supervision from the most senior, respected clinicians you can find; reading books by your favorite mentors; or joining organizations where you will be in the same room with those you admire. I let myself take in deeply from mentors, even when the connection is at a distance. You, too, can recognize this as a form of collaboration as long as you open yourself to feeling supported by the contact.

EXERCISE: MY SUPPORT SYSTEM

List your current support system in each of the three areas.

Increase your professional support this month by adding additional people into your life in at least two out of the above three areas.

People I hire and why: _____

_____

People I attract and why: _____

_____

People I am attracted to and why: _____

_____

Is my support system sufficient for my current needs? _____

_____

Which areas do I need to increase and how will I do this? _____

_____

ADVISORY CIRCLES

If you've spent any time within a large corporation or nonprofit organization, you're probably aware of the important role of the board of directors. Ideally, a board functions as the brain trust of an organization. The chief executive officer selects the best and brightest people he or she knows from a variety of fields from within and outside the organization to provide oversight and direction. In a perfect world, the board operates without any personal or political agenda, save one: They want what is best for the organization.

Advisory circles are the sole proprietor's remedy for the lack of a board of directors. You may have several people you turn to for advice, but I am going to propose that you set up a formal circle of professional, highly positive support, operating on the principles of mutuality and partnership. Your advisory circle will operate as a rotating board of directors, allowing each person in it to guard against insular thinking and gain the benefit of the advice of others whom you respect. Create an advisory group of no more than six people, no fewer than four. Who should be a member of the group? It will help if everyone is in private practice. You might include some therapists, but also consider having a lawyer, an accountant, or a management consultant. Each person should be someone you respect, whose advice and experience will be relevant, and someone you would like to give your support to, in turn.

If the group has six members, everyone agrees to meet a minimum of once a week for 6 weeks. Each meeting will take an hour. The format of each meeting is simple—a different person takes center stage each time. This person takes 20 minutes to present his or her professional story and answer any questions other members may have; then the group gives their best advice. Here's a set of guidelines that works well:

1. The Center-Stage Person's Presentation

Take no more than one third of the allotted time to talk about these points:

- A statement of your vision and goals for your practice (more on this in Chapter 16)
- Your current challenges

- Opportunities you are not currently taking advantage of
- What other people should know about you, in order to best advise you (including how you like to be coached by others)

2. A Time for Questions

The questions are for the clarification of your board and should take another third of the time at most. Don't let the question-and-answer time become the advice-giving time. Keep the two separate. Questions are just to help your circle understand the above points.

3. Discussion, Advice, and Suggestions From the Circle

During this last third of the hour, the center-stage person must sit quietly. The keyword here is *quietly.* The members of your circle will now give you advice, direction, and suggestions, based on wanting the best for you personally and professionally. They will talk about your situation while you listen. You will hear many ideas that you may want to downplay or resist. Listen with an open mind and reject nothing at this time. Take notes. You are free to accept or reject whatever you like later, but first consider all the possibilities without excuses or explanations. When the time is over, thank your circle for their efforts. The next time you meet, it's somebody else's turn and you become part of their advisory circle.

Remember, collaboration and mutuality are the keys to this effort. Everyone agrees to play by the rules and everyone agrees to take a turn at advising and being advised. When advising, everyone agrees to speak from a place of the highest good, without personal agenda. (For this reason, you may not want to have your spouse or close friends sit in on this professional support circle, unless you are sure you can both remain loving and objective for each other professionally.) This support group can become a tremendously important, enriching asset for your business.

This method of advisory circles is one that is used for leadership training of executives. You are in a leadership role, as the owner and operator of your practice.

CHAPTER 16
Crisis-Proof Leadership

A therapist wears many hats in a private practice. You deliver services, do the books, network for referrals, and sometimes empty the trash. But you must also take time to put on your chief executive officer (CEO) hat and be the leader of your small business; even if your business is a sole proprietorship, it needs leadership and direction. Think of your leadership role as caring for the well-being of your business, much like a parent cares for a child. As a leader, it's up to you to make hard choices and see into the future to decide what is the best path for your practice over time. You have to put profitability on an equal footing with professional ethics, service, and integrity.

Executive coach Suzi Pomerantz, says that the owner of a sole proprietorship leads by both possibility and influence. According to Suzi, leading by possibility means that you lead yourself as you learn to be an entrepreneur to stay optimistic and visionary, to see what is possible. Leading by influence means that you see those who surround your practice (your clients, your colleagues, your staff) as people whom you also lead and develop. Seeing leadership this way can help you to set a leadership agenda. You continually transition in your role. As you stretch your business, you encourage and motivate those with whom you have contact. Here are three leadership strategies for you to consider, to help you become more in charge.

- Develop a leadership agenda.
- Maintain the agenda.
- Set your strategic focus.

LEADERSHIP AGENDA

If you were in a leadership role in a large corporation, you would be groomed for leadership. You would be mentored and taught how to behave and think differently from an employee or a manager. You would be trained to become a leader. As the owner of a small business, even though you are ostensibly the CEO of your practice, you may not feel like a leader because you have never been trained to think and act in this way. Leadership training begins with an introduction to a leadership agenda. I learned about coaching business leaders when I enrolled in coach training at CoachU, a large coach-training organization. CoachU's curriculum (CoachU, 2005) included a list of transitions to help people make a shift in their role and begin to set leadership goals.

During the past decade, as I have coached hundreds of therapists and other small business owners, I have adapted the CoachU list of transitions to introduce small business owners to a shift toward leadership. I have refined this list further to set a leadership agenda for you during a time of crisis. Read the leadership agenda below, and consider your areas of focus to help you become more of a leader in your practice. The first area of a leader's attention during a financial crisis is the financial picture.

Leadership for profitability includes shifting:

From	To
Being clueless about money	Developing money maturity
Having no financial tracking	Having regular review of profit and loss reports
Having an unprofitable practice	Taking steps to cut expenses and boost profits
Having no direction for business	Having a plan for consistent, steady, slow growth
Feeling hopeless	Having eyes on the prize
Putting wants first	Putting integrity first, needs second, wants third
Losing money each month	Saving money each month

Leadership for self-sufficiency includes shifting:

From	**To**
Being vague about value	Articulating the results and benefits of your services
Hiding self-worth	Claiming your expertise and skill
Reacting without a plan	Following a plan with a sense of calm
Avoiding setting boundaries	Willing to speak up for the sake of the practice
Seeing only the next step	Seeing five steps ahead
Being unmotivated	Persevering and achieving
Procrastinating	Proudly completing weekly goals

Leadership for fulfillment includes shifting:

From	**To**
Working in the practice	Working on the practice
Always being under stress	Managing time well
Feeling envious of others	Feeling satisfied with self and taking responsibility for choices
Being hard on self	Loving to laugh and seeing humor in self
Living in the past or future	Loving the present; able to "be here now"
Being tired at the end of the workday	Feeling refreshed by work and life
Being fueled by adrenaline	Finding energy from healthy living and fun activities

Rise to the next level in your business development. Use the above list to identify a few goals that will take you from managing the practice to leadership. Read on to see how to hold the goals in mind long enough for them to become integrated into your daily life.

MAINTAIN THE AGENDA

Having an agenda is not the same as maintaining it. The shift you are trying to make may be a stretch and one that needs daily focus and intention. My clients find it helpful to use a process of business affirmations to help them move faster to implementing a big agenda item. Some of the business owners I coach get dramatic results using a business affirmation (a positive statement that you repeat many times to help your mind accept it). They work with an affirmation consistently and find that without any other behavioral change on their part, they move in this direction. Others have less dramatic results, but say that using the affirmation helps them to stay reminded about the agenda item. Still others use the affirmation but don't notice any immediate change. I fall into this camp; I do it for a while and forget about it. Months pass, and then I realize the affirmation I worked with briefly 6 months earlier, "I am refreshed by my work," has become my reality. Try this three-step process, keep some notes about your experience, and watch what happens.

1. *Choose a business affirmation* from the right-hand list of leadership agenda items above.

2. *Write the affirmation once.* Divide a piece of paper into two columns to write your affirmation. Make sure it is succinct. On the left, write the affirmation. The reason for making the statement succinct is that you will be writing it over and over. You can do it by hand or on a computer, but the key to making this work is writing it, not just thinking it.

3. *After writing, listen quietly for any internal negative thoughts.* Write down one negative thought in the right-hand column, opposite the affirmation. Then repeat this process until the page is full. Use the same affirmation each time. Resist any inclination to change it. At the end of the exercise you will have a list that looks something like Table 16.1.

Table 16.1. Negative Beliefs

Affirmation from leadership agenda	Negative thought
I see five steps ahead for my practice.	No I don't.
I see five steps ahead for my practice.	I can't do what it takes.
I see five steps ahead for my practice.	That's for other people, not for me.
I see five steps ahead for my practice.	I'm not smart enough to do this.
I see five steps ahead for my practice.	My practice never stays full.
I see five steps ahead for my practice.	I'm too lazy.
I see five steps ahead for my practice.	That's not me.

Your negative thoughts will read like a stream of consciousness, albeit a highly critical stream. Time after time in the classes I teach, we read out these negative beliefs and everyone is amazed at how similar they sound, regardless of who is reading them and what the affirmation states.

CLEAR AWAY YOUR NEGATIVE BELIEFS.

To counter your negative beliefs, pick one of the following three methods.

- *Run through them.* Exhaust them by using your affirmation to drain away their charge. Write the affirmation over and over again, day after day. Over time you will notice that your mind quiets, tires of protesting, and agrees with the statement. When this happens, begin to notice any changes in your behavior and your thinking about this issue. This may take a day, a week, or a month, depending on the affirmation you have created.

- *Replace them.* Use visualization to give yourself a different picture, a message that counters the negative belief. For example, imagine a clear mental image of the affirmation and hold that picture in mind. Create a piece of artwork, or make a collage from magazine photos, or draw a symbol that represents the affirmation. Look at it often. Meditate on the image. Again, the point is to help your mind create a new sense of what is possible.
- *Refute them.* Make a third column on your paper and use your intellect to answer back to the negative belief. It might look like Table 16.2.

Table 16.2 Refuting Negative Thoughts

Affirmation	Negative thought	Refutation
I see five steps ahead for my practice.	No I don't.	Okay, this is a new skill. It may take me some time to learn how to anticipate and think.
I see five steps ahead for my practice.	I can't do what it takes.	I have done this in other areas of my life. I do long-range treatment planning for clients. I can transfer that skill to my business.
I see five steps ahead for my practice.	That's for other people, not for me.	I always admire this ability in others and if I want, I can adopt this strategy and join the crowd.

Each day, fill in one page. Write the affirmation based on a desired leadership agenda, and then write any negative thought that surfaces in response. Clear away negative thoughts, so that at the end of 30 days you have no negative response when you write or think your affirmation. Use a business affirmation each day this month. Use one of the three methods for clearing away negative beliefs that surface.

EMBRACE YOUR AMBITION

Joe Bavonese, therapist and marketing coach, says that those therapists most likely to sail through a recession or economic crisis are proactive and ambitious. They are comfortable taking some calculated risks because they have a clear sense of what they want to create. They excel at what Joe calls the "inner game of private practice"—using their ambition to help them move through fear or paralysis to action.

But ambition—a strong drive for business success—may be outside your comfort zone of objectives. It was a taboo feeling for me early on in my career. As the daughter of an entrepreneur, I understood the desire for business success, but as a social worker trained to be a helping professional, the idea of ambition did not sit well with me. As I became a business coach, I wondered how to reconcile the desire to be of service with a desire to be at the top of my profession. How would aiming high make practice building easier? I questioned my preconceptions about ambition. What if ambition, instead of signifying something negative to me, such as self-absorption and narcissism, was really a type of fuel that fed big visions?

By not giving free reign to my ambition, I tended to keep a lid on my goals and vision. I didn't allow myself to imagine great things for myself, only good things. I avoided opportunities and potential connections that seemed too large for me, and I didn't allow myself to get too enthusiastic or excited, for fear I would just get disappointed. Without a comfort level with ambition, when I had visionary thoughts about my practice, I kept them to myself. But as I began to play with the notion of ambition as fuel, I could see that it was a natural entrepreneurial emotion and an important energy source that helped to invigorate big dreams. Ambition acted like a stimulant and helped me aim higher, do more, and spread my wings. I don't always act on my feelings of ambition, the same way I don't act on every feeling that goes through me, but I learned to embrace, accept, and enjoy the feelings as they emerged. With ambition, I play a bigger game.

Executive coach Richard Leider, author of *The Power of Purpose*, uses a process of questioning to help raise the stakes for those he coaches (Leider, 2005). The first question he might ask a CEO is: What's the gap between where you are now and where you want to be? The less obvious follow-up question is: How will you know when you get there? Asking yourself the right question is a way to become more ambitious. Some questions to raise your level of ambition might be:

- What unintended results are you getting now?
- How are you contributing to them?
- How do you need to shift your way of being, thinking, and behaving?
- Can you hold yourself to a higher standard?
- If you were to take yourself more seriously, how would you show it?
- How will you celebrate when you become a person who is more of a leader and less of a follower?

EXERCISE: AMBITION AS FUEL

Answering the following questions can help you to normalize this entrepreneurial emotion and allow your feelings of ambition to fuel your goals.

1. What did you learn about ambition in your family or in your history?
2. How might letting your feelings of ambition surface help you in manifesting your vision?
3. What do you fear about letting your natural ambition surface?
4. What needs to shift inside you to understand ambition as a fuel?
5. What steps can you take to get more comfortable with this feeling in daily life professional life?
6. What specific time will you put aside each week for daydreaming, meditating, and being open to thoughts of your business vision, letting all your feelings (including those of ambition) emerge?

FIND YOUR STRATEGIC FOCUS

As you can see, leadership in a crisis means staying highly focused. Jim Collins, author of *Good to Great* (2001), offers a simple exercise to help you find the strategic focus for your small business and then stick with it. His approach can help you set a quick but powerful vision for your practice during a crisis, by knowing what you do best and what is most profitable. Your strategic focus helps you to keep it simple by doing one big thing well, as you ride out a difficult market or a personal problematic situation.

To find your strategic focus, complete my adaptation of Collin's Three Circles exercise (Collins, 2001, p. 95):

1. Draw three equal-sized circles that overlap or intersect with a common center: a Venn diagram (see Figure 16.1).

Figure 16.1: Venn Diagram

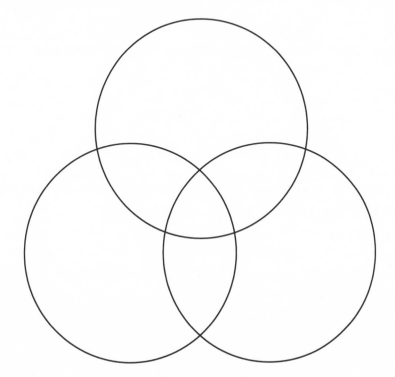

2. Assign colors or letters to each circle to keep them separate.

3. Identify each circle: Circle A is the soul of your practice: Inside this circle, list those services that you're passionate about offering. Circle B contains your brand: Inside this circle, list the aspects of your practice that connote your expertise, reputation, and excellence. Circle C is your economic engine: Inside this circle, list the services or products that are consistently profitable and generative.

4. The point where the three circles intercept—where passion, brand, and profitability overlap, will become the new strategic focus of your business.

Here is a case example of how finding your strategic focus helps develop your practice in a time of crisis.

FROM FLOUNDERING TO FLOURISHING

Carol is a psychotherapist who has been in a private practice for over a decade. Like many other therapists, she has trained in multiple methods and is a generalist: "I see anybody and everybody," she says. As a result of the recession, her practice is floundering. She has many open hours each week and has no sense of what to do. When she contacted me for individual business coaching, my first suggestion was that she tackle the Three Circles exercise.

"In the first circle write the one or two services you offer that convey your greatest passion," I said.

"I love everything I do. How can I choose one or two?" she asked. "I know about a dozen or more methods and work with couples, adults, and children. This is what I do. It's all my passion."

But not every passion is equal, I pointed out. "Usually passion implies getting selective and prioritizing. For example, I might really, really, really like all thirty-two flavors of Baskin-Robbins ice cream, but I am only passionate about Rocky Road. I'll get out of bed in the middle of the night, when it's raining, put on a slicker and galoshes, for a Rocky Road ice-cream cone. If you can prioritize based on passion, you'll reinvent your practice in a needed way. It'll help you to develop a stronger identity about your work, and deepen your connection with the heart of what you offer to others."

Carol agreed in principle, she said stiffly, after a long pause, but not in spirit, I thought to myself. I gave it another try. "A decade ago, your decision about being a generalist and having multiple services and training made sense. The market was up and you had less need to focus your energy or your costs. But today, your practice is hurting. Money, time, and energy are in short supply. Having a kitchen-sink mentality bleeds away resources and profits. Each additional method and service requires time to learn, practice, market, and perfect. Each exerts its own pull. Before you know it, you're tugged in many directions. You need to recommit to a new direction, to get smaller and stronger in your offerings. If you get clear about your three circles, you'll be halfway home."

On our next call, a different-sounding Carol greeted me. I heard a new degree of resolve in her voice. "I don't know if you sensed how difficult this homework would be for me," she began. "I really struggled to complete the circles, but along the way, I had what I can best call a revelation.

"At first I was really annoyed at your request to limit my kitchen-sink mentality," she said. "I counted up the services I offer: fifteen different services for six populations of clients. I know it's a lot, but the more I thought about narrowing my focus, the more upset I became. I finally just sat for about an hour, trying to understand why your reasonable request was creating so much angst for me. Is it okay that I talk about this?" she asked shyly. "I know this is business coaching, not therapy, but it feels very relevant to help you understand me better."

I told her that as a business coach, I had two clients: the business and the business owner. Some of the most productive business turnarounds come when the therapist challenges old beliefs and the client learns to go beyond a set way of seeing herself or the world. I encouraged her to go on. Carol took a breath. "I tried to think why I was so attached to having such a diverse or, as you might say, diffuse practice. I know my practice is vague; it even feels scattered to me, probably because I do so many things in an impulsive way. This has always been true for me, in all areas of my life, starting from child-hood where we moved around from city to city. I stayed scattered and uncertain.

"Even though I've put myself through college to earn a master's degree, even though I always supported myself and paid more than my fair share of household expenses, even though I've worked extremely hard, by staying so scattered and diffuse in my work I've been living out the idea of having no solid home, no grounding."

Carol sounded very sad and her voice broke. "To stay unsuccess-ful and scattered is a form of acting out my childhood. It's my way of still declaring that I'm not really a grown-up, I'm still a child. And my practice isn't really a business, it is just my playground."

GETTING FOCUSED

This simple exercise, getting focused by prioritizing three aspects of your existing practice, can force a business owner to face reality and make needed changes. As a business coach, I heard Carol's decla-ration that she needed to "grow up" and be more mature about her practice as an opportunity for personal self-confrontation and trans-formation.

"I can't help but wonder who you'll become when you take on the full leadership of your business," I said.

Now Carol's voice got low and strong. "I'll become a full adult. My practice isn't a hobby. This is my livelihood!"

"So as the CEO of your practice, will you take me through your three circles?"

Carol responded with confidence. "The first circle is the services I'm passionate about offering (see Figure 16.2). There are three: play-therapy sessions with young children in my office, parenting classes for families I offer through a neighboring church, and couples workshops I give in a rented space. I absolutely love all of these.

Figure 16.2: Carol's Order

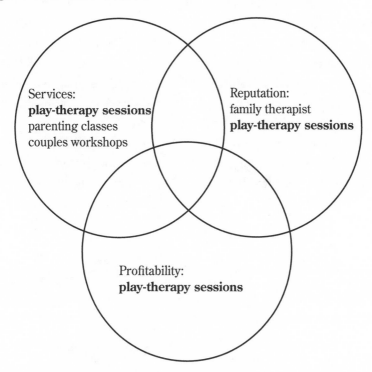

"Before I could fill out the second circle—my reputation and expertise—I checked with some of my colleagues to ask how I was perceived in the local community. They said I'm known as a very good family therapist, in a town where most therapists prefer individual work, but that they most often hear my name come up in reference to child therapy.

The third circle is harder for me to fill in. I don't know what my economic engine is or how to define it." To help Carol find what Collins calls the economic denominator—the most profitable of all her services, which can be repeatedly generated with the least amount of expense—we cost out each service, looking for any obvious or hidden profit drains. Carol made the most money per hour with the couples workshops she teaches, but when she factored in the unpaid hours spent preparing material, registering couples, collecting deposits, finding and renting space, setting up the room, taking down the room, and then resting from the exhaustion of the process, it's clear that the workshops had too many hidden costs to be her economic engine. Her most consistently profitable service (to her surprise) was play therapy, a specialized service of child therapy for which she bills and gets full fee.

Next we looked at each circle for the area of overlap (see Figure 16.3). "This is so interesting," she said. "My favorite service, play therapy, is also what I'm known for in the community, and now I see it's how I made the most money. It all fits together." She chuckled. "It's funny, isn't it? Instead of treating my practice like a playground and being unsuccessful, I'm going to focus on play therapy and be profitable!"

Figure 16.3: Carol's Overlap

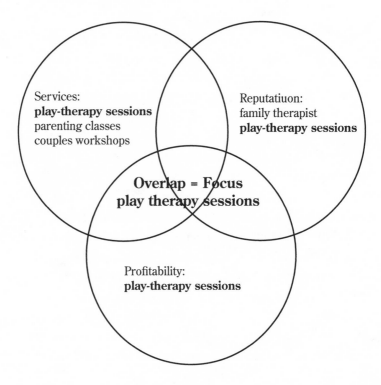

Services:
play-therapy sessions
parenting classes
couples workshops

Reputatiuon:
family therapist
play-therapy sessions

**Overlap = Focus
play therapy sessions**

Profitability:
play-therapy sessions

APPLYING RESOURCES

With her focus in place, I then asked Carol to apply all her resources for the next 6 months to sustaining this one area of focus. She was immediately anxious: "You mean forget about everything else I do? What about existing clients who don't fit that category? What about referrals that come in for other services? I can't afford to turn any clients away!"

I explained patiently that focusing her practice was a process. She could take the time she needed. Carol said she would think about it. But on the next call, she sounded resolute and agreed to use her marketing resources, small advertising budget, and networking contacts to promote play therapy. "I thought about everything we discussed, and I know I'm just scared to change. But it's time for me to put up or shut up," she declared.

"Or maybe just grow up," I suggested softly. I then reinforced her strengths. "It takes courage to be willing to take on a challenge, and in this case, you're taking on a big one."

In this spirit, we got specific with a list of action items. She agreed to say no to all new opportunities that would distract her from her focus, to take on no new trainings, to promote her focus when networking, to change her Web site text to more accurately reflect the core of her retooled practice. She made to-do lists and "stop doing" lists. We set up times to talk twice a month for 45 minutes to review her list of wins, challenges, goals, and action steps.

Now the tedious work began. Month by month, I helped Carol stay on track. Despite thinking this was "cool," implementing her focused action plan was hard. She still longed to offer more services and take additional training. I reminded her of her earlier insight, and we agreed that it's hard to conquer her fears of success. I ask her to consistently do more marketing and networking to build her refocused practice than she wanted—three networking calls in person a week, additional cold calls by phone, sending out weekly letters to potential referral sources, and attending all professional meetings of the local psychotherapy association. She needed support and encouragement to stay on task, especially when there were no apparent results from these activities after 2 months.

At my urging, she used unfilled client hours to plan and practice marketing efforts, and she penciled them into her calendar. I asked her to see problems as opportunities; for instance, when a play therapy association rejected her proposal to present at the national conference, she submitted the same proposal to a private elementary school PTA and was immediately scheduled to present—a great way to meet parents and teachers. I brainstormed with her; we made lists of people she could call and meet, places she could speak, ways to maximize her time, ideas for cutting unnecessary expenses. I commiserated when times were tough. At the end of each coaching call, she had a list of action steps to stay on plan. Between sessions she e-mailed me her wins so I could cheer her on. We celebrated each and every success and I reinforced her strengths, praising her for taking both small and large steps in the right direction.

Finally she saw clear progress as the marketing began to generate dollars. She affiliated with two private schools as a child therapy consultant, on call to observe problem children in the classroom. Referrals began to fill her schedule. She gave talks for two parent associations and joined an association of elementary-school educators, sitting on their advisory board as a child-behavior expert, all of which results in paying clients. Six months into her plan, her client caseload of play-therapy clients was steadily growing. She rented out her office during the hours when she wasn't working, stopped all paid advertising, and continued her networking. For the month of January, her net income was up by a whopping 45%, and her caseload was now holding steady at 15 clients a week.

SUSTAINING SUCCESS

Carol said she was satisfied and could continue on her own from this point. She wanted to take a break from coaching, which is fine with me, since my goal is for therapists to need my services less and less over time. A few months later, she called to say it was too difficult to keep progressing without the accountability and support of our calls, and we resumed coaching. The last week of June, a year from her initial session, she called and said she has big news: she booked her ideal caseload of 20 client hours for the first time in many years. "I can't believe I did this!" She exclaimed. "It means the world to me that I can bring my practice back to life. I really like the clients I am seeing, I am doing my best work in years, and every hour I work, I earn my top fee."

She was ready to stop again, but this time I had one more coaching request: I wanted Carol to develop an ongoing, sustainable support group of peers to help her counter her earlier professional isolation. "It takes a village to raise a business," I said. "As a business owner, you need to be a good parent for the business you birthed. But just as single parenting is a daunting task, being a sole proprietor with little in the way of professional support can be overwhelming. You need more ongoing professional business support than you give yourself."

Carol decided to place an online message board ad, offering to host a support group for senior psychotherapists to meet monthly. She was surprised and delighted at the response, and soon she was hosting a group of six clinicians each month—another act of leadership and commitment to her practice. As Collins wrote in *Good to Great*, a business's adherence to core values, combined with a willingness to change, preserves the business and stimulates progress. He made a distinction between purpose—what a business stands for (which should never change)—and process—how it does things (which should never stop changing).

Being a successful entrepreneur in today's uncertain market means becoming an informed strategist—a leader. Amid the confusion and concern that many are feeling, we have an opportunity to rethink our relationship to our chosen work, stretch our capacities, learn new skills, and affiliate with our peers for much-needed professional business support. We need to do all of this, and more, to ride out the current downward market, stay viable, and ultimately thrive together.

A SIMPLER WAY

In her book, *A Simpler Way* (1996), Margaret Wheatley explained that there is a simpler way to organize human endeavor.

> *It requires a new way of being in the world. It requires being in the world without fear. Being in the world with play and creativity. Seeking after what's possible. Being willing to learn and be surprised.* (p. 5)

The notion of having a creative, playful, ideal practice that is simultaneously profitable and satisfying may seem like a pipe dream when you are wondering whether your practice can withstand yet another slowdown in client referrals, increasing professional competition, or an unpredictable economic marketplace. But as you have seen through the pages of this book, overcoming the challenges you currently face in order to build a thriving practice is not only possible, it is probable if you will take the lead. As we have explored, leadership during a crisis means knowing what to *do,* but more important, it means knowing who to *be.* From this position it is easy and natural to take the steps to create the private practice you desire—your ideal practice.

Buddhists maintain that all efforts at changing the world begin with looking inside and first changing ourselves. Looking inside is a process we understand; when faced with the challenge of change, we understandably want to retreat to our teepees instead of facing the fierce, shifting winds. But this is not a time for inward retreat. It's time to plan and then to act.

We want to hold on to those values that define us professionally and ethically, and stay true to our core philosophy to help our clients develop insight and awareness, build skills, solve problems, and change behavior in constructive ways. But how we deliver our services requires a willingness to rethink traditional wisdom, let go of old models, and take big steps to reshape our practices so that they can stay strong over time. Some business changes require a time frame of several years to effect. That is why we need to start now and look ahead, so that we have sufficient time. Either we will be the architects of our own renewal, or we will feel victimized and "done in" by the marketplace forces. If we see this as a time for leadership, we can determine the best outcomes for our private practices and our collective future, following Darwin's sage advice: "It is not the strongest of the species that survive, nor the most intelligent, but the ones most responsive to change."

REFERENCES

Ackley, (1997). *Breaking free of managed care.* New York: Guilford Press.

Allen, D. (2002). *Getting things done.* New York: Penguin.

Ansoff, I. (1957). Strategies for diversification. *Harvard Business Review,* 35(5), 113–124.

Ansoff growth matrix. (n.d.). Retrieved October 2007 from tutor2u. net/business/strategy/ansoff_matrix.htm

Aron, E. (1999). *The highly sensitive person: How to thrive when the world overwhelms you.* Bridgewater, NH: Replica Books.

Barnes, P., Powell-Griner, E., McFann, K., & Nahin R. (2002). CDC complementary and alternative medicine use among adults. *Advance Data Report,* 343. Retrieved December 1, 2008, from http://www.cdc.gov/nchs/data/ad/ad343.pdf

Bavonese, J. (2007, July–August). How to develop a money mindset. *Psychotherapy Networker Magazine,* V 31. 32–39.

Bavonese, J. (2009, March–April). Secrets of an effective website. *Psychotherapy Networker* Magazine, V 33. 48–49.

Beck, D. and Cowant, C. (1996). *Spiral dynamics: Mastering values, leadership, and change.* Malden, MA: Blackwell.

Begley, S. (2007, December 24). The roots of fear. *Newsweek.* Retrieved October 19, 2008 from http://www.newsweek.com/id/78178

Borkin, S. (2000). *When your heart speaks, take good notes.* Los Altos, CA: Center for Personal Growth.

Cappon, D. (1993). The anatomy of intuition. *Psychology Today, 26.* Retrieved January 1, 2008, from http://www.psychologytoday. com/articles/pto-19930501-000029.html

Celente, G. (2009). Top trends of 2009. Retrieved January 3, 2009, from www.trendsresearch.com

Celente, G. (1998). *Trends 2000: How to prepare for and profit from the changes of the 21st century.* New York: Warner.

Charland, T. (2006). NOW Medical announces agreement with Supervalu: Retail clinics to be owned by local medical providers. Retrieved November 1, 2007, from www.mcms.org/downloads/ Nowrelease.pdf

CoachU. (2005). *Personal and corporate coach training handbook*. Hoboken, NJ: Wiley.

Coachville. (2002). Seven coaches share their success stories. Retrieved July, 2003, from Coachville.com (www.coachville.com/fullpractice/dupe/FP99coachingpackages.pdf)

Collins, J. (2001). *Good to great*. New York: Harper Business.

Covey, S. (2004). *The 7 habits of highly effective people*. New York: Free Press.

Dean, Ben. (2000, spring). Niche criteria for a successful coaching practice. *Division 42 online*, APA. Retrieved May 10, 2002, from www.division42.org/MembersArea/IPfiles/IPSpg00/Marketing/Dean.html

Duggan, W. (2007). *Strategic intuition: The creative spark in human achievement*. New York: Columbia University Press.

Faass Jones, N. (2001). *Integrating complementary medicine into health systems*. Boston: Jones and Bartlett.

Ferguson, M. (1980). Aquarian Change. In J. W. Pfeiffer & A. C. Ballew, (Eds.), *Theories and models in applied behavioral science, Vol. 4* (pp. 223–225). San Diego: Pfeiffer & Co.

Naik, G. (2007, February 23). Faltering family MDs get technology lifeline. *Wall Street Journal*. Retrieved October 1, 2008, from http://idealhealth.wikispaces.com/file/view/FalteringFamilyMDsWSJ.pdf

Giles, C. S. (2007). Ideal practice part 2. Retrieved June 15, 2007 from http://www.csgiles.org/journal/2007/1/15/ideal-micropractice-part-two.html

Gladwell, M. (2002). *The tipping point*. Boston: Back Bay Books.

Gladwell, M. (2007). *Blink. The power of thinking without thinking*. Boston, MA: Back Bay Books.

Godin, S. (1999). *Permission marketing*. New York: Simon & Schuster.

Godin, S. (2003). *Purple Cow*. New York: Portfolio.

Goldsmith, J. (2008). Health care is not recession-proof. Retrieved January 10, 2009, from http://www.thehealthcareblog.com/the_health_care_blog/2008/06/health-care-is.html

Grodzki, L. (2000). *Building your ideal private practice*. New York: Norton.

Grodzki, L. (Ed.) (2002). *The new private practice*. New York: Norton.

Grodzki, L. (2003). *12 months to your ideal private practice: A workbook*. New York: Norton.

Grodzki, L. (2006, September–October). Triage for your practice. *Psychotherapy Networker Magazine*, 62–68.

Grodzki, L. (2008). *Private practice SOS: An e-book*. www.privatepracticesuccess.com

Grodzki, L. (2009, March–April). Recession-proof your practice. *Psychotherapy Networker Magazine*, 34–39.

Grodzki, L. & Allen, W. (2005). *The business and practice of coaching*. New York: Norton.

Homer, J. (2003). *ASTD releases its latest state of the industry report*. Alexandria, VA: ASTD.

Houppert, K. (2008, December 12). The kid tamer. *Washington Post Magazine*, p. w08.

International coach federation coaching survey. (2003). International Coach Federation.

International coach federation global coaching study, executive summary (2008). International Coach Federation.

Klein, J. (2006). New Data Show Most Clinicians Falling Further Behind. *Psychotherapy Finances, 32*, 381.

Klein, J. (2008a). PsyFin readers reveal their marketing tools and strategies. *Psychotherapy Finances, 34*, 410.

Klein, J. (2008b). Social networking sites present new marketing opportunities. *Psychotherapy Finances, 34*, 416.

Laff, M. (2008, August). Steady under pressure training during a recession. T + D. Retrieved March 3, 2009, from http://www.allbusiness.com/economy-economic-indicators/economic-conditions-recession/11575306-1.html

Leider, R. (2005). *Power of purpose. Creating meaning in your life and work*. San Francisco, CA: Berrett-Koehler.

Meyer, J. P., & Allen, N. J. (1991). A three-component conceptualization of organizational commitment. *Human Resource Management Review, 1*, 61–89.

Miller, S. (2005). "Improve your clinical effectiveness 65% without hardly trying." Psychotherapy Networker Symposium, March 17–20. Audio available at: http://www.psychotherapynetworker.org/audio-courses/full-course-listings/362-a212-how-to-improve-your-practice-by-65-without-trying.

Miller, S., Duncan, B., & Hubble, M. (1997). *Escape from Babel: Toward a unifying language for psychotherapy practice*. New York: Norton.

Moltz, B. (2008). Help your small business survive and thrive in 2009. Retrieved January 10, 2009 from fhttp://www.elance.com/p/blog/help_your_small_business_survive_and_thrive_2009.html?rid=1F0ZO

Moore, G. (Feb. 2002). *Going solo: Making the leap. AAFP Magazine*, retrieved from http://www.aafp.org/fpm/20020200/29goin.html

Niebuhr, R. (1934). Serenity prayer. In R. M. Brown (Ed.), *The essential Reinhold Niebuhr: Selected essays and addresses* (p. 250). New Haven, CT: Yale University Press.

Peters, T. (1997, August). "The brand called you." *Fast Company Magazine*. www.fastcompany.com Issue 10: p 83

Pomerantz, S. (2006). *Seal the deal.* Amherst, MA: HRD Press, Inc.

Popcorn, F. (2009). *The new rules of engagement. Brainserve,* Jan. 1. Retrieved Jan. 10 from www.faithpopcorn.com.

Prince, E. Ted. (2009). "Strength in recession." *Magazine of Leadership Excellence,* 8–9.

Sherpa Executive Coaching Survey (2008). Retrieved January 10, 2009, from http://www.sherpacoaching.com/pdf%20files/SherpaExecutiveCoachingSurvey2008.pdf

Shevlin, S. (2002). Beyond insight to vision. In L. Grodzki (Ed.), *The new private practice* (pp. 115–127). New York: Norton.

Straker, D. (2008). Changing minds: In detail. (2008). Straker Syque Press. London. Retrieved (1/30/09) from http://changingminds.org/techniques/questioning/chunking_questions.htm

Stryk, L. (Trans.). (1995). *Zen poetry: Let the spring breeze enter.* New York: Grove Press.

Thompson, C., Koon, E., Woodwell, W. H., & Beauvais, J. (2002). *Training for the next economy: An ASTD state of the industry report on the trends in employer-provided training in the United States.* Report conducted by the American Society of Training & Development.

Top trends. (n.d.). Retrieved January 1, 2009, from http:www.toptrends.nowandnext.com

Truffo, C. (2007). *Be a wealthy therapist.* Irvine, CA: MP Press.

Truffo, C. (2009). "Pink-spoon marketing." *Psychotherapy Networker Magazine,* 42–47.

Vedantam, S. (2007). "Most ptsd treatments not proven effective." *Washington Post,* October 19, 2007, A3.

Walker, R. (2004, December 5). The hidden in plain sight persuaders. *New York Times Magazine.*

Walsch, N. D. (1996). *Conversations with God.* New York: Putnam.

Westerhoff, N. (2008, December 17). Set in our ways: Why change is so hard. *Scientific American Mind.* Retrieved January 1, 2009, from http://pragmasynesi.wordpress.com/2008/12/24/set-in-our-ways-why-change-is-so-hard

Wheatley, M. and Kellner-Rogers, M. (1996). *A simpler way.* San Francisco, CA: Berrett-Koehler.

Wilber, K. (2001). *A theory of everything: An integral vision for business, politics, science and spirituality.* Boston, MA: Shambhala.

CONTACT INFORMATION

Contact the Author

Lynn Grodzki, LCSW, MCC
e-mail: lynn@privatepracticesuccess.com
phone: 301-434-0766
www.privatepracticesuccess.com
www.counselingsilverspring.com

Contact Information for Contributors:

Wendy Allen
www.wendyphd.com

Joe Bavonese
http://www.uncommon-practices.com

Susan Borkin
www.susanborkin.com

Deborah Gallant
www.webpowertools.com

Cathy Lange
www.businessworksinc.com

Avrum Nadigel
www.nadigel.com

Suzi Pomerantz
www.suzipomerantz.com

Casey Truffo
www.beawealthytherapist.com

INDEX